ALAN MOORE

BLOOMSBURY COMICS STUDIES

Covering major genres, creators and themes, the Bloomsbury Comics Studies series are accessible, authoritative and comprehensive introductions to key topics in Comics Studies. Providing historical overviews, guides to key texts, and important critical approaches, books in the series include annotated guides to further reading and online resources, discussion questions, and glossaries of key terms to help students and fans navigate the diverse world of comic books today.

Series Editor Derek Parker Royal (c. 1964–2019)

Titles in the series

SUPERHERO COMICS
Christopher Gavaler

AUTOBIOGRAPHICAL COMICS
Andrew J. Kunka

CHILDREN AND YOUNG ADULT COMICS
Gwen Tarbox

WEBCOMICS
Sean Kleefeld

Forthcoming titles

MANGA
Ronald Stewart and Shige (CJ) Suzuki

ALAN MOORE

A CRITICAL GUIDE

Jackson Ayres

BLOOMSBURY ACADEMIC
LONDON • NEW YORK • OXFORD • NEW DELHI • SYDNEY

BLOOMSBURY ACADEMIC
Bloomsbury Publishing Plc
50 Bedford Square, London, WC1B 3DP, UK
1385 Broadway, New York, NY 10018, USA
29 Earlsfort Terrace, Dublin 2, Ireland

BLOOMSBURY, BLOOMSBURY ACADEMIC and the Diana logo are trademarks of
Bloomsbury Publishing Plc

First published in Great Britain 2021

Cover design: Namkwan Cho
Cover image © Rebecca Clarke

A catalogue record for this book is available from the British Library.

A catalog record for this book is available from the Library of Congress.

ISBN: HB: 978-1-3500-6047-0
PB: 978-1-3500-6046-3
ePDF: 978-1-3500-6049-4
eBook: 978-1-3500-6048-7

Series: Bloomsbury Comics Studies

Typeset by Deanta Global Publishing Services, Chennai, India
Printed and bound in Great Britain

To find out more about our authors and books visit www.bloomsbury.com
and sign up for our newsletters.

To Marcia and Ted Ayres: my supportive parents and gracious, albeit accidental, comics archivists.

CONTENTS

List of Figures x
Series Editor's Preface xi
Acknowledgments xii

Introduction 1
 Do We Need Moore? 2
 The Original Writer 4
 A Guide to This Guide 9

1 Historical and Biographical Contexts 11
 Mage of the Midlands 11
 Thatcherism 14
 The British Invasion 17
 Creator Rights 20

2 Key Texts Part One 25
 Invading British Comics 25
  Origins 25
  2000 A.D.: Short Stories, *Skizz, D.R. and Quinch*,
   and *The Ballad of Halo Jones* 28
  The Bojeffries Saga 35
 Reinventing Superheroes: Britain 36
  Marvelman/Miracleman 36
  Captain Britain 42
  V for Vendetta 45
 Reinventing Superheroes: America 52
  The Saga of the Swamp Thing 52
  Whatever Happened to the Man of Tomorrow? 58
  The Killing Joke 64
  Watchmen 71

Contents

3   Key Texts Part Two   87
     Horrors of History   87
        From Hell   87
        A Small Killing   95
        Big Numbers   98
        Brought to Light   102
     Re-imagining Superheroes   104
        1963   105
        Supreme   110
        Moore's '90s Superheroes   115
     Cultural Commons   117
        "In Pictopia"   117
        Lost Girls   119
        League of Extraordinary Gentlemen   123
     America's Best Comics   128
        Tom Strong   128
        Tomorrow Stories   133
        Top 10   137
        Promethea   141
     Histories of Horror   147
        Lovecraft Cycle: *The Courtyard, Neonomicon,*
           and *Providence*   147
        Crossed + 100   153
        Cinema Purgatorio   155

4   Critical Questions   159
     Themes and Techniques   159
     Intertextuality   162
     Magic   165
     Psychogeography   168
     Englishness   170
     Representations   176
        Race   177
        Sexuality   181
        Sexual Violence   185

5   Social and Cultural Impact   **189**
     Authorship and Ownership   189
     The Revised Superhero   194
     Mature Readers?   197
     Politics and/of Comics   202
     Cultural Remixing   206
     Moore After Comics, Comics After Moore   211

Glossary   215
Works Cited   220
Index   234

FIGURES

2.1   Rewinding time in *2000 A.D.*   30
3.1   William Gull appearing before a modern skyscraper
      in *From Hell*   93
3.2   The conclusion of *League of Extraordinary
      Gentlemen: Tempest* #6   129
4.1   "Bat-fishing," an eccentric tradition, from *The Bojeffries Saga*   175

SERIES EDITOR'S PREFACE

The *Bloomsbury Comics Studies Series* reflects both the increasing use of comics within the university classroom and the emergence of the medium as a respected narrative and artistic form. It is a unique line of texts, one that has yet to be addressed within the publishing community. While there is no shortage of scholarly studies devoted to comics and graphic novels, most assume a specialized audience with an often-rarefied rhetoric. While such texts may advance the scholarly discourse, they nonetheless run the risk of alienating students and representing problematic distinctions between "popular" and "literary." The current series is intended as a more democratic approach to comics studies. It reflects the need for more programmatic classroom textbooks devoted to the medium, studies that are not only accessible to general readers, but whose depth of knowledge will resonate with specialists in the field. As such, each volume within the *Bloomsbury Comics Studies Series* will serve as a comprehensive introduction to a specific theme, genre, author, or key text.

While the organizational arrangement among the various volumes may differ slightly, each of the books within the series is structured to include an historical overview of its subject matter, a survey of its key texts, a discussion of the topic's social and cultural impact, recommendations for critical and classroom uses, a list of resources for further study, and a glossary reflecting the text's specific focus. In all, the *Bloomsbury Comics Studies Series* is intended as an exploratory bridge between specialist and student. Its content is informed by the growing body of comics scholarship available, and its presentation is both pragmatic and interdisciplinary. The goal of this series, as ideal as it may be, is to satisfy the needs of novices and experts alike, in addition to the many fans and aficionados upon whom the medium popularly rests.

Derek Parker Royal (*c.* 1964–2019)

ACKNOWLEDGMENTS

Writing this book has been, in truth, a joint effort with Haley O'Neil-Ayres. Her countless forms of support and encouragement were the project's backbone. She has my sincerest thanks.

I would also like to thank my exceptional colleagues at Texas A&M University-San Antonio. For their encouragement, comradery, and keen editorial eyes, I would like to thank my department faculty colleagues, especially, Ann Bliss, Katherine Bridgman, Nicole Carr, Marcos Del Hierro, James Finley, Scott Gage, Katherine Gillen, Adrianna Santos, and Lizbett Tinoco. I also thank my former Chair, William Bush, for his advice as I took on this endeavor. Much appreciation goes to Julie Hebert, administrative assistant for Department of Language, Literature, and Arts, for her attention to my research and travel logistics. A&M-SA's College of Arts and Sciences Summer Faculty Fellowships and Grants program funded much of this book's research.

My editors at Bloomsbury have been helpful at all stages. I am very appreciative of David Avital, Lucy Brown, Ben Doyle, and others, for their professionalism and editorial guidance from start to finish. The late Derek Parker Royal, editor of the Comics Studies Series, was the person who approached me to write this book and expressed confidence that I could take on the project. I did not know Derek well, but he was personable and a generous editor—he is missed.

This book is also indebted to wide networks of comics scholars and professionals. For their gracious granting of permissions to use copyrighted images, I would like to thank Chris Staros at Top Shelf Productions and Charlene Taylor at Rebellion Publishing. Thanks also go to esteemed comics editor Danny Fingeroth, who invited me to be on a Wizard World panel on "comics in college" that, in a roundabout way, led to this book. Throughout the process of writing this book, I have been fortunate to have met and learned much from many of my fellow comics scholars, and I'm grateful for those interactions. Special thanks go to Andrew Hoberek for his editing on my essays on comics for *Los Angeles Review of Books* and other instances of professional generosity.

Comics scholarly communities are descended from and still closely linked to fan communities. On this note, I want to give recognition to my longtime local comic book shop, The Gatekeeper. Although I have not lived in my hometown of Topeka, Kansas for many years, The Gatekeeper remains my shop: I thank them—in particular the store manager Jim Guinotte—for maintaining my pull list and shipping my comics (including anything with Alan Moore's name on it!) first to Arkansas and now to Texas. As a bonus, my current home of San Antonio has an active local comics scene anchored in several great comics stores, such as Alien Worlds and Heroes and Fantasies. Of course, comics fan communities also thrive online. I posed many research questions and calls for help on the Facebook group for *Back Issue* magazine; its members gave me loads of helpful information, for instance details on the evolution of superhero comics' cover credit boxes. I want to thank especially Andrew Wolf, who kindly sent me scans of old interviews with Moore from *Fantasy Express* and other obscure British fanzines. My experiences while writing this book testify to the generosity of comics fans when it comes to sharing and circulating material and information.

Lastly, support from my family has been essential. I want to thank Ted and Marcia Ayres; John and Sara Ayres and their daughters Gabrielle and Allison; Joe Ayres; Steve O'Neil and Stephanie Muñoz-O'Neil; Patrick O'Neil and Meredith Tack and their son Arthur; and Caitlin and Ryan Shea and their sons Francis and Edward. Special appreciation goes to my partner, Haley O'Neil-Ayres, and our two sons, Felix and Calvin. They have my deepest love and gratitude.

INTRODUCTION

Comics written by Alan Moore made possible not only this book, but also the very idea of this book: that is to say, Moore's contributions to English-language comics over the past forty years helped legitimize the notion that comics merit scholarly attention. Standard accounts of comics' authorization by gatekeeping institutions like universities and museums put Moore's *Watchmen*, done with artist Dave Gibbons, in a triumvirate with Frank Miller's *The Dark Knight Returns* and Art Spiegelman's *Maus*. If these three comics, as Bart Beaty and Benjamin Woo write, were "awkwardly grouped" together by "entertainment industry magazines seeking to establish a cultural trend" (2016: 19), the troika nonetheless acted as comics' major wedge into cultural respectability. Based only on the impact of *Watchmen*, let alone his full professional record, Moore has been an instrumental figure for the formation of comics studies as an academic field.

Yet, Moore's place in comics studies is now noticeably unsettled. Comics studies is past its institutional infancy, but the field's organizational infrastructure and apparatuses—professional organizations and conferences, academic journals and book series, degree programs—are in fact still forming and maturing. Accordingly, at present comics studies' canon of foundational texts remains "loosely defined and fluid" (Beaty and Woo 2016: 9). In a recent assessment of the field, Henry Jenkins points to a wave of "monographs [that] demonstrate the value of a particular approach, a particular author, a particular genre"; these types of books, he explains, will only truly "establish a field" by "getting out of the canon" ("Roundtable" 2016: 62) as it was first conceived. Thus, if in 2012 Eric Berlatsky could confidently assert that Moore's "privileged position in the history of comics is certain" (Berlatsky 2012b: vii), such confidence may no longer hold. As the field solidifies, and now that Moore is retired from comics, his comics' canonical statuses are primed for critical reappraisal.

Here is where this book comes in. *Alan Moore: A Critical Guide* is part of Bloomsbury's Comics Studies Series, a line dedicated to presenting comprehensive overviews of major genres, creators, and themes of graphic literatures. These critical introductions serve as accessible entry points for readers who may be relatively new to the field, but they also perform a broader meta-function: by tracing the critical significances for key topics within comics studies, these guides do needed mapping work. *Alan Moore: A Critical Guide* attends to a major comics writer's corpus, reviewing the critical conversations surrounding it as well as gesturing to new perspectives on it. The intended result not only clarifies our knowledge of Moore's comics and their many significances, but also facilitates reconsiderations of that work and its relation to the comics field.

Do We Need Moore?

Moore has long been recognized as one of the finest English-language comics writers. Moore's author biography (2019) for Top Shelf Productions, one of his primary publishers, claims, "Alan Moore is widely regarded as the best and most influential writer in the history of comics." Likewise, the British Council's entry for Moore (2019) describes him as "the grand elder statesmen" of comics and "one of the indispensable pioneers of the modern comic and graphic" storytelling. When general reader publications cover Moore, they frequently exclaim his stature: representative headlines include "How Alan Moore Transformed the Way I Saw Comics" (Berlatsky 2016), "Legendary Comics Writer" (*Wired* 2009), and "Our Greatest Graphic Novelist" (Barber 2006). Comics scholarship also tends to register and accept Moore's high reputation. In an article on Moore's comics for the journal *ImageText* Sean Carney proclaims, "Due to the overall quality of his prodigious output, Moore is often referred to as the single best writer in the history of the comic book medium" (2006: para. 1). Accordingly, Moore's comics have been of significant interest to comics scholars: Beaty and Woo determine that Moore is one of the most cited comics creators in databases containing comics scholarship (2016: 6–8, 55). This book, if nothing else, is an acknowledgement and response to Moore's long-standing high status in the field.

Alan Moore: A Critical Guide engages the contexts, histories, critical conversations, and, of course, the comics that have contributed to Moore's reputation: its chapters track the development of Moore's career; analyze his comics' thematic preoccupations, characteristic techniques, and major innovations; situate those comics within broader narratives of the comics medium, field, and industry; and synthesize critical perspectives on Moore's comics. This book surveys Moore's comics and their receptions, but it does so with an eye toward their evolving positions within the changing concerns and new directions of comics studies. Indeed, this guide arrives at an opportune moment for scholars and readers of Moore, as well as for comics studies as a scholarly enterprise. Following the final issue of 2019's *The League of Extraordinary Gentlemen: The Tempest*, Moore officially retired from comics—at least if his public statements are trusted. He has reneged prior insistences that he is done with comics. However, this time seems different, primarily because it appears as if comics may now also be walking away from Moore.

The apparent abandonment of Moore is occurring on many fronts. First, in recent years industry leaders have quit courting him, a shift seen in Marvel Comics' purchase of *Miracleman* and DC Comics' franchising of *Watchmen*. Such moves exacerbate rather than alleviate Moore's grievances with those companies' control of his older work. Once DC and Marvel accepted that no professional relationship with Moore was forthcoming, it would seem they have committed themselves to making his older work as lucrative as possible. Given those companies' financial incentives, their actions may be justified: the market appears healthier for cannibalizations of Moore's older work than new comics from him. In 2017, the premiere issue of *Doomsday Clock*—DC's crossover maxi-series between its franchised superheroes and *Watchmen*—was the third best-selling comic book of the year. Issues of Moore's newer series from recent years, by contrast, rarely appeared in the top 100 best-selling comics lists for their release months, perhaps reflecting the diminished draw of his name.

Another shift is an overdue reassessment of racial and sexual representations in Moore's comics. This turn was presaged by the Black feminist blogger Pam Noles, who in 2007 began a series of critiques of Moore and collaborator Kevin O'Neill for their inclusion of the appallingly racist Golliwog character in their *League* series. Marc Singer develops Noles' critique in a more formally academic context, arguing that *League*'s "reactionary politics and imagery," from racist imagery to misogynist tropes, "are hardly limited to the Golliwogg" and that if "Moore and O'Neill sometimes present these characters and ideologies as subjects for critique, they are just as likely to indulge in them" (2019: 124). Singer ends his analysis of ideological blind spots in Moore's aesthetics by lamenting how scholars seem unwilling to confront such aspects of Moore's work as it is found not only in *League* but throughout his comics. His call for renewed scrutiny on this front, then, may signal a less reverential critical consensus.

Critics are also questioning Moore's heretofore rarely disputed reputation as a writer of unparalleled talents. Writing for *Slate*, Douglas Wolk calls Moore "comics' Orson Welles: a genius formalist with a natural collaborative impulse and a habit of taking on overambitious projects. His work is alternately groundbreaking and painfully lazy; he often coasts on his cleverness for a quick paycheck" (2003). The rest of Wolk's profile has other similarly backhanded compliments, and it concludes that ultimately Moore's legacy is the modest accomplishment of "genre comics" done "with a lot of craft." Wolk wrote that piece back in 2003, but its impression of Moore as a savvy but overrated stylist has become more commonplace within comics scholarship. For instance, Beaty and Woo maintain that Moore's comics are emblematic of middlebrow culture (2016: 56), deploying "middlebrow" for its historically pejorative connotations. Moore's dubious legacy, for Beaty and Woo, is to have entrenched mere "quality comic books" as "an upper limit on comics' rise" (2016: 64) in prestige.

In his book, *Reading Comics*, Wolk muses, "It's not at all correct to say that the last twenty-five years of the history of comics are the history of Alan Moore's career, but it's fair to say that it sometimes seems that way" (2008: 229). This statement smacks of exhaustion, not admiration, implying that it is now time to rethink comics history and Moore's place within it—and create new futures for comics shaped by revised critical narratives. By presenting an overview of Moore's now-complete comics career and charting key lines of scholarly inquiry into Moore's oeuvre, this book both reaffirms the significance of Moore's comics and gestures to a project of reassessment.

The Original Writer

A single-author study for a comics writer presents immediate conceptual problems. While there are plenty of examples of the solo writer-artist—prominent within the "graphic memoir" genre and underground "comix" tradition—by and large comics' creative labor is distributed across a handful of contributors: typically, a writer, pencil artist, inker, letterer, and colorist. In some cases, an editor might be considered part of the core creative team. Early in his career, Moore followed the writer-artist model, but the majority of his work and certainly all his major works are collaborations in which Moore is credited strictly as the comic's writer. How this volume treats comics authorship, generally and in the specific case of Moore, therefore requires attention. In short, must this book necessarily overlook or devalue contributions from Moore's artistic partners?

This question reflects a long-running argument over comics as "a writer's medium" or "an artist's medium." Within this debate, formalist studies tend to privilege comics' visual elements and the artist's role. Scott McCloud's landmark *Understanding Comics* justifiably excludes "words" from its definition of comics, conceding that "a great majority of modern comics do feature words and pictures in combination" but, since comics can be wordless, too much emphasis on verbal elements is "restrictive" (1993: 21). Similarly, Thierry Groenstein's *The System of Comics* rebuts the notion that "comics are essentially a mixture of text and images" in order "to demonstrate the primacy of the image" (2007: 3) for comics. Such accounts also reflect how comics' graphic features tend to define the medium in a popular imagination—the word "comics" conjuring images of panel shapes and vibrant art. Yet, in the academic study of comics, visuals frequently seem to be a secondary consideration.

Within comics scholarship, art and visual design tend to take a backseat to narrative and other literary or literary-cultural concerns. Thomas A. Bredehoft writes, "scholars, publishers, and even comics creators habitually privilege the 'writer' of a particular comics work over the artist or artists" (2011: 98). Yet, Bredehoft contends, "to the degree that [this hierarchy] privileges language over the image," it is "in conflict with the essential nature of the medium" (2011: 98). Art's subordination in comics studies arguably can be put at the feet of institutional forces. Bart Beaty's *Comics versus Art* shows that university "art departments, and in particular art history departments, lagged in the adoption of courses and research on comics" resulting in "a tendency to drive attention away from comics as a form of visual culture" (2012: 18). Instead, Beaty notes, "the literary turn in the study of comics prevailed, with hundreds of essays published on generic, thematic, formal, and narrative concerns raised by a host of comics and works in the domain of popular culture" (2012: 18). The dominant approaches to comics scholarship, Beaty argues, derive from literary and cultural studies and therefore reflect the preoccupations and methods of those fields in ways that can distort our understanding of comics as a specific cultural form.

Other structural factors contribute to this swing toward the literary. Referring to comics' path to cultural legitimacy in the mid-1980s, Beaty and Woo recount how "various actors in the comic book field began drawing quite self-consciously on literary principles of value" as a way "to elevate individual works as well as the entire art form" (2016: 53). An indicator of this shift was the growing purchase for the neologism "graphic novel," a term that gestures toward literariness to shed the presumably embarrassing and juvenile connotations of the term "comics." In Beaty and Woo's framework, Moore's high reputation is in fact part and parcel of a longer transformation in which critics, fans, and industry professionals have bid for comics' prestige by positioning the writer's role as paramount, done to draw on the cultural status value of "literature." Paul Williams documents this process in *Dreaming the Graphic Novel: The Novelization of Comics* (2020).

Beaty and Woo intimate that Moore is complicit with comics' literary turn; they claim that the "road from 'great comic book artist' to 'great graphic novel(ist)'" is one that "runs through a small handful of comic book writers, and chief among them is Alan Moore" (2016: 54). However, Moore's own views on comics creation underscore its collaborative character. In an essay first serialized in 1985, recently republished as the slim illustrated book *Alan Moore's Writing for Comics*, Moore clearly rejects any "images versus literature" conflict for defining the comics form. In his essay, Moore bristles at competing tendencies to use vocabularies taken from either film or literature to talk about comics. On one hand, Moore argues that if "cinematic thinking has undoubtedly produced many of the finest comic works of the past 30 years . . . any emulation of film technique by the comics medium must inevitably suffer by the comparison" (2010e: 3). Yet, on the other hand, if comics are "viewed in literary terms, in an effort to draw comparisons between comics sequences and conventional literary forms" the result is "novels without scope, depth or purpose" (2010e: 3–4). Undue emphasis on either comics' visual or verbal aspects thus misses comics' formal hybridity. Consequently, Moore advocates for devising a critical vocabulary crafted specifically for comics.

Moore also routinely stresses the artist's role in the creative process. According to Moore, in comics story and art must "be equal" (Lawley and Whitaker 2012: 43); in this spirit, he says, "I'm only ever doing half a piece of art. [My collaborator's] only ever doing half a piece of art. It's when they go together that it starts moving" (Roach et al. 2012: 11). Taking such claims further, when describing the process behind *Watchmen*, Moore proposes a figurative slippage between comics creation and procreation: "I couldn't have done the *Watchmen* without Dave Gibbons, and he couldn't have done it without me. That was the result of an almost sexual union" (De Abaitua 2012: 77). Moore has also taken the sides of artists in some contentious disputes over comics authorship, in particular vigorously maintaining that, despite writer and editor Stan Lee's fame as impresario of Marvel Comics, artists like Jack Kirby and Steve Ditko were the creative engines behind

Marvel's classic characters and stories. Now, if in other moments Moore may seem to champion the primacy of the writer for comics authorship or overplay his own contributions—he contradicts himself often across his public comments over the decades—in the main Moore sees comics as a collaborative art.

Nevertheless, Moore is frequently presented as if he were the sole author of his comics. For instance, Avatar Press' publications of some of his more obscure comics add his name in the possessive to the titles, which by implication diminishes the many contributions of Moore's artistic collaborators. (Ironically, the Afterword to *Alan Moore's A Small Killing* includes artist Oscar Zárate's assertions of his primary authorship for the graphic novel.) To be sure, this book's title, *Alan Moore: A Critical Guide*, itself risks projecting a misleading impression of comics creation.

Yet, if Avatar's foregrounding of Moore's name in their publications is likely a marketing decision that hinges on Moore's name recognition in the comics marketplace, comics scholars have their own rationale for disentangling Moore from his creative partnerships. Annalisa Di Liddo refers to the creation of comics "as an organic, almost alchemical act, which is in itself hybrid and not entirely definable" (34). Still, she clarifies that Moore's scripts give not only "the necessary technical suggestions about perspective and angles, or about the positions of objects and characters in each panel" but also contain "historical notes, commentaries, and descriptions of the possible sounds and smells one might have found on the scene" and address "what nuances colors might have" (Di Liddo 2009: 32). Moore's biographer, Lance Parkin, likewise stresses that Moore's work is done in collaboration, but insists that "it is not always the two-way exchange of ideas that word implies" (2013: 125). Moore is a collaborator, but one who takes deep involvement in his comics' visual designs.

This intense creative involvement in his comics' visual aspects yields consistencies throughout Moore's body of work even though his artistic collaborators' styles can vary considerably. Parkin argues that though "Moore has worked in collaborative media with over a hundred different artists, each with their own style" (2013: 1), across comics written by Moore "there are always connections and commonalities" that disclose "they're clearly all the product of the same creative mind" (2013: 2). The British Council's page for Moore similarly insists, "it is important to recognize that, though his career has rested on a series of collaborations with a disparate group of artists, Moore is best seen as an auteur. His forensically detailed scripts play to the strengths of his various collaborators but are always essentially the product of Moore's literary and visual imagination" (2019). Moore himself says of his process: "I always work in full script—and not only full script, fuller than normal scripts. My scripts are gigantic. They are huge amounts of detail and description" (Khoury 1999). His *Watchmen* script, for instance, devotes an entire page of instructions to artist Dave Gibbons for the first panel alone. Moore's dizzyingly dense scripts do not make his artists mere executors of his vision—and Moore insists that "the artist is quite free to ignore" his script's elaborate details (Khoury 1999)— but his intricate and discursive scripts nonetheless suggest a strong hand with visuals that in turn develop consistencies across his body of work that cut across his collaborations.

For that reason, comics penned by Moore reflect an intelligible creative vision. To borrow a sentiment from Marcel Proust's *Le temps retrouvé* (*Time Regained*): "For the writer as much as for the painter, style is a matter not of technique but of vision." Questions of technique matter, but this book's critical focus is on the artistic vision discernible across comics bearing Moore's name.

Reconciling this emphasis with comics' collaborative nature is possible. M. Thomas Inge insists that one need not jettison entirely the notion of a distinct author in order to account for collaborative creation: "On a practical level, recognizing that the concept of the solitary genius, or of the divinely inspired author, is a myth calls for no drastic change in the ways we teach and write" (2009: 630). According to Inge, we need not abandon the category of "author" altogether in order to "allow more for a social and contextual concept of authorship," one that gives "a more realistic and less romantic view of literary production" (2009: 630). Inge's pragmatic view leads us to treat Moore as *an author* of his comics, whose recurring themes and techniques form "a coherent oeuvre" (Carney 2006: para. 2), but not *the author*. We might therefore most accurately describe this book not as a "single-author study" but as a "single-collaborator study," one that traces patterns and themes across partnerships. The book follows the career of a single individual collaborator, but effectively deploys the name "Alan Moore" as proxy for "Alan Moore and given collaborators" over the course of that career. Its analyses treat the verbal elements typically ascribed to the writer within the contexts of comics production, recognizing that their creations and effects only occur in conjunction with their visual expressions.

To be sure, my training as a literature scholar does mean this book chiefly employs the methods and approaches of literary and cultural studies: namely, "close reading, historical contextualization, and engagement with various strands of critical theory" (Singer 2019: 30). If such approaches risk obscuring comics' visuality, as critics of comics' literary turn contend, literary-minded analyses of comics also have affordances—especially for a study of a comics writer with a reputation for a distinctly "literary" sensibility. On this point, after Singer extols the benefits of comics studies' "multidisciplinary and interdisciplinary character" and the essential need for "diversity of perspectives" (2019: 30) within the field, he defends the tools of literary criticism. These tools, he argues, "have value not because they are part of some venerable and unitary tradition . . . but because they continue to perform important intellectual work" (2019: 30). Some of the best examples of comics scholarship grounded in models of literary studies, moreover, trouble our understandings of their own key terms that have served as referents, points of contrast, and sources of status anxiety for comics. Such terms include "literature" itself. To this point, in *Considering Watchmen*, Andrew Hoberek—with a nod to Charles Hatfield's likeminded approach in *Alternative Comics: An Emerging Literature*—explains that his analysis of the "formal dimensions" to Moore and Gibbons' comic "self-consciously interrogates—rather than tak[es] for granted—the concept of literature" (2014: n. pag.). Importing literary criticism's tools, then, need not necessarily subsume comics within the traditions, values, and assumptions of literary studies.

A Guide to This Guide

This book's readings not only interpret individual texts but also assemble those comics into a vision of Moore's overall body of work, thereby establishing recurring themes and tracking the developments of his comics career. Readings also relate Moore's comics to relevant contexts, from broader trends in the comics industry to historical events and concerns. Furthermore, the book engages the relatively large amount of scholarly as well as journalistic or popular criticism on Moore's comics, contending with various critical perspectives on Moore, key sites for consensus and dissensus, and emergent directions for the academic conversations surrounding Moore and his work. This wide-ranging portrait of Moore's career develops over a series of chapters that can be read linearly, unfolding as a narrative account, or can be read selectively since chapters are divided into discrete sections and subsections that allow readers to turn directly to specific topics and texts.

These varied topics and texts, to be clear, are limited to Moore's *comics*. Moore is a very prolific writer and artist, working not only in comics but also in prose fiction and nonfiction, film, music, performance art, and more. However, since this book is part of a Comics Studies Series, it focuses on Moore's career in comics and only references his diverse non-comics work in terms of its relation to his comics. Furthermore, for reasons of space and scope, this study excludes comics originally written by Moore for other media but adapted by others into comics, such as *The Birth Caul*, *Fashion Beast*, and others. This book limits itself to Moore's comics conceived as comics.

After this Introduction is a chapter entitled "Historical and Biographical Contexts." As its title suggests, this chapter offers a snapshot of the life of Alan Moore, chronicling the personal and professional experiences that have shaped him as a comics writer. The chapter also addresses germane historical developments and contexts. After the grounding provided by that chapter, the book turns to its centerpiece: "Key Texts." These two expansive chapters feature critical readings of Moore's most significant comics plus briefer explications of some minor works and juvenilia. Key Texts locates major themes and tells a story of Moore's career through his comics.

The next two chapters draw from and build upon ideas and themes developed in the Key Texts chapters' analyses. "Critical Questions" is divided into sections that trace issues and critical debates that cut across Moore's comics career and corpus. Lastly, "Social and Cultural Impact" examines how Moore's comics have shaped the comics field and reverberate in other discourses and spheres. Collectively, the chapters act as a guide for charting past and future excursions with Moore in the comics field.

CHAPTER 1
HISTORICAL AND
BIOGRAPHICAL CONTEXTS

This chapter begins with a biographical sketch of Moore, followed by sections devoted to historical contexts that deepen our understandings of Moore's comics and their significances. The chapter's overviews are elaborated throughout the book and other relevant contexts will be introduced, but the information included in this chapter grounds much of the subsequent analyses.

Mage of the Midlands

Alan Moore was born on November 18, 1953, in a hospital outside Northampton, located in the East Midlands of England. His father, Ernest, was a laborer and his mother, Sylvia, worked at a local printer. A few years after Alan was born, Sylvia and Ernest had another child, Mike. The Moore household also included his grandmother and occasional other boarders. Of his childhood council home, Moore recalls, "We got electric light but didn't have an indoor flush toilet; we had an outhouse without a cistern at the bottom of the yard, and there was no light in there" (Khoury 2008: 13–14). Such conditions had little impact on his well-being or happiness; according to Moore, he had "no idea that there was any other sort of way that people lived" (Khoury 2008: 14). He loved his neighborhood and its sense of community, and he is grateful for the upbringing they provided him.

Moore's accounts of his childhood can seem romanticized, but they signal his affiliation with working-class experience and identity. He sees comics as part of this heritage. In a 1984 interview he drolly recalls, "Comics, when I was growing up, were part of a working class tradition. Mothers gave them to their kids to pacify them. Instead of a Valium, it would be a copy of *The Topper* or *The Beezer*"—or reprints of American comics (Lawley and Whitaker 2012: 27). Along with his initiation into comics, Moore's working-class background provided him a set of values; or, at least, values that Moore associates with his class identity: communitarianism balanced by self-sufficiency, and equality underwriting individual autonomy. Such values feed into his comics.

Reading was encouraged in the Moore household, and young Alan did so enthusiastically and widely. He was bright. Upon transfer to a middle-class school, however, Moore confronted his lack of privilege: he was no longer the most academically talented student, and he saw that his diminished status was chiefly due to material disadvantages. As a result, he lost interest in school and felt stirrings of resentment and rebellion. Drawn to the counterculture of the late 1960s and early 1970s, Moore explored the music and popular arts of the hippie fringe, which overlapped with subcultures built around fan communities for genre fiction and comics. He also embraced the era's drug culture, becoming an avid user of marijuana and psychedelic drugs. But, after bringing LSD to school he was expelled. His institution's vindictive headmaster wrote letters to other academies warning them of Moore, ensuring that he was unable to enroll elsewhere and thus ending his formal education. In short order, he was out of his family home, working odd jobs to make ends meet, and, by 1973, married to the person who would be his first wife: Phyllis Dixon.

While moving through a series of low-paying jobs, he was active in arts collectives. Within such groups, Moore made contacts in the music and arts scenes of Northampton and its region. He dabbled in music, prose and poetry, visual arts, performance pieces, and comics. After learning that Phyllis was pregnant with what would be the first of two daughters, Moore recognized that he was at a vocational turning point. With Phyllis' support, he turned to art fulltime. Among other creative endeavors, Moore began writing and drawing comic strips for local underground publications. His interests in music and cartooning converged when he was hired to make a regular strip for the rock magazine *Sounds*, putting Moore on a path toward a professional comics career.

Although he initially intended to work as a solo writer-artist, by the early 1980s Moore was concentrating on his writing. Part of this decision likely stemmed from his gradual move away from underground or alternative comics to more mainstream fare. Independent publishers and the music press catered to audiences receptive to Moore's manic art style, but the more mainstream comics genres like fantasy, superheroes, and science fiction tended to feature more polished and realistic art unsuited to Moore's artistic sensibility. Moore thus focused his energy on writing; his entrance into mainstream comics as a writer would seem to be confirmed by 1980, when he sold his first scripts for *2000 A.D.*, home to the UK's top comics talent in a booming comics market.

Moore's contributions for *2000 A.D.* would continue over the next few years, eventually moving from one-off short stories and fill-in features to longer-form serialized narratives. Around this time, Moore began work on two serialized features for a new comics anthology, *Warrior*, that would dramatically change the direction of his career: *Marvelman* and *V for Vendetta*. Despite significant publishing delays, the two series would spur changed perceptions about genre comics' formal and thematic possibilities. *Marvelman* and *V for Vendetta* also opened the door to American comics: in 1983, DC Comics—one of US comics' "Big Two" publishers—invited Moore to write *The Saga of the Swamp Thing*. Success on this title led to higher-profile work at DC, including Moore's masterpiece with artist Dave Gibbons, *Watchmen*. However, conflicts over the working conditions at large corporate publishers led Moore to cut ties with DC by the end of the 1980s.

From about 1988 to 1993, Moore worked outside comics' dominant publishing channels. At this time Moore took on several ambitious, eclectic comics projects—all departures from popular genres like superheroes or fantasy—and published them via independent presses, book publishers interested in an emerging market for graphic novels, and his own self-financed publishing operation called Mad Love. These endeavors, however, would prove hard to sustain financially.

The early 1990s were a transitional, turbulent time in Moore's personal life as well. In 1973, Moore had married Phyllis Dixon, and the couple soon welcomed two daughters, Leah and Amber. During the mid-1980s, Debbie Delano joined Alan and Phyllis to form a polyamorous unit. By the early 1990s, however, Phyllis and Debbie decided to continue their relationship apart from Alan; daughters Leah and Amber lived with their mother and Debbie. While all parties adjusted to these changes, and Moore would later begin a new romantic relationship with American comics artist Melinda Gebbie (they married in 2007), the period of separation from Phyllis and Debbie was tumultuous.

During the first few years of the 1990s, furthermore, Moore became heavily interested in the occult and various esoteric traditions. On his fortieth birthday in late 1993, Moore publicly declared himself a practicing ceremonial magician. Moore's enthusiastic turn to magic facilitates refinement of his theories about language, art, and collective imaginations, all of which he thinks through using magical concepts. His ideas about the occult and art, moreover, filter into his comics.

Around the same time as his conversion and fervent commitment to magic, Moore returned to comics' popular genres. In 1993, Moore began a series of superhero projects for the upstart publisher Image, chiefly as a way to finance his more offbeat projects but also because he embraced the company's creator-owned mission. In 1997, Moore won the prestigious Eisner Award for Best Writer, which jointly honored his work on the independent project *From Hell* and the Image superhero series *Supreme*. This moment might be taken to symbolize Moore's signature ability to reconcile idiosyncratic tastes and endeavors with commercial tastes and appeal.

At the outset of the twenty-first century, Moore was kicking off a prolific new period. In an agreement with the popular artist-writer and publisher Jim Lee, Moore developed a publishing imprint, America's Best Comics, distributed through Lee's company, Wildstorm. But, shortly after Moore's arrangement with Lee was struck, DC bought Wildstorm in a move that Moore believes was intentionally done in order to bring him back into the DC fold. Moore fulfilled his ABC responsibilities, yet most of his ABC creations remain DC's intellectual property. This experience, compounding his legal battles with DC over rights to *Watchmen*, was chastening and infuriating.

DC's allegedly underhanded purchase of ABC, along with other and similarly aggravating experiences with the comics industry—including perceived censorship and the licensing of Moore's comics for film adaptations against his wishes—have contributed to Moore's increasingly misanthropic public persona. His comics from the past decade or so frequently reflect his anger: in its late volumes, the long-running *The League of Extraordinary Gentlemen* series evolves into a caustic denunciation of the shallowness of commercially driven popular culture. Other late-career comics, a body of work that centers on the horror genre, collectively suggest a frightening, despairing portrait of the contemporary world. Moore's disenchantment with comics has led him to focus more projects outside comics, like prose fiction, performance, and film. And in 2019 he retired from writing comics altogether, bringing his remarkable comics career to a bitter end.

Thatcherism

For a historically minded writer like Moore, one whose work often directly engages with historical events and narratives, situating his comics in relevant historical contexts is essential. And for Moore, indeed for a wide swath of British comics writers of Moore's generation, *the* historical context centers on a single, transformative historical figure: Prime Minister Margaret Thatcher. Moore himself acknowledges the sway of Thatcher and her policies on his breakout comics of the 1980s, many of which tended toward dystopian genres and apocalyptic themes. Looking back at his comics from the 1980s, he recalls, anger at "this insane right-wing Boadicea running the country . . . tended to reflect in my work" (Robinson 2011). Lance Parkin uses suitable comic book lingo when he calls Thatcher "Moore's arch-nemesis" (2013: 247). Moore even dramatizes hostility for Thatcher in the final act of his superhero comic *Miracleman*, when his titular superpowered protagonist—in a scene that smacks of wish-fulfilment—deposes Thatcher and installs an egalitarian new world order at odds with her market-based, individualist politics.

What is Thatcherism and how does it relate to Margaret Thatcher, Prime Minister of Great Britain from 1979 to 1990? Historians Ben Jackson and Robert Saunders open their volume of essays on Thatcher's legacy by declaring, "Margaret Thatcher was one of the most controversial figures in modern British history" (2012: 1). They add, Thatcher "was the only Prime Minister of the twentieth century to give her name to an ideology," which is to say Thatcherism, even though "there is no agreement on what [Thatcherism] was or who believed in it" (2012: 1). Even if "Thatcherism" is not an explicitly articulated political program, most analyses of it agree that as a politico-economic ideology Thatcherism uneasily reconciles unrestrained markets with strong state authority. In part due to Thatcher's own assertive political style and charisma, these ideological values migrated from the political realm into the terrains of culture and society. Thatcherism is a politics, a sensibility, and a cultural phenomenon.

Perhaps because it threatens their values, most of Thatcherism's diagnosticians have been from the political Left; their accounts thus skew critical. A prominent site for influential critical analysis of the Thatcher phenomenon as it was occurring was the socialist academic journal *Marxism Today*. In 1983, just four years after Thatcher's election, the journal's editors Stuart Hall and Martin Jacques put together a book of essays entitled *The Politics of Thatcherism*. In their introduction, Hall and Jacques define Thatcherism by its reactionary and regressive agenda: "Its project has been to reverse the whole postwar drift of British society, to roll back the historic gains of the labour movement and other progressive forces, and to force-march the society, vigorously, into the past" (1983: 11). As Hall and Jacques' reference to "postwar" indicates, their critique understands Thatcherism as an undoing of a specific political order enshrined after the Second World War.

That political order was the decades-long consensus built around Britain's postwar welfare state. The welfare state was an extension of and reward for wartime solidarities. Its features included high marginal taxation rates to dampen economic inequality; robust social provisions, including a National Health Service providing medical services free at the point of use; and a mixed economy with nationalized key industries. The welfare state was put in place by the Labour Party after its electoral victory in 1945, but many of its institutions and precepts were accepted by centrists in the two major parties: Labour and its opposition the Conservatives. Moore was born in 1953, which was the time of the welfare state's consecration as the new political common sense for the UK. Thatcherism, later, was dedicated to overthrowing this egalitarian-minded status quo.

Moore was certainly not the only comics creator in the 1980s to turn their attention (and ire) to Thatcher and Thatcherism. James Chapman's *British Comics: A Cultural History* (2011) identifies a number of British comics that took Thatcher as target for satire and critique. Moore's breakout comics from the 1980s reflect the generally anti-Thatcher environment of the British comics scene. *V for Vendetta* is patently a critique of Thatcher-era England and, as Andrew Hoberek notes, though set in the US *Watchmen* can be read as a displaced "vision of the transformation of the United Kingdom under Margaret Thatcher" (2014: n. pag.). Thus, three of Moore's major comics of the 1980s—*Miracleman*, *V for Vendetta*, and *Watchmen*—stage conflicts against Thatcherite values.

Yet, Thatcherism's influence on Great Britain and Moore's comics does not end when she leaves office in 1990. One of Stuart Hall's early essays on Thatcherism, "The Great Moving Right Show," prophetically notes that Thatcherism "no longer looks like a temporary swing of the pendulum in political fortune" (1988: 39). Instead, Hall concludes, Thatcherism represents a political reshuffling, creating "a new balance of political forces" (1988: 56). The endurance of Thatcherism has exceeded Hall's weary prognostication. When Labour returned to power in 1997, it incorporated and internalized so much of Thatcherism's fundamental precepts about the primacy of market logics that the party narrowed the gap between it and post-Thatcher Conservatives. "New Labour" made no real effort to undo the Thatcher's government privatized industries, lowered taxes, and reduced social services, nor did it give much rhetorical pushback to

Thatcher's cultural elevation of individuality, competition, and material accumulation. For this reason, even as Moore wrote comics into the 1990s and the new millennium his politically minded work remained in dialogue with Thatcherism and its bipartisan inheritance, a political hegemony often called "neoliberalism."

Moore not only recognizes Thatcherism as an ideology that persists beyond Thatcher's time in office, but also sees it in relation to trends that trace back for centuries. In a 1998 interview, Moore uses the term "aesthetic Thatcherism" to name a long historical process of art's commodification, during which artists "started to believe we were entertainers, and it was just a job" (De Abaitua 2012: 93). Here Moore anachronistically refers to Thatcherism to convey art's diminishment by crass commercial imperatives. Moore thus aligns Thatcherism with values and tendencies that are hostile to what he sees as the truer aims of cultural production. And since this notion of "aesthetic Thatcherism" cheapens and diminishes art, for Moore, Thatcherism—its aesthetic, cultural, and political energies—must be intensely resisted.

Despite Moore's hostility toward Thatcher and Thatcherism, the relation between his comics and the politico-cultural shift of the 1980s is actually vexed. Indeed, commentators have noted how Thatcher's influence has been so profound that even many of her harshest critics, unwittingly, internalized her values. Hoberek makes such a case for *Watchmen*: "Moore's critique of Thatcherism from the point of view of his countercultural and anarchist politics actually shares the distrust of all institutions that was at the heart of eighties conservatism and a nascent neoliberalism" (2014: n. pag.). Moore, then, is not immune from Thatcher's push to the right: the political and cultural transformations of Britain inform and complicate the politics of his comics. In a broader sense, moreover, Moore's confrontations with Thatcherism in his comics are proxies for a wider investment in British, specifically English, cultural experience and national identity, which have been informed if not dominated by Thatcherism and its legacies for the past forty years.

The British Invasion

One irony of Thatcherism is that for all the hostility felt by artists toward Thatcher, that contentiousness and sense of outrage often led to the creation of vibrant, powerful, and lasting creative work. Such was the case within British comics, which had a renaissance in the late 1970s and early 1980s.

Comics dovetailed and dialogued with other underground and youth subcultures, audiences shifted, comics creators pushed creative boundaries, and publications like *2000 A.D.* become hotbeds for innovation. American publishers, including large corporate ones driving the industry, took notice. US publishers' mass hiring of UK talent led to a so-called British Invasion.

A starting point for the influx of British creators into the American comics market is the founding of Marvel UK in 1972. Initially, Marvel UK reprinted American superhero comics for the British market, typically repackaging stories in anthology formats. As the decade went on, Marvel aimed for a stronger foothold: Chapman writes, "In the mid-1970s, however, seeking to establish itself as a third power alongside [British publishers] IPC and D.C. Thomson, Marvel launched several original titles for the British market" (2011: 182). Part of Marvel UK's expansion was a new superhero series, *Captain Britain*, though that title had trouble finding an audience since "the American parentage of 'Britain's greatest superhero' was to provoke the ire of British readers" (2011: 183). Moore's *Captain Britain* run with Alan Davis, however, centered English questions.

By Moore's recollection, Marvel UK's offerings were mostly uninspired. He recalls that editor Bernie Jaye "had been given a pitiful budget" (Khoury 2008: 56), but since she was widely liked and respected, Moore and others were willing to do supplemental pieces at low cost. Moore contributed prose stories starring an original Marvel UK noir hero, Night Raven, as well as reviews and opinion essays. One of those essays, "Blinded By the Hype" (2012a), is notable for its critique of legendary Marvel writer-editor and company figurehead, Stan Lee. Moore laughs that he was able to get away with printing that "Affectionate Character Assassination," as the essay's subtitle has it, because "Marvel USA didn't read the Marvel UK product" and the "only relationship between Marvel UK and Marvel America at that time seemed to be that they had the same name" (Khoury 2008: 56–7). Even if Marvel UK overall was a middling endeavor, its interest in the British comics market and scene anticipates the later mass recruitment of British creators by American publishers.

Moore is perhaps the central figure for this British Invasion. Bart Beaty and Benjamin Woo name Moore as "the trailblazer for the cohort" and suggest that assessments of Moore's comics "can perhaps be applied to the British Invasion writers as a whole" (2016: 57). Moore's professional involvement with US comics began in 1983, when he received an unexpected phone call from Len Wein, a respected figure in American superhero comics who was at the time working as an editor for DC Comics. Wein was calling about an opportunity to write *The Saga of the Swamp Thing*. In Moore's memory of the call, Wein said "that he'd read the stuff that I'd been doing in *Warrior* and elsewhere and was interested in giving me a trial on the series and seeing if I could come up with anything" (Khoury 2008: 83). Moore accepted the offer. While several British artists preceded Moore at DC, the critical and commercial success of his *Swamp Thing* amplified interest in British creators—especially British comics writers.

A direct result of Moore's success on *Swamp Thing* is arguably the British Invasion's most mythologized moment: DC's appointment of editor Karen Berger as company liaison to the UK. Berger had joined DC's editorial office in 1979, despite having basically no familiarity or interest in comic books. But, she impressed senior editorial staff and was hired by Wein as his own replacement on *Saga of the Swamp Thing*, which put her working with Moore. Berger eventually became an ambassador of sorts for DC to the British comics scene. She recalls of the appointment to the UK: "[w]hen I was out there, my feeling was, 'There's so much talent here, why don't we really make use of them and work with them in developing projects for DC?'" (Carpenter 2016: 472). According to Dan Mazur and Alexander Danner, "Berger continued to recruit writers from *2000 AD* and other British comics magazines, officially launching the British invasion of American mainstream comics" (2014: 175). These creators transformed the tones and looks of US comics.

While the British Invasion included artists—for instance, Dave Gibbons, Brian Bolland, Dave McKean, Alan Davis, and Steve Dillon—ultimately its biggest impact and legacy came from its writers. The most notable three writers of this cohort are Moore, Neil Gaiman, and Grant Morrison. Greg Carpenter's book, *The British Invasion*, in fact casts the entire phenomenon as an intensely personal psychodrama played out between these three men, all of whom, in Carpenter's account, meta-textually project their views on writing, the comics industry, and each other through their comics. Carpenter's book provides some sharp readings of these writers' comics, but it limits our understanding of the British Invasion's significance. By focusing intensely on the comics of Moore, Gaiman, and Morrison, and reading those comics in strong biographical terms, Carpenter reduces the British Invasion to a drama of interpersonal relationships and professional rivalries.

Beaty and Woo are closer to the mark when they examine the British Invasion as an index of changes to the comics field. In Beaty and Woo's account, Moore is "chief among" a "small handful of comic book writers," most of them British, who "planted the seeds of a 'long revolution' within American comic books" (2016: 54–5). This revolution has had many effects, namely a shift in discourse from "comic book" to "graphic novel" and, accordingly, from critical attention to the visual aspects of comics to their literary dimensions. Beaty and Woo make the case that, due to the British Invasion, "media discourse (including that of comics critics) routinely treats collaboratively authored comics art as if it sprang fully formed from the heads of its writers" (2016: 54). Comics' visual components, post-British Invasion, become subordinated to literary and narrative aspects.

This critical privileging of the writer relates to one other key feature of the British Invasion's long revolution: revisionism. Moore's comics embrace the revisionist imperative to use self-referential and meta-textual techniques to comment on comics themselves. Beaty and Woo, underscoring the role of writers in the British Invasion, note that "it is at the level of content, rather than form, that these [revisionist] comics are most explicitly 'about' comics" (2016: 58). The revisionist method interrogates comics history, but "a reader must be exceptionally well versed in the history of comics in order to appreciate the revisions that are being made" (2016: 59). Revisionist narratives revitalized comics storytelling, but potentially at the cost of accessibility. The legacies of revisionism, and the British Invasion broadly, are therefore mixed and contested.

Creator Rights

Creator control, entailing creative freedom as well as legal ownership, is a central preoccupation of Moore's career. As Hoberek puts it, Moore's interviews and comic books alike make assertions for "his own creative agency and ownership in an industry structured around the work-for-hire employment of creative talent" (2014: n. pag.). In a similar vein, Marc Singer offers a compelling interpretation of *The League of Extraordinary Gentlemen* that attends to the series' "dependence on copyright law, and its self-conscious struggles for creative autonomy" (2019: 94). In these and other comics from Moore, we see a narrativizing of the broader push for creative rights, recognition, and compensation, a movement that Moore joined with simultaneous enthusiasm and acrimony. While the British Invasion did not launch the fight for creator rights—a labor conflict that effectively started with the birth of the industry—the cultural legitimation that came with the British Invasion gave the movement new energy and urgency. The revisionist techniques associated with the British Invasion, moreover, displaced the fight into comics texts.

Moore outlines a deep history for creators' rights in an essay, "Buster Brown at the Barricades," featured in the politically minded fundraising anthology *Occupy Comics*. According to Moore's overview, disreputable and even criminal elements were integral to the US comics industry's founding. Moore cites Gerard Jones' popular comics history *Men of Tomorrow* when he notes that Harry Donenfeld, instrumental for the creation of DC Comics and thus the American comics industry, was an "erstwhile alleged rum-runner and pornographer" (2014b: n. pag.). Donenfeld's big hit for DC was Superman: the character created by Jerry Siegel and Joe Shuster is the prototype for the whole superhero genre. In a disgraceful precedent, however, DC's legal "appropriation of their character by means that some have seen as dubious would seem, unfortunately, to have laid a template for the business practices which have prevailed within the comics business ever since" (2014b: n. pag.). "Buster Brown" contends that industry practices such as work-for-hire and corporate authorship are acts of theft perpetrated by publishers that literally began as criminal operations.

An essential context for Moore's interventions in comics creators' rights struggle is the growth of the "direct market," beginning around the mid-1970s. During this time, Charles Hatfield writes, owners of specialty comics shops innovated how they did business by "going 'directly' to major publishers DC and Marvel and buying nonreturnable comics at deep discounts. . . . With this arrangement in place by 1975, a hobby hitherto centered on the trade of collectible old comics began to take in an increasing influx of new product" (2005: 22). The direct market led comics publishers to cater more intently to fan communities and to the expansion, and eventual bursting, of a collectors' market centered on speculations of a comic book's rising value.

Yet, if the direct market's evolution moved toward the interests of large publishers and mainstream fan communities and tastes, its roots are with countercultural, often self-published, "comix" of the 1960s and 1970s. Hatfield notes that comix "were the first movement of what later came to be known among fans as 'creator-owned' comic books" (2005: 16). Even as the direct market became enmeshed with corporate comics practices, it functioned as a space for elevating small publishers of creator-owned comics. At least initially, then, the direct market preserved and popularized much of the rebellious and independent spirit of the underground comix scene.

The direct market ultimately becomes a nexus for several trends—the collector's market; self-published, independent or alternative comics; and an increasingly influential comics fandom—that together contribute to spirited debates over creators' rights that grew louder and louder throughout the 1980s. Robert N. O'Nale Jr. (2014) names three self-publishing comics creators who took instrumental roles in the creators' rights movement: Dave Sim, writer-artist behind the mock-epic *Cerebus the Aardvark*, and Kevin Eastman and Peter Laird, the creative team responsible for the surprising pop culture phenomenon, *Teenage Mutant Ninja Turtles*. O'Nale recounts two comics creator summits held, the first organized by Sim in 1986 and the second convened by Eastman and Laird in 1988. These meetings included figures from the alternative comics realm, including writer-artist and later comics theorist Scott McCloud.

At the summits, O'Nale writes, "creators gathered . . . to discuss the problems of the industry and propose solutions that they could utilize as a united front" (2014: 970). The outcome of these gatherings was a document, *A Bill of Rights for Comics Creators*, also called the *Creator's Bill of Rights*. This document gives "12 concise, one-sentence statements of rights" including "The right to full ownership over what we fully create" and "The right to full control over the creative execution of that which we fully own" (O'Nale 2014: 970). *The Comics Journal* published the *Bill of Rights* in its September 1990 issue. O'Nale, on one hand, questions "how effective the Creator's Bill of Rights was at creating an effective, permanent change to the industry" but, on the other hand, maintains that "the document itself represents a small portion of an important movement by comics creators to take back their industry for themselves" (2014: 970). While one might quibble at O'Nale's closing intimation that the industry was ever the creators to take back, the comics creators' rights project was an indication, and precursor, of real changes in the comics industry.

To be sure, DC and Marvel, the major US publishers—and the primary beneficiaries of policies like corporate authorship—began responding to the changing climate. In his official history of DC Comics, Les Daniels notes how, in 1981, DC's new corporate leadership introduced a royalty plan that "gave percentages to writers and artists on all comics that sold beyond the break-even point" as well as "additional royalties for the creators of new concepts" (2013: 173). Yet, Daniels' authorized company history inflates the significance of this move, declaring it to be "a big step in a business where talent had traditionally received no share of the proceeds for their creations" (2013: 173). Daniels' careful language here avoids explicitly recognizing that while creators may receive *royalties* for "new concepts" they still did not own their creations. Moore makes this point in a 1988 interview: "The idea of creators owning their own creations is something that DC Comics, even in its new enlightened mode refuses to entertain. They've set up a new concern called Piranha Press, which they optimistically hope will attract work of the quality of *Love and Rockets* and *Maus*, yet DC will continue to own rights to all characters" (Sharrett 2012: 58). To this day, at Marvel and DC corporate ownership remains the norm.

Concerns over infringements on creator rights in fact led Moore to end his professional relationship with DC and swear off corporate publishers altogether. His frustrations were two-pronged. In addition to his exhaustion with industry practices hostile to labor, like corporate authorship and work-for-hire, Moore was attuned to threats of censorship. By the late 1980s, boundaries regulating content appearing in comic books were falling away, which in turn produced calls for new ratings systems to preserve the regulation of content "standards." Publishers' announcements to rate and classify books based on subjective evaluations of content were met with anger from comics creators: a petition signed by Moore and more than twenty other comics professionals denounced such measures as a form of self-censorship. In a 1987 essay, "The Politics and Morality of Rating and Self-Censorship," Moore announced that he will no longer work for publishers that, as he sees it, are firmly at odds with his ethical commitments to free expression. Moore's ire over the threat of censorship went hand-in-hand with his anger over unjust contracts and the inability to own rights for work produced at the company—so he refused to abide the rules.

If the creators' rights movement gained momentum throughout the 1980s, its impact arguably reached its apex with the 1992 founding of Image Comics, an upstart publisher that challenged the duopoly of Marvel and DC. Image was comprised of several art studios, publishing together as a collective under the Image banner. The consortium was formed by a group of hugely popular comics artists. These artists brazenly walked off best-selling titles to launch their creator-owned properties, in many cases also taking on writing and editing responsibilities. Although the Image titles were driven by their arresting, splashy art and outrageous new takes on the superhero, Moore was attracted to it as a symbol of the mainstreaming of the creators' rights movement. He would contribute scripts to several Image books, including *Spawn* and *Youngblood*, two major hits of the time. While it briefly seemed as if Image seriously threatened the dominance of Marvel and DC and was poised to upturn the established industry order, as

Daniels writes, it was not long until "some of the young Turks had problems turning in their drawings while simultaneously running their businesses and enjoying their success. Books appeared late, retailers took losses, and Image played its part in the industry slump of the 1990s" (2013: 258). By the late 1990s and into the new century, several Image creators were once again working for DC and Marvel in some capacity.

The overall, long-term legacy of the creators' rights movement, then, is ambiguous. In terms of Alan Moore's comics career, however, its impact is inarguable. A key figure in the movement, the outspoken Moore puts his money where his mouth is by refusing to work for DC or Marvel and not accepting royalties for adaptations licensed from his comics without his approval. Moore has also derived creative energy from the push for greater rights. In many cases, Moore's comics allegorize or otherwise contend with questions of creative ownership and rights. For Moore, artists' working conditions cannot be disassociated from their creative output.

Yet, at the same time, the relative failures of the creators' rights movement seem to have contributed to Moore's disenchantment with the medium and intense hatred of the industry. In the Introduction to his collection of interviews between Moore and various interlocutors, Eric Berlatsky observes that reading Moore's comments made "over a thirty-year period" illuminates, among other things, Moore's "initial enthusiasm toward, and then disillusionment with, the comics industry" (2012b: xiii). In a 2009 interview included in Berlatsky's book, Moore laments, "I love the comic book medium. It is one I shall never abandon. But the industry . . . [is] dark satanic mills" (Musson and O'Neill 2012: 194). More than a decade later, Moore's "love" for the medium may have faded. By 2016, Moore often critiqued the new cultural legitimacy for superhero narratives—it "looks slightly unhealthy" (Marchese 2016: n. pag.)—and admitted he is no longer "genuinely excited" about comics. The creators' rights movement's failure to break corporate comics' stranglehold on comics production is surely a factor for Moore's malaise with the medium itself, a dissatisfaction that not only underpins his caustic comments about the state of comics today but also seems to have directly contributed to his 2019 retirement from comics.

CHAPTER 2
KEY TEXTS PART ONE

Key Texts attends to Alan Moore's most important comics. Criteria for inclusion in these two chapters include comics' quality, impact, and markers of artistic evolution or a professional milestone. The organization of these two chapters is chiefly but not strictly chronological, for texts are also grouped thematically. Key Texts' chapters tell a story of Moore's career via glosses of his major works.

Invading British Comics

This initial section covers Moore's arrival on the British comics scene in the late 1970s and early 1980s. Moore, active in artistic collectives and underground music circuits, first wrote and drew comics that resemble the American comix tradition—itself connected to musical and artistic subcultures. Moore's early work shows a countercultural sensibility, even when married to popular genres and commercial tastes—a reconciliation that persists throughout Moore's comics career.

Origins

Alan Moore's comics career emerges out of a counterculture tradition. Maggie Gray rightly reminds us that Moore's early career as a cartoonist "developed in the context of the hippie counterculture and the British underground comix scene of the 1970s" (2017: 2). Moore's creative spirit was nurtured in art collectives like the Northampton Arts Lab and its successor, the Northampton Arts Group. In terms of comics output during this gestational period, Moore was "limited to a handful of single-tier, four-panel comic strips that were printed in a local underground monthly, *ANON*, the self-proclaimed 'Alternative Newspaper of Northampton'" (Millidge 2011: 42). "Anon E. Mouse," written and drawn by Moore, appeared in *ANON*'s first five issues, but, presaging future friction with publishers, Moore was frustrated by "heavy editorial interference" (Millidge 2011: 42). After placing cartoons in underground papers like *Dark Star* and Oxford's *Back Street Bugle*, as well as for larger outlets like the music weekly *New Musical Express*, Moore submitted samples to one of *NME*'s competitors, *Sounds*. In response, the magazine offered to make Moore's *Roscoe Moscow*, a half-page parody strip done under the pseudonym "Curt Vile," a regular feature. After sixty-one episodes, Moore ended *Roscoe Moscow* and replaced it with *The Stars My Degradation*, whose title is a riff on the classic 1957 science fiction novel by Alfred Bester, *The Stars My Destination*.

The Stars My Degradation maintains *Roscoe Moscow*'s parodic edge but turns attention from the earlier strip's emphasis on popular music toward lampoons of the science fiction and fantasy genres. *Stars* also features send-ups of popular British and American comics like *2000 A.D.* and the popular Marvel superhero series *Uncanny X-Men* (Moore had skewered superheroes before, in *Roscoe Moscow* and in *Dark Star*). Both strips for *Sounds* bear the strong influence of the counterculture comix movement; referring to *Roscoe Moscow*, Moore admits that it "owed more than a little to Art Spiegelman's *Ace Hole*" (qtd. in Parkin 2013: 65). Still, Moore's *Sounds* strips give glimpses of what will become trademark techniques and styles. Gray identifies *Roscoe Moscow*'s "high reflexive metafictional approach that gleefully destabilised the comic and highlighted its artificiality" (2017: 213). The self-referential satire found in *Roscoe Moscow* and *The Stars My Degradation* is continuous with the genre deconstruction that later cements Moore's critical reputation. Moore wasted no space in his *Sounds* strips, cramming each panel as well as the gutters between panels with sight gags and other marginalia, anticipating the bombardment of visual information and references in *Watchmen*, *League of Extraordinary Gentlemen*, *V for Vendetta*, and other later works. Ultimately, these two strips provided Moore's first real opportunity for steady comics work, itself significant, and signal creative developments to come.

Constantly seeking cartooning work during the late 1970s, Moore sent samples to his local free newspaper, *The Northants Post*. The editor liked Moore's pitch and, desiring a strip suitable for children, suggested that he develop a strip about a little cat. *Maxwell the Magic Cat* debuted in *The Northants Post* in 1979. For the strip's artwork, Moore abandoned his intricate stippling and overflowing panels for clean-line work and sparse compositions, often figures against empty backgrounds. Though the cartoon is at face value a simplistic children's comic, Moore infuses his strip with a bleak tone and cruel vision of the world that belies its superficial innocence.

Artist Eddie Campbell, one of Moore's acclaimed comics collaborators, says that though "Maxwell was to be in the idiom of a children's funny-animal comic" the strip "is permeated by a kind of psychotic daftness" (1986: 5) that reflects the spirit of the 1980s. Such mordant humor registers in Moore's penname, Jill de Ray, which Campbell explains "echo[es] the name of Gilles de Rais, a 15th Century French nobleman executed for the murder of over 140 children" (1986: 5). Moore's evocation of a notorious child-killer in his pseudonym for a purportedly children's comic gestures toward the irreverent comedic spirit behind *Maxwell*.

One can detect in *Maxwell* previews of his later, more ambitious comics. The introduction to the second collected edition of *Maxwell* stakes out the territory of the strip's accomplishments: "So the combination of straight (?) gags, explorations and exploitations of the strip form, and topical issues, comprised the Maxwellian repertoire, and always in those five flaming panels!" (Georgiou 1987: vii). As this description indicates, *Maxwell* attends to the mechanics of comics. An early strip moves through four text-less panels featuring an image of a static Maxwell against a white background; however, Maxwell's placements in the successive panels' borders changes. Some panels break up the image so that the cat's body appears at top while his head pokes up from the bottom. Maxwell thus appears to scrolling vertically within the panels. The punchline is the sliding Maxwell saying to the reader, "Perhaps someone could try giving the top left corner of the page a good swift thump??" (1986: 23). Intended humor derives from the strip's replication of a malfunctioning television screen's steady roll and riffing on an easy repair technique. The gag's comparison cues Moore's early interest in comics that foreground comics' formal affordances.

Moore wrote and drew *Maxwell the Magic Cat* until 1986, discontinuing it after the *Post* ran an editorial he found homophobic. By that point, he was a successful comics writer. When he started *Maxwell* in 1979, however, he was a fledgling professional. Moore's hunger for work and experience during this early period meant that he would accept projects even if he were not terribly enthusiastic about them. Examples of such halfhearted work are Moore's contributions to two transmedia franchises: *Dr. Who* and *Star Wars*. Neither of these mass media powerhouses counts Moore as a fan. He admits, "I have no interest in *Star Wars*; I have no interest in *Doctor Who*" (Khoury 2008: 71). Still, he was "happy to get any work that [he] could" (Khoury 2008: 71). "Black Legacy," Moore's first script for a June 1980 issue of *Dr. Who Weekly*, was drawn by David Lloyd—Moore's future co-creator of *V for Vendetta*—and he proceeded to provide back-ups for *Dr. Who* until late 1981.

Around this time, Moore also sold scripts to *Empire Strikes Back Monthly*, UK home for Marvel's *Star Wars* comics. This series title had changed from *Star Wars Weekly* to reflect its new publishing schedule as well as new branding for the 1980 sequel to the first *Star Wars* film. However, Moore found the debut *Star Wars* to be "utterly dreary" and did not "see any of the subsequent follow-ups" (Khoury 2008: 71). His disinterest is detectable in his *Star Wars* stories. Despite being solidly crafted and readable on their own merits, they do not capture the films' sensibilities and tone. In Moore's "Tilotny Throws a Shape," for example, Leia encounters amorphous sentient beings that are able to manipulate matter and claim to have "invented time and edges" (2017b: 221); the beings seem to be celestial deities of some sort. Moore's script also hinges on time paradoxes and metaphysics. All of these mind-bending narrative elements clash with *Star Wars*' style of operatic space fantasy.

Though Moore's *Star Wars* and *Dr. Who* material is minor, this licensed work coincides with his ongoing production of comix-style strips. When looked at in the context of Moore's total career, then, this overlapping of edgy, independent comix with work-for-hire scripts for licensed properties at a corporate publisher presents a tension that will persist throughout Moore's career: the tenuous reconciliation between comics' artistic possibilities and commercial, populist appeals.

2000 A.D.: *Short Stories,* Skizz, D.R. and Quinch, *and* The Ballad of Halo Jones

Moore's big break into British comics might be dated July 1980. That month saw Moore's debut in the pages of *2000 A.D.*, the legendary British science fiction comics anthology. *2000 A.D.*, founded in 1977, is a British comics institution known for cultivating comics talent. Dan Mazur and Alexander Danner write that the anthology "ultimately helped to launch the careers of many of the biggest names in science-fiction and fantasy comics" (2014: 166). Moore's initial contributions to *2000 A.D.* were scripts for two features, *Tharg's Future Shocks* and *Tharg's Time Twisters*, both of which had reputations as spaces for up-and-coming creators to hone their craft.

Moore used the *2000 A.D.* strips to cut his teeth as a comics writer, experimenting with technique and formula. Such experimentation often yielded fruitful results. For instance, Moore cites "The Reversible Man" from the *Time Twisters* feature in 1983's *2000 A.D.* #308 as "one of the best stories"

(Khoury 2008: 65) of his career. *Time Twisters* is distinguished from *Future Shocks* in that its entries focus on temporal disjunctions of some kind, an emphasis that usually lends itself to tales of time-travel or distortion. "The Reversible Man," drawn by Mike White, approaches the feature's theme askance: in four pages, it narrates in reverse the life and death—or, death and life—of a typical man, whose goofy inverted name, "Lamron Namron," belies the strip's melancholic tone. Beginning with a black panel signifying his death from a stroke, the strip then depicts his corpse spring to its feet before cycling, backward, through pivotal life events.

This defamiliarizing narrative device invests seemingly quotidian moments with affecting poignancy. For example, the panel featuring Lamron's accidental meeting of his future (or, past) wife—they bump into each other on a train platform—transitions to a panel of them standing apart, reading their newspapers in silence, overlaid with the caption "I never saw her again." This reversal makes visible the significance of seemingly incidental events: by not bumping into someone, he loses a life-partner (Figure 2.1). "Reversible Man" also anticipates Moore's interest in formal symmetries. Final panels move from Lamron's birth to blackness, with a transitional caption that reads, "I can't breathe any more. I can't . . ." (2011g: n. pag.). The strip ends as it begins: a black panel. These identical bookending panels stress the story's temporal estrangement, obscuring lines between birth and death. Future comics like *Watchmen* extend such compositional symmetries.

Eventually, *2000 A.D.* "promoted" Moore from one-off short stories to his own serialized narratives. The first of Moore's *2000 A.D.* serials was *Skizz*, a collaboration with artist Jim Baikie. *Skizz* debuted in the same 1983 "prog" (the magazine's quirky parlance for "issue") as the "Reversible Man" episode of *Time Twisters*; moreover, that prog appeared the same day that *Sounds* published its last installment of *The Stars My Degradation*. According to Gray, this publishing convergence symbolically marks Moore's transition "into the mainstream British comics industry" (2017: 238). For *Skizz*, Moore had an editorial mandate to capitalize on the hit film *E.T.*: create a strip about a kid and a cutesy alien. Yet, Moore dispenses with *E.T.*'s sentimentality, shifting the setting from a leafy American suburb to the benighted streets of post-industrial Birmingham, England. The key context for *Skizz* is the unemployment and social dislocation that define the early years of Margaret Thatcher's premiership. In this way, *Skizz* resembles not *E.T.* but *The Boys from the Blackstuff*, a seminal five-episode social drama that aired on BBC2 in the autumn of 1982.

Figure 2.1 Rewinding time in *2000 A.D.* Art by Mike Williams. "The Reversible Man." Copyright © Rebellion *2000 A.D.* Ltd. All rights reserved. Used with permission.

Skizz takes the basic narrative framework of *E.T.* but injects a social conscience and focus on English working-class experience that recalls *Boys from the Blackstuff*. One of Skizz's human allies, Cornelius, an unemployed pipefitter, speaks the refrain "I've got my pride" throughout the narrative, a likely homage to memorable *Blackstuff* catchphrases like "Give us a job" and "I can do that!" *Skizz's* backdrop resonates with its main plot about a stranded extraterrestrial who is met with suspicion and violence from the British government, represented by a shadowy investigative unit. The indignities and assaults faced by Zhcchz, whose name's pronunciation is approximated phonetically as "Skizz," are counterpoised with downtrodden but resilient working-class human characters: Skizz and his human allies all experience hardship from an uncaring, antagonistic state.

Hope for Britain's future as well as Skizz's well-being comes in the form of Roxanne "Roxy" O'Rourke, a punkish fifteen year old. The story's human protagonist, Roxy befriends and aids the stranded alien. Roxy protects Skizz from the "special emergencies commission," a government task force led by the brutal Jan Van Owen. Though he is never explicitly identified as an Afrikaner, Van Owen's foreignness is marked in his name, dialect, and comments about "his country." His attempts to subdue Skizz and weaponize his technology therefore relate to the racist, colonialist violence of apartheid. Van Owen is put at odds with an ethnically diverse English working class, who, by virtue of their affinities and alliance with Skizz, are likened to alien outsiders in their own country. In a crucial scene, Van Owen tries to intimidate Roxy's friend Loz in a billiard hall. But Loz reverses Van Owen's refrains about "back home" by countering, "John . . . you're not in your country now" (Moore 2005b: 74). Baikie punctuates this scene with a panel depicting Van Owen confronted by Loz and a cadre of multiethnic youths. Van Owen's grimacing face is foregrounded and turned toward the reader. Here, then, an old colonial sourly turns away from Britain's multicultural future.

The conflict between Van Owen against Roxy, Skizz, and their working-class compatriots represents a struggle over Britain's condition that is the narrative's real focus. Skizz regularly comments on the backwardness of his surroundings, evidenced by the hostility he glimpses in the culture, such as the televised professional wrestling that he recoils from at the start of the third installment. Such brutishness, however, contrasts with the tender affection between Skizz and Roxy, as well as Roxy's friends' commitment to aid Skizz in his quest to return home. Elements of decency and solidarity are even found within the British state. A scientist performing cruel tests upon a captured Skizz eventually protests, asking Van Owen of a particularly invasive procedure, "Look, is this really necessary?" (Moore 2005b: 55). The scientist acquiesces to Van Owen's authority, but qualifies, "for the record, I'm only doing this under extreme protest" (Moore 2005b: 56). Other state representatives express disapproval of Van Owen's methods, even if they give in or mount ineffectual resistance, such as a bureaucrat's threat to write an unflattering report (Moore 2005b: 71). Such bristling from Van Owen's partners make British politics, like its culture, into a site for internal conflict. *Skizz* thus leverages its realist setting and social theme to pursue a perennial science fiction premise: what direction might the future take?

Shortly after *Skizz* came Moore and Alan Davis' *D.R. and Quinch.* The title characters originated in a one-off *Time Twisters* story, but they proved popular enough with readers that they were put in a semi-regular series. *Time Twisters* introduced the titular teen ne'er-do-wells as immature college students from outer space: Ernie Quinch, a massive, tusked alien who "like[s] guns and starting fights" and whom his psychiatrist deems a "psychotic deviant," and his friend, former reform schooler Waldo Dobbs—known as "D.R.," for "diminished responsibility"—who is smaller and gremlin-like in his appearance, albeit with a rockabilly pompadour. During a summer break from school, this outrageous duo goes on a time-travelling joyride across the history "of this utterly worthless filth-pit planet called Earth." The strip's humor derives from its depiction of epochal events in Earth's planetary history—dating back to the extinction of dinosaurs—as consequences of D.R. and Quinch's reckless behavior. Their antics often involve weapons of mass destruction, from their use of a "thermo-nuclear bazooka" to instigate continental drift to the final and complete destruction of the planet in the future. Earth's geological formation, the rise of human civilization, and the planet's total obliteration, then, all turn out to be a mindless college prank.

As this summary likely indicates, irreverent humor is perhaps the comic's defining feature. "D.R. and Quinch Get Drafted!," for one, ridicules the imperialistic jingoism resurgent in Britain following the neo-imperialist Falklands War of 1982. While D.R. and Quinch initially recoil at being drafted by the Ministry of War, when visiting the enlistment office they glimpse the army's arsenal. Davis' wide rectangular panel depicts the grinning duo surrounded by exotic artillery; Moore's caption with D.R.'s narration reads, "He showed us a vast quantity of dangerous weapons. Many of these were so utterly horrible that I had not dared to believe they could exist. I felt totally patriotic" (2010b: n. pag.). Yet, the very same scene also parodies countercultural anti-war protest with a gaggle of aging hippie aliens who are "burning our draft cards and, like, chanting things" (2010b: n. pag.). The strip's satire of jingoistic nationalism, then, is offset by the parody of symbolic acts of resistance, which are mocked as unfocused ("chanting things") and, in the imagery of middle-aged protestors, outdated. Any discernible critique of militarism in the "Drafted!" strip, moreover, is deflated by the finale, in which D.R. sips a drink and stares into space in a reflective mood: "I suddenly saw the answer to all this senseless violence that afflicts us all. But, like, I didn't write it down or anything. And, like, y'know how it is—next morning I had totally forgotten what it was, man" (2010b: n. pag.). This closing gag explicitly articulates the comedic ethos of the strip: any gesture toward sincerity must be undercut and rendered moot.

In this spirit, while the titular characters are avatars for the strip's anarchic spirit, clashing with and undermining various forms of authority and respectability, they too are routinely humiliated and undermined. Any suggestions that D.R. and Quinch are admirably anti-establishment enemies of hypocrisy are punctured by the pair's own backbiting, venality, and foolishness. A certain social irresponsibility—for which Moore now expresses regrets—derives from this comedic ethos, one that refuses to maintain or legitimate any position other than the imperative to mock, a posture that risks making false equivalences and leaving unjust power structures untroubled. If nothing else, however, *D.R. and Quinch* is touchstone for the underappreciated importance of satire and self-referential comedy in Moore's body of work. Despite *D.R. and Quinch*'s limitations, it demonstrates a strong parodic current running throughout Moore's career.

By general consensus the best of Moore's *2000 A.D.* serials is the space fantasy *The Ballad of Halo Jones*, which Moore co-created with artist Ian Gibson. This series debuted in *2000 A.D.* prog 376 (July 1984) and ended in prog 466 (April 1986); its run is divided into three distinct books that narrate the journeys of their titular, everywoman heroine. To make her interstellar wanderlust meaningful, Book One is dedicated to Halo's point of departure: a giant, floating housing project known as The Hoop, which is moored to the Atlantic Ocean off the United States' eastern coast. The oval design of The Hoop functions as visual metaphor for the endless, pointless repetitions that constitute life for its inhabitants, a monotony that fuels Halo's desire for escape.

In Book Two, Halo has a series of misadventures as a server on a luxury space liner, and in Book Three she is recruited into an intergalactic expeditionary force, a sort of spacefaring French Foreign Legion. For these tales, physical action is heightened and the use of confusing futuristic lingo lessened, changes seemingly designed to placate two specific reader complaints from Book One. These changes do not compromise quality, though, and across its books *Halo Jones* hits many generic, tonal, and thematic registers: social comedy, action-adventure, and gritty drama. Moore and Gibson meant for the saga to span nine books, but other obligations, creative differences, and frustration with *2000 A.D.*'s work-for-hire policies left that ambition unfulfilled.

As it stands, though, *The Ballad of Halo Jones* might best be seen as an early example of Moore's commitment to multidimensional female protagonists. Insight into Moore's views on gender representation can be found in "Invisible Girls and Phantom Ladies," an essay on sexism in comics serialized in *The Daredevils* #4–6, approximately one year before *Halo Jones* debuted. In his essay, Moore critiques comics' histories of shallow characterization for women and gratuitous images of gendered violence. Moore ends the piece by pointing out the paucity of female creators on mainstream comics titles, despite no shortage of talented women working in the field.

Ballad of Halo Jones directly contends with questions of gender politics. When Halo joins the staff for a luxury space-cruiser at the start of Book Two, she reacts in shock at her revealing cocktail outfit: "But . . . showing my *feet* and everything! I mean, on the Hoop, if a woman did *that*, I mean . . . well, we just didn't do it" (Moore 2010a: n. pag.). This comment reflects how the material deprivations of the Hoop are multiply punishing for women, insofar as those hardships also intersect with and compound patriarchal notions of masculinity that in turn lead to displaced violence against women.

The feminist principles of Moore's *Daredevils* essay also register in Halo's characterization. Not only was a capable, rounded, nonexploitative female lead for an adventure comic series itself a rarity, but Moore and Gibson also insist on Halo Jones' universal representativeness. Both writer and artist have noted how they conceived Jones as a relatable everywoman figure. Book Two of *Halo Jones* even articulates this characterization explicitly. A prologue to the second installment is set in an "Institute of Para-Historical Studies" several centuries after the main narrative. The instructor, Dr. Brunhauer turns to "an obscure historical figure," Halo Jones. At the end of his talk, Brunhauer declaims his conclusions: "You see, I've spent 15 years researching this woman—and do you know what I've found out? It's this . . . *she wasn't anyone special*. She wasn't that brave, or that clever, or that strong. She was just somebody who felt crammed by the confines of her life. She was just somebody who had to get out. And she did it!" (Moore 2010a: n. pag.). Along with the description of Halo Jones as "obscure," this dialogue drives home, perhaps excessively, that the hero is unexceptional.

At the same time, the fact that research institutions study Halo's life and she has accrued enough mythology to create (mis)conceptions about her undermines her alleged ordinariness. Indeed, Brunhauer queries his class to recall "her most famous quotation," which turns out to be "Anybody could have done it!" (Moore 2010a: n. pag.). How many anonymous common folks have "a most famous quotation"? In her narrative's future, then, Jones stands contradictorily as a figure of historical fascination and historical amnesia. Thematically, however, this paradox imbues heroic significance and dignity to otherwise overlooked people. And at another level, Jones' purported typicality makes her a figure for reader projection. Within the context of the misogynist genre history Moore outlines in "Invisible Girls and Phantom Ladies", *Halo Jones*' attempts to induce its chiefly male audience toward cross-gender character identification is noteworthy in its own right. Such overtures toward more feminist representation of women in comics persist as a significant part of Moore's contribution to the comics field, despite— as later chapters address—criticisms that his own comics indulge in graphic representations of violence against women.

The Bojeffries Saga

One other notable early series is *The Bojeffries Saga*, co-created with artist Steve Parkhouse, which was born out of Moore's desire to do comedy— though the strip's exact form would not take shape until Parkhouse joined the project. The pair decided that *Bojeffries* would key in on the eccentricities of Englishness, a cultural identity they associated with idiosyncratic traditions and peculiar everyday details from their childhoods. Monstrosity became Moore and Parkhouse's vehicle for capturing the strangeness of Englishness: *Bojeffries* is a horror-comedy, a comical account of an oddball family of vampires, werewolves, and other monsters who inhabit an urban English community likely modeled on Moore's Northampton. *Bojeffries* debuted in 1983, with later entries sporadically released by various publishers across roughly three decades.

Critics frequently attribute *Bojeffries*' relative obscurity, at least within the American market, to its Englishness: the comics is immersed in English culture, customs, and sense of national identity. Gary Millidge claims "the strip is almost impenetrable to an American audience" (2011: 90). Moore similarly maintains that it seems "surrealistic to Americans" but, for him, it "describes the flavor of an ordinary working class childhood in Northampton. And the inherent surrealism in British life" (Khoury 2008: 60). One of the aspects of *The Bojeffries Saga* most often assumed to vex Americans is its use of language: Millidge cites Moore's "phonetic approach to conveying the characters' various dialects" (2011: 90) as a source of confusion for non-British readers. Yet, language in *Bojeffries* is weirder than mimetic representations of accents and speech patterns.

Consider the initial episode, "The Rentman Cometh," in which the Bojeffries patriarch, Jobremus, uses "duzzy" as colloquialism. Moore has clarified that this "evasive semi-swear" word was "peculiar to [his] first wife's father, who would use it instead of saying 'bloody,' or something like that" (Boyle 2014: n. pag.). *Bojeffries* plays with and ironizes language, stretching its boundaries and capacities for conveying meaning. In a 1984 interview, Moore addresses *Bojeffries'* "colloquial, idiomatic language" by emphasizing, "I love language—slang, jargon, poetry—how silly it can be, and how powerful and evocative" (Lawley and Whitaker 2012: 35). Rather than stressing the strip's representations of accents and dialects, then, Moore here turns to language's versatility and effects in the abstract. The strangeness of the Bojeffries clan mirrors the strangeness of language itself.

Reinventing Superheroes: Britain

From 1982 through 1988, Moore produced a body of superhero comics that constitute his breakthrough moment. While not all of Moore's major comics from this period sit fully or neatly within the superhero genre, they nonetheless can be organized in various ways around the figure of the superhero. To say that these revisionist superhero comics are the foundation of his critical reputation is no overstatement. The next two sections attend to this body of superhero comics.

Marvelman/Miracleman

Editor Dez Skinn launched *Warrior*, a black-and-white anthology, in March 1982. Eager to tap into new tastes and trends in British comics, Skinn formed Quality Communications, with *Warrior* as its flagship. This audacious monthly series was guided by two main principles: feature new stories in British comics' most popular genres and be a showcase for top talent. *Warrior* attracted writers and artists with the lures of greater creative freedom and opportunities for ownership rights.

Skinn was adamant that *Warrior* revive an old British superhero: Marvelman. When Steve Moore declined helming this relaunch he referred Skinn to his friend but no relation Alan Moore (Parkin 2013: 81), which led to a pitch and from there a script. Moore teamed with Garry Leach, a detail-oriented artist who was the only penciler with interest in the project that Skinn could find. Because Leach's perfectionism threatened deadlines he was soon replaced by frequent Moore collaborator Alan Davis. Later artists to work with Moore on the strip include Rick Veitch and Jon Totleben. Along with these artistic shufflings, the strip would also switch publishers. Financial disputes between Moore and Skinn resulted in *Marvelman* going on hiatus, ending with a cliffhanger in 1984's *Warrior* #21. The anthology was canceled shortly thereafter, so Skinn sought to license *Marvelman* to American publishers, eventually landing at Eclipse Comics. Eclipse began reprinting the stories from *Warrior*, resizing and coloring the black-and-white magazine pages. Fearing a lawsuit from Marvel Comics, however, Eclipse renamed the series and hero *Miracleman*. My analysis will use the two names interchangeably, depending on the context of the reference.

As background, the original premise for Marvelman was lifted from the American superhero Captain Marvel, created in 1939 by C. C. Beck and Bill Parker. In 1954 the UK publisher L. Miller and Son, Ltd. hired Mick Anglo to create a derivative hero, Marvelman. Anglo's *Marvelman* is a wish-fulfilment fantasy in which a goodhearted youth uses a magic word to transform into an adult with vast powers, including super-strength and flight. Young Micky Moran turns into Marvelman by saying "Kimota," a phonetic reversal of "atomic." This premise is lifted directly from Beck and Parker's hero, young Billy Batson, who uses the magic word "Shazam" to transform into the brawny adult superhero Captain Marvel. Also like Captain Marvel, Micky shares his powers with other youngsters, creating a makeshift "Marvel Family" comprised of teens and preadolescents inhabiting muscular bodies of superpowered adults. Anglo's ebullient and earnest, if silly and juvenile, Marvelman tales ran until 1963 when his publisher went bankrupt.

When the character reappeared in *Warrior*, then, the property had been dormant for nearly two decades, a publication gap narrativized by Moore and Leach. At the outset of the story, set in early 1980s Britain, an adult Mike Moran is happily married but struggling professionally as a freelance journalist; moreover, he is plagued by migraine headaches, half-remembered dreams of flying, and a word that remains elusively on the tip of his tongue. The word finally returns to him while reporting on an antinuclear proliferation protest that turns into a hostage situation. In the midst of danger, "the word is there, swimming before him, blurred through the fog of pain and nausea, but as recognisable as destiny" (Moore 2014d:

20). Upon at last recalling "Kimota!," Mike is transformed once again into Miracleman, instinctively acting to foil the hijack attempt while declaring, jubilantly, "I'm back!!" (Moore 2014d: 23). Notably, an aside in the action shows Miracleman pause and mutter to himself, "Eighteen years. Eighteen years, trapped in that old, tired body" (Moore 2014d: 22). This seemingly throwaway line foreshadows the idea that Miracleman is not Mike's mind and personality transposed into a superpowered body. Miracleman instead is a separate consciousness sharing dimensional space with Moran. Their memories and consciousnesses may blend, but they are nonetheless two distinct entities, a division with grave implications as the narrative unfolds.

Miracleman stands out for its transformation of an anachronistic hero into a more complex character, a move facilitated by relocation to a verisimilar modern setting. Ironically, the touted "realism" of *Miracleman* obscures its parodic qualities. Moore in fact cites the influence of Harvey Kurtzman and Wally Wood's "Superduperman," a 1953 spoof of Superman and Captain Marvel from the comics magazine *Mad*. Brian Cremins (2014) attends to the impact of "Superduperman" on *Miracleman*, noting how Moore adopts Kurtzman and Wood's use of exaggeration first to pinpoint and then to undercut the superhero genre's central features. Moore's extreme reinvention of Marvelman obviously contrasts, directly and indirectly, with the silly charm of the simplistic original series. Such contrasts, per Cremins, suggest that nostalgia for the consumer culture of one's childhood distorts perceptions of those products. Moore's "dramatic parody" amounts to a return to a comic book associated with childhood, which then in turn facilitates an interrogation of its genre's subtexts and ideological underpinnings from the vantage of adulthood.

To this end, again, Moore uses a signature strategy of parody: exaggeration. A trademark feature of superhero tales that Moore amplifies for parodic effect is violence. An early example of *Miracleman*'s engagement with comic book violence is Mike Moran-Miracleman's reunion with Jonathan Bates, formerly his superhero sidekick named Kid Miracleman. After the mysterious incident that retired the Marvel Family and caused Moran's amnesia, part of the series' elaborate backstory, Bates became an entrepreneur. Yet "Bates," Moran realizes, is in fact Kid Miracleman incognito, pretending to be human while secretly using his enhanced abilities to acquire wealth and power. His refusal to trigger a body-switch for two decades has kept the actual Bates' consciousness as a perpetual child in limbo. This revelation prompts a fight between the former superhero partners. The fight sequence that ensues foregrounds the danger such a fight poses for bystanders, showcasing the deep fear and trauma for ordinary people that a superpowered slugfest would actually inspire.

This scene foreshadows even greater violence: in the final act of Moore's run, Kid Miracleman seeks revenge on Miracleman with a notoriously graphic rampage across London. Artist John Totleben renders in hideous detail the decapitations, filletings, and disembowelments that Kid Miracleman inflicts upon London's citizenry. The images of this butchery are gratuitous in terms of their excess and explicitness—but not for being purposeless or done for shock value. Parody, dramatic or comic, exaggerates to reframe the familiar. In this spirit, the controversial goriness of Totleben's disturbing artwork dials up the frequently bloodless or unseen violence of superhero urban battles. An effect of this intensified violence is to draw attention to the brutality latent within but elided by typical depictions of superhero conflicts: the horror of superhero combat is made visible here. This move upends superhero comics' standard depictions of action and freewheeling urban destruction, unsettling the vicarious pleasures of those genre conventions.

Coextensive with *Miracleman*'s challenge to superhero comics' uncritical representations of violence is the series' skeptical orientation toward the power fantasies latent in the superhero figure. Dr. Emil Gargunza, one of Miracleman's antagonists, was a traditional "mad scientist" for the Anglo series; in Moore's retelling, Gargunza is an Argentinian geneticist recruited by Nazi Germany. In 1941, Gargunza, sensing Axis' defeat, defects to England where he is enlisted into a secret program within the Royal Air Force's intelligence division. A few years later this shadowy organization is charged with handling the remains of a crashed alien spacecraft found in the fields of Wiltshire. This momentous event initiates Project Zarathustra, the endeavor ultimately responsible for creating Miracleman and the Miracle Family. Miracleman's existence, then, is owed to his archenemy whose scientific expertise is aligned with Nazi eugenics, making the phenotypically White, virile, and lithe Miracleman a plain Nazi epitome. The Nietzschean allusion of Project Zarathustra, moreover, telegraphs the fascistic dimensions to the very idea of a superhuman. By making legible the overlap between the superhero and the Nazi *Übermensch* ideal, *Miracleman* suggests that despite superhero narratives' investments in justice the genre still internalizes, and often validates, fascistic notions of authority through strength and domination.

Miracleman thus finds fascistic undercurrents at the core of the superhero genre, a point reinforced as the Anglo stories are folded into Moore's narrative. In the revisionist backstory, Gargunza discovers that the downed starship's dead pilot is a member of an extraterrestrial species capable of harvesting multiple physical bodies for individual consciousnesses, so its mind can transfer to new embodiments suitable to various environmental conditions. When uninhabited, these spare bodies go into extradimensional limbo. Gargunza uses the alien genetics and technology to build superpowered bodies for his human test subjects, kidnapped runaways including Moran. While running tests, Gargunza puts the children into induced comas; inspired by a *Captain Marvel* comic book, he devises a superhero fantasy in their dreams to establish a "pseudo-logical" explanation for their powers. This move narratively reorients Anglo's *Marvelman* stories as fabrications deviously crafted by Gargunza to control his subjects. Allegorically, this reframing suggests that the naïve stories of Anglo—signifiers for a bygone era of comics storytelling—were cover for a more sinister reality. Anglo's *Marvelman* retroactively becomes a metonym for superhero comics' covert interpellations of readers into quasi-fascist ideologies of power, authority, and masculinity.

Moore's *Miracleman* conscripts Anglo's *Marvelman* to question the unstated logics of the superhero, especially the inherent assumption that a singular figure can determine, enforce, and perhaps impose what is just. Volume III of *Miracleman*, which began publication in 1987, pursues this critical thread most fully. This third volume, entitled *Olympus*, introduces another member of the Marvel Family, Miraclewoman. The narrative explains that Miraclewoman bided her time when Miracleman first reemerged but now seeks him out to end a cold war between two transdimensional species. Ultimately, Miraclewoman herself negotiates a settlement between the two sides by convincing them to begin sexual experiments with each other, arguing that the erotic and creative are more powerful than the thanatic and destructive. Miracleman and Miraclewoman embrace this insight, beginning their own sexual relationship and, along with it, a more proactive, procreative approach to superheroism. The final factor here is Kid Miracleman's atrocity in London. Chapman notes of Kid Miracleman's slaughter: "[w]ith its horrific images of indiscriminate killing (cadavers hanging from lamp posts, bodies impaled on the hands of Big Ben, the River Thames choked with the bodies of the dead), [the scene] has been read as an allusion to the Holocaust" (2011: 193). Miracleman and Miraclewoman rebuild London—and the world—as they see fit, responding to Kid Miracleman's fascistic terror with fascism's totalitarian ambitions.

The narrative turn here resituates the superhero figure within twin frameworks of utopia and dystopia. Upon the ashes of London Miracleman and Miraclewoman construct Olympus, an enormous and futuristic ziggurat. Olympus' name and architecture evoke temples of the ancient world, but it is retrofitted with the smooth, exotic contours of alien techno-ornamentation and topped with a gaudy "MM" insignia that brands it like a superhero's costume and paraphernalia. From Olympus Miracleman and Miraclewoman impose a new world order. They first eliminate nuclear weapons and power plants, then terraform the planet, "transporting ozone from a lifeless gas-giant" thereby "renew[ing] the stratosphere" (Moore 2015c: 101). Their environmental strategies intersect with political moves: Miracleman abolishes currencies and markets, declaring, "From August, everything is free; national surplus teleported to those nations most in need until they master self-sufficiency. Each soul shall have free clothing, food and shelter, entertainment, education, all requirements for a worthwhile life . . . with greater luxuries for those who wish to work providing the above" (Moore 2015c: 102). As Miracleman puts it, he and his allies "calculated costs and allocated profits, and we were accountants of utopia" (Moore 2015c: 102). Their regime rehabilitates criminals, cures diseases, and solves other social ills—all that seemed endemic to Thatcher's England. Miracleman and Miraclewoman's triumph is signified by their shimmering and thunderous super-sex, climaxed in the skies above London.

Miracleman builds a utopia, but it is disquieting. When Miracleman expresses ambivalence about his and Miraclewoman's measures, she responds, "Did humans ask such agonised questions about the free will of cows, or the destiny of fish?" (Moore 2015c: 100). Such condescension toward humanity is reinforced when Miracleman invites Liz Moran to undergo a process that will make her superhuman. Liz's refusal puzzles Miracleman, prompting him to prod, "You don't understand what you're turning down" to which she interrupts, "and you've forgotten what you're asking me to give up" (Moore 2015c: 116). This biting comment clearly refers to Miracleman's lost humanity. Indeed, earlier, Mike Moran exiles himself to interdimensional limbo so Miracleman can exist permanently, an act construed as suicide. Notably, in the series' first volume, a clue that Kid Marvelman is evil is the revelation that he betrayed and locked away his human counterpart. By severing his own ties to humanity, then, Miracleman seems to move closer to his fiendish enemy.

Moore's *Miracleman* ends with the eponymous character wearing a militarized version of his costume featuring pelisse with cape, a tunic, and epaulettes. Atop Olympus, sipping ambrosia and gazing at the horizon, Miracleman is his brave new empire's omnipotent ruler, transcending the superhero genre's standard typology of "hero" or "villain" or even "anti-hero." He instead resembles the totalitarian dictator's fantasy of himself as a benevolent, godlike leader. Rather than being altruistic preserver of the status quo, typical role of the superhero, Miracleman remakes the world with his power. With its ambivalent ending, *Miracleman* resonates with other Moore texts, like *Watchmen*, that question centralized authority and contend political underpinnings of the superhero genre.

Captain Britain

Miracleman's skewed perspective on the superhero genre surfaces, albeit more subtly, in another Moore comic from this period. Shortly after launching *Marvelman*, Moore joined Alan Davis on *Captain Britain*, published by Marvel Comics' UK division. Moore and Davis' run commenced in 1982's *Marvel Superheroes* #387, though the strip soon migrated to a new anthology, *The Daredevils*, before moving to yet another anthology, *The Mighty World of Marvel*.

Prior to Moore's hiring, Davis and writer Dave Thorpe gave Captain Britain a new costume, modeled on the military regalia of Buckingham Palace guards with a Union Jack motif, part of a revamp for the stagnant character. Thorpe and Davis retained the Arthurian elements to Captain Britain's backstory—his mentor is Merlyn, from a mystical realm, Otherworld—but layered in touches of British surrealism *à la* Lewis Carroll and Jonathan Swift. Such folkloric and literary influences were mobilized toward topicality. Disputes over the political content of these tales, however, led to Thorpe's departure. Still, Thorpe and Davis built a narrative architecture inherited and elaborated by Moore when he took over writing the comic book, mid-storyline.

Thorpe's run leaned on a conceit of alternate worlds: Captain Britain operates within a multiversal consortium, the Captain Britain Corps. Moore would later identify Captain Britain's home-world within this multiverse as Earth-616, a designation Marvel retained for its canonical continuity. As leader of the Corps, Merlyn sends Captain Britain to Earth-238, where the UK is run by a government patterned on the neo-fascist British National Party. In this parallel world, Captain Britain confronts Saturnyne, agent of the Dimensional Development Court, which has deemed Earth-238 so backward "it was holding back the development of all the other Earths" and hence needs "the push that would transform it into a properly evolved world" (Moore 2002a: n. pag.). The onset of this accelerated enlightening process,

The Push, is where Moore picks up the narrative; in so doing, Moore gradually transforms Thorpe's story into a covert meditation on national identity.

As the Push goes into effect, Moore reintroduces Mad Jim Jaspers, a Mad Hatter-esque villain with reality-bending powers. Jaspers capitalizes on the world-transformative energies of the Push, harnessing them with his considerable mental powers. The result is a physical projection of Jaspers' madness: Earth-238 is literally overrun by illogic. Furthermore, Jaspers reveals that he was once a politician who campaigned against masked heroes. Jaspers' anti-superhero legislation cuts the path for Earth-238's neo-fascist regime in the first place. A tool of Jaspers' conspiracy is his relentless android, the Fury—another *Alice in Wonderland* allusion—which assassinated the heroes already discredited by his demagogic politicking. Amid the Push's chaos, the lethal Fury disintegrates Captain Britain, but this death is short-lived. Next issue, Merlyn reconstitutes Captain Britain, atom by atom, a resurrection that visually represents Moore's creative process: as he puts it, "I feel I can't do anything with a character until I've destroyed and rebuilt him from the ground up" (Lawley and Whitaker 2012: 31). The rest of Moore's run attends to the aftermath of Jaspers' onslaught, during which an interdimensional court holds Saturnyne guilty for the madness outbreak on Earth-238. As she stands trial, the Jaspers of Earth-616 introduces his own anti-hero legislation, prompting Captain Britain and allies to prevent Earth-238's fate from reoccurring on his home-world.

Moore's completion of Thorpe's narrative set-up makes the apparent moment of salvation for the dystopian Earth-238 its actual doom, as the Push's transformative energies are hijacked by Jaspers. Moore undercuts the apparent *dues ex machina* of the Push, a panacea that by virtue of being imposed not only strips the citizens of Earth-238 of their agency but also absolves them of responsibility. Furthermore, the Kafkaesque tribunal before which Saturnyne later stands, in which the levers of justice are gummed up with bureaucracy and warped by conflicts of interest, suggests that the Court is hardly less authoritarian than the fascist government of Earth-238 that it meant to enlighten with the Push. By structuring his extension of Thorpe's narrative around unintended, disastrous outcomes of the Push, Moore suggests that political and social progress must be organic and popular: revolution from below, not top-down imposition or coercion.

In a similar vein, "Jaspers' Warp"—as the full Thorpe-Moore-Davis storyline is known—seems to endorse civic responsibility and vigilance. This duty is embodied by Captain UK, a refugee from Earth-238. Living anonymously on Captain Britain's Earth-616, she is again called into action when she sees Jaspers' demagoguery repeating itself. Moore introduces Captain UK as a nondescript Londoner; yet, captions explain over panels of her mundane routine, "She has terrible nightmares about death and blood and merciless things without faces. So do lots of other people. And like them, she has to squash them into the back of her mind and get up, and get dressed, and go to work" (Moore 2002a: n. pag.). Although Captain UK is a superpowered hero, these captions frame her experiences—"So do lots of other people," "And like them"—as commonplace. Emphasizing the typicality of Captain UK, Moore hearkens *The Ballad of Halo Jones* by suggesting that his heroes are not exceptional but representative. And by intervening in Jaspers' plot, Captain UK, Captain Britain, and their cohort of heroes perform what is in fact meant to be a shared civic responsibility, an ethic that sits in contrast to the Court's hierarchical administration as well as Jaspers' irrational lawlessness.

The conceit of alternate worlds with countless Captain Britain counterparts speaks to other political questions, namely the politics of national identity. Karin Kukkonen examines the "multiverse" as narrative device in superhero comics: "The multiverse is a set of mutually incompatible storyworlds. In principle these storyworlds can be viewed as counterfactuals; changing particular elements of the characters' situations, they relate to one other as 'what if'-versions" (2010: 55). We can turn from Kukkonen's description of comics "storyworlds" as counterfactuals to Catherine Gallagher's linkage of counterfactual narrative to national identity: "Historical counterfactuality seems . . . to be stimulated by a desire for national character" (2018: 193); indeed, "counterfactualism and national-character creation continue to go hand in hand" (2018: 236). *Captain Britain*'s counterfactual narrative examines national identity—perhaps an obvious point, since the hero's name and costume make him a plain emblem for nationhood. While "Britain" is a geographical, not national, designation, the term rhetorically unifies peoples of at least three nations with an identity. And colloquial interchangeability for "Britain," "England," and "UK" reflects national identity's fluidity, captured in the varied monikers of the Captain Britain Corps.

Captain Britain, then, uses comics' multiverse trope to dramatize the inflections of national identity. Members of the interdimensional Captain Britain Corps include Captain UK, Captain England, Captain Albion, and, alluding to the dystopian Britain of George Orwell's *1984*, Captain Airstrip One. Captain Empire, Captain Commonwealth, among others, also make cameos. Tellingly, Captain England and Captain Albion—signifying, respectively, an ethnic-national identity and a mythologized organic culture—are antagonistic figures. The more cooperative, heroic members are Captain Britain and Captain UK, who, in contrast with the Anglocentric Captain England and the archaic Captain Albion, embody versions of national identity rooted in heterogeneity and collectivity. Captain Britain is no idealized hero—he is in fact a bit of a toff—but his instincts are honorable. His partnership with Captain UK, which culminates with a kiss, seems to endorse a heterogeneous national identity associated on one hand with a multiethnic, multinational construct, Britain, as well as, on the other hand, a coalitional political entity, the United Kingdom.

Like *Miracleman*, then, Moore's *Captain Britain* focuses on genre tropes. In both cases, Moore zeroes in on superhero conventions. *Captain Britain* marshals the genre's types, tropes, and clichés—in particular, its alternate worlds device—toward a commentary on national identity.

V for Vendetta

Moore and David Lloyd's *V for Vendetta* debuted alongside *Marvelman* in *Warrior* #1, but it was canceled mid-story in 1985. After Moore became a star in US comics, DC Comics provided an opportunity to finish the narrative. Beginning in 1988, DC reprinted the *Warrior* episodes of *V for Vendetta*, colorizing the black-and-white strips using a muted, subtle palette. Following the reprints, DC published the story's previously unseen conclusion. Like *Miracleman's* sporadic and protracted publication schedule, the halted and resumed serialization of *V for Vendetta* means its development spans the decade.

Vendetta is not a straight superhero story, but mixes superhero elements with other narrative styles, notably from the future dystopia genre. Still, superhero elements are present and the revisionist sensibilities and formal innovations that characterize Moore's superhero work animate the series.

V for Vendetta depicts a fascistic near-future England. An enigmatic protagonist, called V, has superhero qualities: flamboyant costume with mask and cape, secret identity, theatrical mien, hidden lair, and enhanced physical capabilities. V even recruits a sidekick of sorts, Evey, the narrative's point-of-view character. Moore explains that "originally [*Vendetta*] was just thought of purely in terms of an adventure strip" or "an unusual take upon the superhero strip" (Khoury 2008: 74), but he and Lloyd realized that it "*could* be a love story, it *could* be a political drama, it *could* be, to some degree, a metaphysical tale. It could be all these things and still be a kind of

pulp adventure, a kind of super-hero strip, a kind of science-fiction strip"
(Khoury 2008: 75). The result is a hybrid genre comic.

Countless influences inform *V for Vendetta* and its inscrutable
protagonist. In "Behind the Painted Smile," an essay originally published
in *Warrior* #17, Moore shares a free-association exercise he conducted in
order to catalogue the various "concepts that [he] wanted to reflect in *V*":

> Orwell. Huxley. Thomas Disch. *Judge Dredd*. Harlan Ellison's
> "Repent, Harlequin!" Said the Ticktockman. "Catman" and
> "Prowler in the City at the Edge of the World" by the same author.
> Vincent Price's *Dr. Phibes* and *Theatre of Blood*. David Bowie. The
> Shadow. Nightraven. Batman. *Fahrenheit 451*. The writings of the
> *New Worlds* school of science fiction. Max Ernst's painting "Europe
> After The Rains." Thomas Pynchon. The atmosphere of British
> Second World War films. *The Prisoner*. Robin Hood. Dick Turpin
> . . . (Moore 1990d: 270)

The parataxis of this list mirrors the comic's onslaught of quotations and
allusions. Annalisa Di Liddo writes, "The allusions and quotations are open
for the readers' detection—but the amount is overwhelming, and their
nature is re-elaborated and reshuffled to such an extent that an estranging,
almost whirling effect of polysemy is guaranteed" (2009: 41). *Vendetta*'s
storm of references include classic books and movie posters lining the walls
of V's lair, and V's quoting of Shakespeare. Other citations are subtler: tonal
and thematic nods to various texts and traditions.

References accumulate and collide so incessantly that they lose
definition, a blending visually captured in Lloyd's art, which dispenses with
hard line work for its figures. In a similar vein, Book Two, "This Vicious
Cabaret," opens with a musical prelude: the narrative is told in panels with
captioned lyrics, accompanied by a musical score. *Vendetta* not only cites
its diverse sources of inspiration and influence but also absorbs other forms
into its comics body.

These references together are marshalled toward a political allegory for
1980s Britain. Specifically, *Vendetta* rebukes the conservative turn taken
by British, especially English, political culture during Margaret Thatcher's
premiership, and its mixing of sources and blending of genres relates to
its anti-Thatcher stance. To be sure, reading *V for Vendetta* as a political
parable for Thatcher's UK does risk overgeneralization. Parkin addresses this
potential for flattening out *Vendetta* by rightly clarifying that "Thatcherism

changed radically between 1981 and 1988" (2013: 323), or the span of time from Moore's conception of the book for *Warrior* until his completion of it at DC Comics. For this reason, Parkin explains, *Vendetta* neither is a direct "response" to any particular political event or development, nor is it an extrapolated "projection of where British politics might head after 1982" (2013: 325). However, *Vendetta* can still be read as a rejoinder to Thatcherism in that its dystopian future speaks to and is continuous with the Thatcherite present. In this respect, *Vendetta* is a "nuanced, personal response to a specific period of British political life" (Parkin 2013: 323), one that diagnoses a new British political conjuncture as dystopian, capturing what it *feels* like to live in Thatcher's Britain.

One specific political event, however, acts as a reference point that can help clarify the comic's confrontation with Thatcherism in a way that also accommodates the series' genre-blending. The controversial Clause 28 of the 1988 Local Government Bill "stated that local authorities should not 'intentionally promote homosexuality or publish material with the intention of promoting homosexuality'" (Parkin 2013: 243). Thatcher's government supported this Bill, but its passage, notably, came with Labour votes and inflammatory rhetoric from both parties. At the time, Moore was living in a nonconforming polyamorous romantic relationship, which in his view put him in solidarity with targeted queer communities. His disgusted response to Clause 28 and the political atmosphere surrounding it was to spearhead a protest comic entitled *AARGH!*—or *Artists Against Rampant Government Homophobia!*—an anthology featuring a remarkable roster of comics talent.

Clause 28 as a specific piece of legislation arrived too late in the composition of *V for Vendetta* for it to influence the comic directly, but the climate surrounding the bill and Moore's revulsion at the clause's political legitimation of existing cultural homophobia offers an entry point for unpacking the politics of *V for Vendetta*. Moore alludes to Clause 28 in his introduction to the series' collected edition, first published in 1988, suggesting that he sees passage of the Bill as emblematic of the political culture that inspired *Vendetta*. From this view, queerness is axis for *Vendetta*'s confrontation with Thatcherism and a logic for its blending of genres and references.

Queer reading communities, notably, have adopted V as a representative hero. For all intents and purposes, V is a "male" character: male pronouns are used by others to refer to V, and Lloyd's rendering of the character's physique plus the iconic Guy Fawkes mask—never removed in the series—seem to code the character as male. Despite this self-presentation, V is not the typical emblem of white heteronormative masculinity historically presented by the superhero figure. The perpetually masked face of V means that it could look like anyone, particularly the face of someone singled out for oppression. As Di Liddo notes, "V's face might belong to any of the people the dystopian system has marginalized" (2009: 115), populations that the lyrics of "The Vicious Cabaret" ominously note are now absent in England: "There's mischiefs and malarkies / but no queers / or Yids / or darkies / within this bastard's carnival / this vicious cabaret" (Moore 1990d: 92–3). And in fact according to backstory provided in the narrative, V is literally a marginalized figure.

The first book of *Vendetta* details V's revenge against anyone associated with medical experiments conducted at a facility called Larkhill. This military-run laboratory detains prisoners with minoritized racial, ethnic, and sexual identities. The project ends after the mysterious prisoner from room five—the cell door uses the Roman numeral "V"—concocts napalm and mustard gas from on-site gardening chemicals. Ellen Crowell argues that "V's foray into the domestic art of gardening" (2009: 29) cues homophobic stereotypes of genteel aestheticism, but the revelation that gardening chemicals were used to build bombs means that "such thinking is swiftly undercut. . . . Moore, like V himself, deploys homophobic stereotypes, including the association of art with passivity, to explode them" (Crowell 2009: 30). Characters and readers alike learn this backstory via the diary of a Larkhill scientist killed as part of V's revenge. As investigators examine this journal's contents they note missing pages, asking, "What was on the missing pages, eh? His name? His age? Whether he was Jewish, or homosexual, or black or white?" (Moore 1990d: 85). Here, V is aligned with victimized populations but not identified as one; he thus embodies marginalization in the abstract.

Put differently, V is a queer character. Used in this context, queerness is a term that retains its association with gay identity and the gay rights movement, but expands to encompass a broader subversive nonconformity to dominant, hegemonic categories and expectations. From this sense of queerness comes queer theory, which Ramzi Fawaz—writing about the superhero as a queer figure—defines as "a body of knowledge that concerns itself with the ways queer or nonnormative figures generate alternative desires, bring into view unexpected objects of passionate attachment, and facilitate the production of novel forms of kinship and affiliation"

(2016: n.p.). Queer theory links "the heterogeneity of local, intimate, erotic attachments to the broader scales of political desire, aspiration, and affiliation in public life" (2016: n.p.). By affiliating V with marginalized identity generally and homosexual identity more specifically, *Vendetta* nods to the political potentials in the notion of "queer" as non-normativity.

Yet, a reading gaining traction among fan communities posits that V is queer in a more overt way, specifically the ways in which the text might in fact code V as transgender. This trans reading of V emphasizes the Larkhill researchers' interest in hormone treatments, as well as the changing impression of V's unmasked face by one of the scientists who tortured him: at the time of V's imprisonment, this scientist declares, "His face is very ugly" (Moore 1990d: 81), but years later, she sees his face again and whispers, "It's beautiful" (Moore 1990d: 75). Taking such moments to signify some form of embodied transition may be a bit strained; significant, though, is that queer reading communities locate these resonances (Nunnally 2017: n. pag.). And there are other reasons for embracing V as trans icon. The opening scene of *Vendetta* contrasts the dressings of V and his future coconspirator, the teenaged Evey: he donning his mask and cape, while she prepares for sex work by dressing in miniskirt and heavy makeup. This paralleling suggests that V's superhero-like presentation is akin to Evey's gender performance of sexualized and commodified femininity.

Other moments figure gender performance, queerness, and nonconformist sexual identity into the narrative. One party official, David Almond, is sexually impotent, and in a fairly heavy-handed moment he violently rejects his wife's advances as he obsessively polishes his gun. The unstable leader of the ruling fascist party, who has the doubly gendered name Adam Susan, is a virgin who loves the government's supercomputer system, Fate. Of course, homosexuality itself is repeatedly marked as an oppressed identity, making openly queer characters either absent or victimized. Nevertheless, the presence of queer nonconformity inhabits *V for Vendetta*, with no example being more profound than the story of a lesbian inmate killed at Larkhill. The defiant autobiography of Valerie, written on bath tissue in Room IV at Larkhill, is secretly passed to V in the adjacent room: her tale of resilience against oppression inspires him and is a resource of hope for his insurgency.

V later reuses Valerie's letter in a cruel, elaborate hoax that he concocts for Evey. After tricking Evey into thinking that she has been captured by the fascist government V holds her captive and tortures her, physically and psychologically. Valerie's letter, strategically left in her cell to replicate V's own experience, gives Evey the resolve to resist her faux torturer's demands. Evey emerges from the other side of this merciless training having abandoned any illusions that freedom is possible under the current regime; her consciousness raised, she is now mentally prepared to join V's revolution. Evey's torture leaves her emaciated and bald. While her ragged appearance clearly evokes images of Holocaust prisoners, her baldness and angularity in Lloyd's drawings also give her an impression of conventional masculinity. At the end of this sequence, V takes Evey to a rooftop during a rainstorm for a ritualistic cleansing. Her nude, frail body is desexualized, in contrast to her gender performance at the narrative's outset. V instructs her in this moment to "become transfixed. Become transformed . . . forever" (Moore 1990d: 172). This language perhaps calls to mind "transition" as Evey steps into her newly realized subjectivity and embodiment. In fact, by replicating his own experiences for Evey's reeducation, down to the same inspirational letter from Valerie, V in a sense invites Evey to assume his own ostensibly masculine identity.

Such moments that telegraph trans queerness and the queer-positive narrative threads in *Vendetta*—from heroic gay figures like Valerie to its alignment of totalitarianism with homophobia—complicate a binary political conflict that animates the main narrative: anarchism versus fascism. Moore said in 1984, "I perceive two absolute principles of politics: fascism and anarchy. All the others are just subdivisions. The only question in politics is, '*Should* we be ruled?' That's what's being discussed in *V for Vendetta*" (Lawley and Whitaker 2012: 34). Moore's theorizations of these political categories go relatively unspecified in *Vendetta*; instead, they represent more general political impulses or tendencies. According to Moore, for him "anarchy" refers to a leaderless society: "All it means, the word, is no leaders. An-archon. No leaders" (Killjoy 2009: n. pag.). Moore posits this anarchist ideal as one centered on full individual responsibility for one's flourishing matched with respect for the equivalent autonomy of others. Anarchy, for Moore, represents a natural condition; "structures of order" are "alien" and "the idea of leaders is an unnatural one" (Killjoy 2009: n. pag.). Correspondingly, while the features of British fascism in the comic can be inductively articulated based on textual representations—it hinges on racism, patriarchy, and isolationism—Moore positions fascism in *Vendetta* to reflect his view that fascism, conceptually, reduces to "complete abdication of personal responsibility" (Killjoy 2009 n. pag.) and therefore is anarchy's opposite extreme. *Vendetta* plainly favors anarchism, though its advocacy is counterweighted by V's moral transgressions as well as the complex motivations and interior lives of fascist characters.

Despite seeming to set up a conflict between diametrical political orientations, fascism and anarchism, *Vendetta's* queerness questions that opposition. V and his fascist opponent, Adam Susan, are mirror versions of each other. After all, V's playbook for rebellion include violence and mass murder, surveillance, propaganda, and intimidation—all of which are done first by Susan's fascist government. Consider too Evey's imprisonment, torture, and subsequent radicalization: she comes out of the experience transformed, thus casting subjection to violence as the catalyst to a raised consciousness. Once Evey declares that she would rather die than sign a false confession, her jailor—V in disguise—admits, "Then there's nothing left to threaten you with, is there? You are free" (Moore 1990d: 162). At this point, Evey is allowed to leave her cell to discover that she is in V's secret headquarters. V justifies the torture, explaining that he did it "Because I want to set you free" (Moor 1990d: 167). V's language of freedom contrasts with fascist leader Adam Susan, who sees only the "freedom to starve. The freedom to die, the freedom to live in a world of chaos" (Moore 1990d: 38). Freedom, for Susan, is a danger in a hostile world. Susan's and V's values are at odds, but both hold that acts of coercive violence are necessary as the tools to bring about liberation through ideology.

Salvation, for V and Susan alike, is obtained by violence upon physical bodies. Ideology, fascist or anarchist, interpellates its subjects through coercive violence upon physical bodies, and likewise ideology is mapped onto physical bodies. V, for example, is frequently talked about as if he were more idea than human being. After V dies, Evey refuses to remove his mask: "If I take off that mask, something will go away forever, be diminished because whoever you are isn't as big as the idea of you" (Moore 1990d: 250). If V is a human body transcended into an idea, the fascism of Norsefire is an idea that aspires to embodiment: the Norsefire government uses anatomical names for its ministries, such as the Mouth for its propaganda department and the Finger for its secret police. In both cases, ideology colonizes the body and the body is metaphor for the ideology.

Mirroring V and anarchy with Susan and fascism schematizes the comic's political conflict. That fundamental political conflict, however, ultimately turns out to be something of a red herring. On this note, Moore acknowledges that *Vendetta's* "real story" is not the plot, but what occurs "in the subtext . . . between the lines" (Lawley and Whitaker 2012: 32). The idiom "between the lines" is felicitous, for it not only indicates the prioritization of connotation over denotation but also cues the weakened figure lines of Lloyd's art. Even when colorized, the absence of hard, inked borders around Lloyd's drawings and dialogue balloons stress the comic's thematic murkiness. Long-standing distinctions are rendered as illusions—a move that also syncs with the comic's blurring of genre lines. Here we return to the motif of queerness, for queerness' resistance to binary choices dovetails with *Vendetta*'s rejections of categorical purities, generic as well as political.

The queer bodies and resonances featured through *V for Vendetta* index a hidden alternative to the equally violent and consumptive—if not morally equal—binaries of fascism and anarchy. To be clear, though *Vendetta* problematizes V's anarchism by making him a pitiless terrorist, V's stirring discourse of emancipation and alignment with the oppressed mean the text's political sympathies ultimately favor V's (and Moore's) anarchism. Likewise, if *Vendetta*'s fascists indeed get rounded, nuanced characterizations, they still are depicted as unsavory or at least compromised figures. But, as Todd A. Comer puts it, the true power and liberating potential of V's anarchism in the face of authoritarian oppression is not in "V's 'badass' status as an un-killable idea" but rather in his "connection to gay sexuality" (2012: 110). *V for Vendetta* rebukes the Thatcherite conservatism of its historical moment by turning to the impure contaminations of queer mixture and play as a true alternative; similarly, the comic's extreme intertextuality suggests the liberating possibilities for the medium when fixed generic and aesthetic borders are dismissed and violated.

Reinventing Superheroes: America

Moore's literate, revisionist superhero narratives in *Captain Britain*, *Miracleman*, and *V for Vendetta* not only raised his profile in the British comics scene, but also drew the attention of American publishers. In 1983, Moore began writing for DC Comics, one of US' comics "Big Two" publishers. This work involved scripts for some of DC's flagship superhero characters, including pop culture icons Superman and Batman, and includes a true comic book masterpiece: *Watchmen*.

The Saga of the Swamp Thing

In 1983, DC Comics editor Len Wein contacted Moore with an offer to take over writing responsibilities for a middling horror comic, *The Saga of the Swamp Thing*, whose titular marsh monster Wein himself co-created with artist Bernie Wrightson in 1971. Moore would have been unknown to most US comics readers, but at this point in their history DC was attempting to win back considerable market share lost to industry leader Marvel Comics and, relatedly, shed its reputation as a staid, establishment publisher. For these reasons, DC was increasingly recruiting British comics talent who, it was believed, could bring fresh perspectives to their stable of characters. Moore would go on to write *Swamp Thing* for over forty issues; his primary collaborators were Stephen Bissette, John Totleben, and Rick Veitch. Quickly hailed a classic, Moore's *Swamp Thing* run changed his career.

DC gave Moore room to experiment and he made substantial changes from the onset. Shockingly, in *Swamp Thing* #21 Moore rewrote the character's origin: originally presented as a human scientist named Alec Holland transformed by radioactive chemicals into a mossy bog-creature, in Moore's hands Swamp Thing learns that it is swamp flora that absorbed lingering particulates of consciousness from Holland's irradiated corpse. Swamp Thing is not a man turned into a plant, but a plant that thinks it was a man. This revelation reorients the character and drives the rest of the series narratively and thematically; it encapsulates Moore's transformation of *Swamp Thing* from cult title done in the style of midnight horror features into a work of literate, contemplative horror. The origin change also speaks to Moore's reputation as a master revisionist.

On this note, while Moore's *Swamp Thing* is famous for its erudite take on contemporary horror, the comic is also of a piece with Moore's superhero revisionism. *Saga of the Swamp Thing* blends horror conventions with elements from superheroes and other genres to create a hybrid narrative. If nothing else, Moore's drastic retooling of the character and his origin is often taken as prototypical case of the revisionist method that Moore brought to bear on superhero characters.

The genre identity of Moore's *Swamp Thing*, then, is murky. Moore has fed this confusion. At the time of writing *Swamp Thing* he generally spoke of the comic in terms of horror. In a 2003 documentary, however, he refers to *Swamp Thing* as only "ostensibly a horror comic" (*Mindscape* 2008), and in a 2008 interview he stresses how he saw the character and comic in terms of DC's superhero line: "So we started to build up the supporting cast, Swamp Thing's relationship to the DC universe" (Khoury 2008: 88). Such statements run contrary to commonplace accounts that position *Swamp Thing* as straight horror. For example, in a 2005 retrospective review of Moore's run, the pop culture website *ign* defensively asserts that *Swamp*

Thing "is not a superhero book" and its quality suffers when it verges "into the 'simple' realm of capes and masks" (George 2012: n. pag.). Yet, Moore recalls that he "thought that Swamp Thing would probably do better as a character than [sic] do better as a title creatively and commercially, if he was more integrated in the DC universe" (Khoury 88). Such comments highlight *Swamp Thing*'s brand of genre mixture.

To this point, consider the roll call of characters from DC's stable who appear as guest stars during Moore's *Swamp Thing* tenure. In Moore's second issue, Swamp Thing contends with the Floronic Man, a plant-themed villain of minor hero the Atom. Later guests include the Justice League of America, DC's preeminent super-team; numerous "supernatural," magical, or horror-themed characters, such as The Demon, Deadman, Phantom Stranger, the Spectre, and Dr. Occult; well-known, commercially viable characters like Batman, Superman's archenemy Lex Luthor, and the Green Lantern Corps; and, finally, science fiction-tinged characters like Adam Strange, Metron, and Darkseid. These guest stars and more appear in nearly half of Moore's issues. Lance Parkin in fact cites their inclusion as source of creative friction on the book, for Bissette objected to the use of so many superheroes (2013: 155). Moore himself bristled at the editorial mandate that some issues feature narrative links to the 1986 company-wide maxi-series *Crisis on Infinite Earths*. Nevertheless, these crossover ties as well as the parade of superhero guest stars situate Swamp Thing's story firmly within DC "shared universe" of superhero comics. Far from a standalone horror title with its own self-contained narrative rules and an atmosphere separate from DC's superhero line of comics, Moore's *Swamp Thing* is immersed in DC's mainstream continuity.

Moore's choices for guest stars are significant. The majority of characters to appear in his *Swamp Thing* straddle generic lines. For instance, the Demon, the Spectre, and Deadman's physical appearances—respectively diabolic, ghostly, and skeletal—visually cue horror, but all three complement their terrifying visages with costumes redolent of superhero bodysuits, blending horror and superhero aesthetics. Issue #27, which ends an arc featuring the Demon, is dedicated to that guest star's creator, Jack Kirby: renowned as a superhero artist, Kirby's character designs often bear the influence of the monster comics he drew prior to the 1960s superhero boom. Moore describes his guest star selections as an attempt "to create a DC supernatural milieu" that would "relaunch the idea of other supernatural characters as a viable alternative to mainstream super-heroes" (Khoury 2008: 89). The characters' utility is to reimagine the superhero in terms of horror.

From this angle, even the appearances of traditional superheroes speak to *Swamp Thing*'s generic hybridity. When the Justice League appears in issue #24, the opening page depicts the League's satellite fortress overlaid with captions: "There is a house above the world, where the over-people gather. There is a man with wings like a bird. . . . There is a man who can see across the planet and wring diamonds from its anthracite. There is a man who moves so fast that his life is an endless gallery of statues" (Moore 2009d: 111). Andrew Hoberek reads this passage for its uncanniness, noting that its account of the super-fast superhero The Flash's subjectivity "hint[s] at the existential horror of being someone for whom the rest of the world seems to be frozen in place" (2014: n. pag.). This sense of estrangement recalls "an old science-fiction device, employed by authors who represented the subjective reality and ironic downsides" of superpowers (2014: n. pag.). Moore therefore recasts DC's iconic superheroes using tropes from horror and science fiction.

Science fiction elements, moreover, flourish late in Moore's run with the guest appearances of intergalactic explorer Adam Strange. The title of the story introducing Strange in issue #57, "Mysteries in Space," is homage to *Mystery in Space*, a science fiction anthology once published by DC and in which Strange appeared. This reference, plus appearances by the otherworldly brothers Cain and Abel, narrators of DC's horror-mystery anthologies *House of Mystery* and *House of Secrets,* are *Swamp Thing*'s acknowledgments that DC's publication line has long exceeded superheroes and that superheroes themselves intersect with other genres.

Despite *Swamp Thing*'s genre hybridity, the comic certainly fits within a horror tradition. At the time of its publication, Moore and DC certainly publicized *Swamp Thing* as a horror title. In a 1984 interview Moore confirms his interlocutor's description of *Swamp Thing* as "essentially a horror book" (Lawley and Whitaker 2012: 36). A 1984 featurette video produced by DC to promote *Swamp Thing* features Moore explaining that his creative approach is "to focus upon the reality of American horror" because "to really frighten people you have to somehow ground the horror in their own experience" ("Swamp Thing Interview"). This strategy, he details in a later, retrospective interview, meant "link[ing] up the elements of fantasy horror from our imaginations . . . with real life horrors—racism, sexism, pollution, the collapse of the environment—and thus lend these social issues some of the weight that fantasy fiction could offer" (*Mindscape* 2008). *Swamp Thing* leverages visceral fears of horror to contend allegorically with social dilemmas and anxieties.

The scale and type of these allegories vary considerably. Issue #40, for example, shifts the setting from the Louisiana bayou to Maine for a werewolf story in which Swamp Thing is largely a supporting character. This issue focuses on a woman named Phoebe, who is introduced on the first page at a market. A caption narrates how the cashier separates Phoebe's purchase of tampons into a separate bag, "as if to protect her other groceries" (Moore 2010c: 134). The cashier's attempt at discretion, suggesting internalized distaste and embarrassment over menstruation, parallels with intercutting panels that describe and depict ancient Native American rituals of punishment and isolation for menstruating women. Although this anxiety over women's bodies is thus presented as cross-cultural and transhistorical, its present manifestation is tied to a patriarchal and consumerist contemporary culture. During this sequence, Phoebe's surroundings are littered with advertisements for domestic products ("good news for housewives!"), disposable douche, and a pornography store—all expressions of sexist and commodified constructions of femininity.

Phoebe, it turns out, is a werewolf. Swamp Thing confronts her, and when he asks, telepathically, "What . . . are you?" she responds, "I am woman" (Moore 2010c: 146). If Phoebe's transformation, induced monthly by a full moon, risks positing menstruation as monstrosity, the constant gendered insults directed at Phoebe as well as the targets of her rage once transmogrified—she first attacks her misogynist romantic partner before rampaging through the porn shop and grocer—make clear the comic's critical intent. Phoebe hates her lycanthropy—described in the title as "The Curse," itself a play on a colloquialism for menstruation—and in the end kills herself with the kitchen knives advertised at the tale's outset. This suicide is construed as an emancipatory release. The horror figure of the werewolf is leveraged toward a critique of cultural fears over women's bodies that in turn subject women to several forms of patriarchal and misogynist violence.

"The Curse" exemplifies Moore's revisionist strategy of repurposing genre tropes toward social commentaries. Other stories do similar moves with pollution, racism, and gun violence. While these comics were received as groundbreaking at the times of their publications, Tim Callahan suggests that they have not aged well: he refers to them as heavy-handed, "oppressively pedantic" and at times cloying (2010d: n. pag.). Still, *Swamp Thing*'s parables exemplify Moore's view that horror succeeds when it functions as social commentary: the visceral horrors of the genre are most meaningful when attached to the real horrors of modern experience.

Another key element of *Swamp Thing* is its emphasis on embodied subjectivity. Moore explains that a major affordance of his revised origin for Swamp Thing was the opportunity to explore nonhuman subjectivity. After Swamp Thing gets past any invested belief in his humanity, he is able to get in touch with a "new identity as this totally unprecedented swamp creature" (Khoury 2008: 88). This character examination feeds into the political consciousness of the series: Colin Beineke, for instance, reads Moore's *Swamp Thing* for its demonstration of "ecological thought and consciousness" (2011: para. 1). Along with its overt eco-politics—warnings against toxic waste, nuclear energy, and pollution and forms of environmental decay—through its hero *Swamp Thing* attempts to represent a plant consciousness. Swamp Thing sits in a line of Moore characters, also including Miracleman and *Watchmen*'s Dr. Manhattan, whose subjectivities, values, and indeed entire worldviews are not human and thus do not conform to human standards.

Unlike the disconcerting uncanniness of Miracleman's and Dr. Manhattan's estrangement from humanity, Swamp Thing's vegetable consciousness has utopian energies—ironic since Swamp Thing is the only "horror" character of the trio. In issue #47, Swamp Thing encounters the Parliament of Trees, a council of flora that mediates an elemental collective consciousness for plant life known as The Green. During his time with the Parliament, Swamp Thing recognizes his own previously narrow understanding of self: "I see now . . . how limited . . . how human . . . I have been in my thinking" (Moore 2010d: 124). This plant consciousness is communal, amorphous, and effectively eternal. One tree pithily clarifies the distinction between human and plant subjectivity by asserting, "Flesh . . . speaks . . . Wood . . . listens" (Moore 2010d: 120). The utopian potential of this alternative subjectivity is made clear via Swamp Thing's romance with his love interest in the series, Abby Holland. Starting in issue #34, "Rite of Spring," the two begin a sexual relationship. Sexual intercourse occurs when Abby eats a tuber growing off Swamp Thing's body, an act that unites Abby's consciousness with the mind of Swamp Thing, which in turn puts Abby in tune with the Green. Artists Bissette and Totleben depict this encounter as a hallucinatory expansion of consciousness. In this way, *Swamp Thing* continues Moore's interest in fantastic subjectivities and their ideological potentials and it anticipates Moore's millennial explorations into alternative embodiments and their possibly emancipatory affordances.

As its speculation of vegetable consciousness may indicate, *Swamp Thing* broke away from the pulpy traditions of US horror comics. In a similar vein,

Moore and his artists brought a distinctly literary sensibility to the series. Di Liddo argues that *Swamp Thing* is a space for Moore "to experiment with new linguistic formulas" that include an "ironic distortion of language" (2009: 54). Such stretching of language rings of literary modernism, a resonance noted by Hoberek, who argues the touted "realism" of *Swamp Thing* should be understood not in terms of content, but its representation of subjectivity, thereby making the series' "realism" a formal or technical matter.

This overtly "literary" mixture of horror, fantasy, and superheroes found in Moore's *Saga of the Swamp Thing* became the template for comics published by Vertigo, a DC imprint launched in 1993. Founded by Karen Berger, Moore's editor on *Swamp Thing*, Vertigo distinguished itself with creator-driven, offbeat comics series that often drew upon superhero sources but pitched them in related genres—noir, horror, fantasy, science fiction, and so on. Tracing Vertigo's lineage back to Moore's *Swamp Thing* makes Moore indirectly responsible for the many game-changing comics to come out of Vertigo, from Neil Gaiman's *Sandman* to later books like Garth Ennis and Steve Dillon's *Preacher*, Warren Ellis and Darick Robertson's *Transmetropolitan*, and *Y: The Last Man* by Brian K. Vaughan and Pia Guerra. Moore's *Swamp Thing* has been folded retroactively into Vertigo's history: recently collected volumes of the series anachronistically bear the Vertigo logo.

Saga of the Swamp Thing changed the direction of Moore's career in comic books. The series' boosted sales and genuine critical acclaim—including recognition from review outlets beyond the insular world of comics— gave DC confidence to put Moore on high-profile projects with relative creative freedom. While the positive professional relationship would not last, *Swamp Thing* began an approximately five-year tenure at DC in which Moore produced several milestone comics.

Whatever Happened to the Man of Tomorrow?

"Whatever Happened to the Man of Tomorrow?" first appeared as a crossover between Superman's monthly titles, starting in *Superman* #423 and then concluding in *Action Comics* #583. Both issues are cover-dated September 1986. This two-parter was not the first time Moore wrote Superman: in 1985 DC published Moore and Dave Gibbons' "For The Man Who Has Everything" in *Superman Annual* #11 as well as "The Jungle Line," illustrated by Rick Veitch, in *DC Comics Presents* #85. While Superman is the ostensible protagonist in both those comics, Batman, Wonder Woman, and Robin feature in the former and Swamp Thing costars in the latter. *Whatever Happened*, however, focuses on the narrative world of Superman: the hero, his villains, and allies.

Yet *Whatever Happened to the Man of Tomorrow?* is also continuous with Moore's previous Superman comics, for all of them perform meditations on the character. The plot of his collaboration with Gibbons, "For The Man Who Has Everything," has the alien tyrant Mongul using a spore-like lifeform called the Black Mercy—"something between a plant and an intelligent fungus" (Moore 2011b: 16)—to incapacitate Superman. The Black Mercy feeds on its host's "bio-aura," and in symbiotic return "gives [its host] their heart's desire. . . . It's telepathic. It reads them like a book, and it feeds them a logical simulation of the happy ending they desire" (Moore 2011b: 16). Superman's mind enters a dream-world in which his destroyed home planet of Krypton lives. Much of the narrative's action focuses on Batman, Robin, and Wonder Woman's efforts to contain Mongul and awaken Superman from his coma, which is to say that Superman, until the end, is on the plot's periphery.

Similarly, the Superman-Swamp Thing story, "The Jungle Line," depicts Superman suffering from a fugue-like fever dream after being exposed to a Kryptonian fungus. Notably, the first half of the comic uses captions to narrate the action: this third-person narrative voice refers to Superman only as "he," and, on one occasion, "the man of tomorrow," one of Superman's many hyperbolic nicknames. The refusal to identify Superman as Superman has a distancing effect that parallels his slippery sense of self, an effect of the fever-induced hallucinations. This estrangement is also captured in the nonlinear storytelling and jarring images of a disheveled, unshaven Superman drawn in Veitch's scratchy style. When Swamp Thing appears at midpoint, captions shift to first-person narration giving access to Swamp Thing's consciousness. After Swamp Thing cures Superman, the third-person narrative captions return, including one placed over a triumphant image of the Man of Steel with the declarative sentence, "He is Superman" (Moore 2011c: 147). Captions in "The Jungle Line" thus invite the reader to identify with Swamp Thing as an observer of Superman and position Superman's deathly fever as the Man of Steel's struggle to reclaim his true identity.

In "For The Man Who Has Everything" and "The Jungle Line" Superman is incapacitated and in need of rescue. Both stories also end up being about identity: "He is Superman," as "Jungle Line" concludes. "For the Man," likewise, begins with a catatonic Superman "living" in a mental realm created by the Black Mercy. After Superman awakens, his uncharacteristic rage is defamiliarizing to readers and fellow characters alike: he towers over Robin, darkened by shadow, and demands, "Who . . . did this . . . to ME?" (Moore 2011b: 30), to which a frightened Robin stammers an answer. Superman confronts Mongul, and—his face shadowed yet eyes emanating an eerie red glow—whispers "Burn" (Moore 2011b: 34), delivered in dialogue lettered in smaller print to signify quiet intensity. After scorching Mongul with his heat vision, Superman is poised to deliver a lethal blow. However, he glances at a statue of his parents that, it is implied, reminds him of his core values. At this pivotal moment, Superman's allies return and help him to subdue Mongul. The story's narrative arc shows Superman first as unexceptional and ineffectual, next as vicious and lethal, before finally returning—and reaffirming—him to his usual position of responsible, merciful strength.

Like its predecessors, *Whatever Happened to the Man of Tomorrow?* is a Superman story that examines its famous hero. Moore also decenters Superman in *Whatever Happened*, as its title suggests, by making Superman an absent presence—at least, that is, absent from a frame narrative that structures the story. This frame narrative is set in 1997, a decade in the future at time of publication, and it depicts a slightly aged Lois Lane Elliott being interviewed by a reporter from *The Daily Planet*, who is writing a feature entitled "The Last Days of Superman." The journalist asks Lois "about the years leading up to Superman's disappearance and presumed death" (Moore 2011j: 207), so the events of those years are told in flashback with Lois providing narration and commentary.

Here is where the publishing context for *Whatever Happened* is responsible not only for the story's genesis but also for its surprising poignancy. Moore's story was commissioned as a coda of sorts to the twelve-part maxi-series *Crisis on Infinite Earths*, by writer Marv Wolfman and artist George Perez. *Crisis* itself was produced in conjunction with DC's fiftieth anniversary. Wolfman and Perez's interdimensional adventure was a celebration of DC's rich and vibrant history, but was also a moment of closure and a sort of internal "housecleaning" that sought to make the narrative world of DC's superhero comics more accessible to new readers. *Crisis'* narrative collapses DC's multiverse of timelines and alternate realities into one composite universe with a streamlined continuity and modernized characters. The moment of *Crisis* signifies DC's redefinition of itself.

Whatever Happened functions as both tribute and farewell to the continuity and style of what became known as the "pre-*Crisis*" type of

Superman, and DC generally, comic book. To 1980s audiences, these comics—whose heyday was the so-called Silver Age running from roughly 1956 to 1970—were defined by their unsophistication and absurdity. Visuals in *Whatever Happened* reinforce its connection to DC's Silver Age past: Moore's artistic collaborator is Curt Swan, generally accepted as the definitive Superman artist of the 1960s. *Whatever Happened* is also Swan's last major contribution—his Swan song, if you will—to *Superman*. Moore's script celebrates the zaniness of DC's Silver Age narratives, including nearly all their iconic aspects. Yet, Moore juxtaposes the bright, simplistic optimism associated with Superman's Silver Age and visually cued by Swan's art with the darker, more cynical sensibilities of the late 1980s and 1990s.

In short, the narrative of *Whatever Happened to the Man of Tomorrow?* allegorizes the transition from pre-*Crisis* styles and sensibilities to the ironic, edgier reinterpretations of that Silver Age material that characterizes 1980s comics. When Lois, in the frame narrative, recounts her memories of Superman's last days she begins by describing a period of relative calm. This tranquil period of Superman's life is disrupted when old enemies, all of whom are historically associated with Superman's classic Silver Age period, begin returning. However, these foes perpetrate attacks far deadlier and depraved than their past crimes: Bizarro, an inverted mirror-image of Superman, exterminates the entire population of his obverse Earth, Bizarro World, before killing himself; the Toyman and the Prankster, whose names indicate their meddlesomeness, torture and murder Superman's friend Pete Ross; and a militia of Metallo robots storms *The Daily Planet* in a tactical siege. Meanwhile, the remains of Brainiac fuse to the body of Lex Luthor, forming an unnerving mechanical-organic hybrid—"the new Brainiac-Luthor team" (Moore 2011j: 217)—plotting Superman's death. Superman runs a gauntlet of these increasingly dangerous enemies.

Twin auras of confusion and fatalistic doom hang over these events. As Superman says at Pete Ross' funeral, "I have bad feelings about this. Bizarro, the Prankster, the Toyman . . . they were all just nuisances before. What turned them into killers?" (Moore 2011j: 215). The situation becomes grim enough that Superman fears for the lives of his surviving friends—Lois, Lana Lang, Jimmy Olsen, Perry White, and a few others—so he moves them to a secure location, his Fortress of Solitude at the North Pole. At the Fortress, Superman is greeted by other allies from his quirky Silver Age past. When Krypto the Super-dog arrives, complete with red cape flowing from his collar, Lois' narration recalls that the super-canine's "arrival struck an ominous note" (Moore 2011j: 223). The caption with this foreboding narration accompanies a ludicrous image of a flying, costumed animal, a collocation that captures the story's convergence of older and emergent storytelling styles in superhero comics. Characters, from Superman to outrageous examples like Krypto, who carry with them legacies of naïveté and silliness are tinged with darker, more menacing shades. As allegory, the story offers elegiac resignation in the face of new market trends and shifting reader preferences.

At the end of the tale, the puppet-master who has been manipulating Superman's enemies into more diabolical and deadly versions of themselves is revealed to be Mr. Mxyzptlk, arguably Superman's wackiest classic antagonist. Mxyzptlk is a floating imp who periodically travels to Earth from the incomprehensible Fifth Dimension. His stories involve him beguiling Superman using his genie-like magic powers, seemingly only for his own juvenile amusement. Yet, by Moore's narrative logic, Mxyzptlk's appearance and mischievousness were only a ruse: "Did you honestly believe a fifth-dimensional sorcerer would resemble a funny little man in a derby hat?" (Moore 2011j: 247), he shrieks, as he turns from vaudevillian sprite into a gangly, gargantuan goblin. This monstrous appearance and the violence it holds were apparently always buried beneath Mxyzptlk's silly visage and hijinks.

Mxyzptlk embodies the dialectic of the story's allegory: a sinister violence lurks within a seemingly harmless, kitschy exterior. This relation is also evoked by the clean-line work and traditional page compositions of Swan's art, a contrast between style and content that enters into dialogue with the scores of older, less self-aware comics drawn by Swan and others in a similar style to the one repurposed here. *Whatever Happened* implies dark themes were always present in older comics, but as subtext; what the revisionist narrative does is make that subtext visible, not only in the pages of the revisionist comic itself but also in the re-readings of the older comics being revised. But why elevate subtext to text? What is the motivation behind this change?

Here, consider Mxyzptlk's own enigmatic motives. If previously nonlethal villains are deadly only under Mxyzptlk's sorcerous influence, what drove Mxyzptlk from naughty to ultraviolent? According to the villain himself: boredom. Mr. Mxyzptlk explains,

The big problem with being immortal is filling your time. For example, I spent the first two thousand years of my existence doing absolutely nothing. . . . Eventually, simple inertia became tiresome, so

I spent the next two thousand years being saintly and benign, doing only good deeds. When that novelty began to fade, I decided to try being mischievous. Now, two thousand years later, I'm bored again. I need a change. Starting with your death, I shall spend the next two millennia being evil! After that, who knows? Perhaps I'll try being guilty for a while. (Moore 2011j: 247)

In this moment, Mxyzptlk is describing comics trends as much as he is explaining his own behaviors and moods. A way of being is novel until it is not and a new way emerges, a sentiment that applies to Mxyzptlk's personality overhauls and to patterns in comics publishing.

Of course, tastes and trends are not naturally occurring phenomena: they are collectively determined by communities of creators and readers who coproduce comic book content as well as its meanings. We get insight into Moore's thought on this issue from his 1987 pitch for *Twilight of the Superheroes*, a proposed crossover for DC's superheroes that ultimately never materialized. In one of the pitch's discursive asides, Moore asserts that "the large and largely incomprehensible tides of public favor or dismissal that determine the success of a title are often influenced by very subtle things far below the waterline" (1988c: n. pag). Since, Moore suggests, reader needs are usually subconscious, cultural products often fulfill psychological and emotional demands that audiences did not know they require. Like comics readers, Mxyzptlk is only semi-aware of the reasons driving his changed needs and preferences. Mxyzptlk also stands in for the other half of the trend equation, the comics creators, whose work meets their audience's subconscious desires: as resident of the Fifth Dimension Mxyzptlk exists on a higher plane and his magic allows him to control reality. He is the one who "rewrites" Superman's foes in violent terms. Mxyzptlk's desire for novelty plus his reality-shaping wizardry align him at once with comics reading practices and creator innovations, which work together toward comics production and meaning-making. This dialectic is subject to periodic sea changes, allegorized by Mxyzptlk's *volte-face* to vicious evil.

The shift to darker styles in the 1980s, like Mxyzptlk's transformations, reflects new needs and circumstances. Despite its memorialization of Silver Age styles and sensibilities, *Whatever Happened* positions the grim and gritty turn not only as invigorating and inevitable, but also as authentic—in the sense that darker stories do not betray the characters but foreground elements previously submerged. The revelation that Mxyzptlk is motivated by an obscure impulse to disrupt and renew the status quo creates symmetry with information disclosed by Lois at the start of her flashback. Lois initially notes that the years immediately preceding Mxyzptlk's assault on Superman's life were "quiet," for his enemies were captured or hiding; in short, "it seemed like there was nobody left to fight" (Moore 2011j: 207). This calmness translates, meta-textually, as creative stagnation: the revisionist turn, Moore therefore suggests, jumpstarts a stalled narrative.

Yet, Moore makes clear, these shifts are temporary. Mxyzptlk admits that his evil will not last forever, and that he will change again once boredom returns. Furthermore, the final pages plainly indicate that Superman, whom Lois insists to her interviewer lost his powers before dying, in fact lives on as Lois's husband Jordan Elliott. While a "classic," Silver Age Superman may be presumed dead, the story's finale suggests, the truth is that version of the character remains, only hidden from view. And images of the Elliotts' infant son crushing coal into diamonds with his bare fists—a famous Silver Age gag for Superman—reinforces the idea that a sensibility that seems lost will inevitably return. Driving this point home, Superman's new identity, Jordan Elliott, is a reworking of Jor-El, the name of Superman's biological father on Krypton, and his son with Lois, Jonathan, is named after Superman's adoptive father on Earth. Just as Superman's paternal progenitors live again, in a sense, so too may the Silver Age. If *Whatever Happened*, on one hand, is a narrative capstone, its open-ended conclusion—with Superman literally holding a door open while breaking the fourth wall—welcomes the return of older sensibilities, which Moore himself will later do in *Supreme*.

Whatever Happened to the Man of Tomorrow? displays the tension that structures much of Moore's superhero work: the negotiation between, on one hand, Moore's knowledge and genuine affection for superhero stories and, on the other hand, his interest in subverting the genre's conventions by sifting below the surface, uncovering and exploring the genre's questionable ideological underpinnings. If *Whatever Happened* performs and validates the ironic "deconstruction" and darkened tone of revisionist superhero comics from Moore and his contemporaries, its valedictory nostalgia for Superman's Silver Age also expresses ambivalence over what is lost amid comics' revisionist turn.

The Killing Joke

Batman: The Killing Joke is a collaboration with artist Brian Bolland. The graphic novella is Moore's second Batman story—first is "Mortal Clay" (2011e) from 1987's *Batman Annual* #11—yet in truth *Joke*'s actual main character is the Joker, Batman's most prominent villain. Moore sketches parallels between Joker and Batman, commonalities that emerge via flashbacks that seem to depict the tragic circumstances that turned the Joker into a vicious, clown-faced killer. In Moore's telling, the Joker was an unsuccessful, anonymous comedian who agrees to abet a burglary of a chemical plant out of financial desperation. On the eve of the crime, his pregnant wife dies in a freak accident. Despite his grief, the comedian is pressured into following through with the crime, only for the burglary to be interrupted by Batman. Amid the ensuing fracas the reluctant burglar is immersed within chemicals that alter his physical appearance into Joker's trademark bleached skin, green hair, and ruby rictus smile. After this cruel turn of events, the Joker gives his mind to madness since in "a world as psychotic as this . . . any other response would be crazy!" (1988a: n. pag.). Against popular depictions of the Joker as an avatar of purposeless evil, Moore's Joker is a troubled victim, though any sympathy for him is negated by the appalling acts he commits in *Killing Joke*.

The comic begins with Batman visiting Joker, who is incarcerated at Arkham Asylum for the Criminally Insane. Batman is inspired to make this excursion, so he explains, after thinking about the violent relationship between the two men and wanting the peace of mind from "a genuine attempt to talk things over" (1988a: n. pag.) in order to avoid their otherwise seemingly unavoidable mutually destructive path. However, Batman soon learns that Joker has again escaped the asylum.

On the loose, Joker invades the home of Commissioner James Gordon and, in an infamous panel, shoots Barbara Gordon—the commissioner's adult daughter and formerly the superhero Batgirl—point blank in the abdomen. This scene ends with Joker undoing the blouse of the injured Barbara while his gang kidnaps her father. Later, Joker subjects Commissioner Gordon to physical and psychological tortures at an abandoned circus fairground. One of these torments includes projecting a series of photographs of an agonized Barbara, naked and bleeding from her gunshot wound. The violence of this scene is sexualized: Commissioner Gordon is stripped nude save for a BDSM-style leather, studded collar, and the gendered violence depicted on-panel, rooted in the imposition of power, functions without question as a representation of sexual assault.

Joker's purpose is to break Commissioner Gordon, psychologically. He explains, "Madness is the emergency exit . . . [for] all those dreadful things that happened" (1988a: n. pag.). Since the villain's aim is to prove that his madness is an understandable response to an unjust world, the climactic showdown between Batman and Joker is a physical expression of a psychological conflict. During a lull in Batman and Joker's fight, Gordon yells out, "I want him brought in . . . And I want him brought in by the book! . . . By the book, you hear? We have to show him! We have to show him that our way works!" (1988a: n. pag.). This demand sets the stakes of this fight as the validity of a prevailing social order, one ground in lawfulness that is itself associated with neuro-typical notions of sanity and rationality.

Needless to say, *Joke*'s sexual politics are vexed. Critics and fans of the Barbara Gordon character bemoan that a heroic female character is sacrificed to advance a psychosexual conflict between three men. Moore has expressed regret at the book's excessively "nasty things" (Khoury 2008: 123). The controversial representations of sexual violence central to *Joke*'s legacy are revisited in Critical Questions, while the remainder of this section focuses on the engagements with comics continuity that make *Joke* a companion piece to Moore's *Whatever Happened* Superman story.

These questions of continuity may seem quixotic, but actually bear on how to read *The Killing Joke*. For decades, *Joke* was held as canonical for DC's continuity. As a result, writers and artists who did not want to abandon the character of Barbara Gordon redeveloped her: in the hands of writers like John Ostrander, Gail Simone, and others, Barbara adopted a new superhero identity, Oracle, and fought crime as a computer hacker. Barbara, then, remained in *Batman* comics, and as Oracle her character became one of the few prominent superheroes with a visible disability. But a side-effect of this character development for Barbara Gordon in the years after *Joke* is that it solidified *Joke* as part of the DC universe's official timeline: its narrative events "happened." But, a close reading of *Joke* shows how its narrative interrogates continuity and chronology themselves, troubling how the story's events relate to Batman's serialized history and canonical timeline.

Despite its emphasis on origins, *The Killing Joke*—akin to *Whatever Happened to the Man of Tomorrow?*—might be read as "the last Batman-Joker story." If nothing else, the graphic novella shares with Moore's farewell Superman story a thematic investment in genre history, putting engrained associations of superhero comics with childishness and absurdity in dialogue with the 1980s' darker revisionist wave. Like *Whatever Happened*, even as *Joke* features hallmarks of superhero revisionism—its subdued tone, so-called adult themes, and graphic violence—these moves are made, narratively, with an eye on the genre's more lighthearted past. This contrast is sharpened by the presence of Batman, "a character who, in the view of the wider public that exists beyond the relatively tiny confines of the comic audience, sums up more than any other the essential silliness of the comic book hero" (Moore 1989a: n. pag.), as Moore once wrote.

Killing Joke's conversation with the kitsch legacies of Batman, and superhero comics in general, are announced in background icons glimpsed in panels throughout the story. Early on, Batman reflects on his enemy and their years of conflict. During this scene, Batman is surrounded by the memorabilia on display in his lair, the Batcave. The third panel in this scene gives a close-up shot of one such item, a framed photograph of Batman and his allies. Strikingly, this portrait is a reproduction of an illustration entitled "Greetings from the Bat-family!" that first appeared in 1961's *Batman Annual* #2 as a pin-up. The original image was drawn by Sheldon Moldoff, but attributed to Batman co-creator Bob Kane, whose name often appeared on ghosted artwork. Because the image in *Killing Joke* is an exact reproduction—it even includes, bizarrely, the Kane signature—Batman and others appear in the cartoony style of Moldoff, which contrasts with Bolland's realistic illustrative art. Furthermore, characters featured in the image—Batwoman; a pre-Barbara Gordon version of Batgirl; Ace the Bat-Hound; and an impish sprite called Bat-Mite—are characters that were excised from DC continuity by *Crisis on Infinite Earths* a year or so prior.

The next scene is the notorious moment in which Barbara Gordon is shot. Just before, Barbara and her father—like Batman in the preceding scene—are reminiscing about memories of the Joker. Commissioner Gordon clips and inserts a newspaper article about the Joker's recent escape into a scrapbook of Joker crimes. After gluing the new headline into the book, Jim flips to the front of the binder, lingering on the first reported encounter between Batman and Joker. The newspaper photos shown in this panel, akin to the Bat-family photo in the scene before, are drawn in the crude style of Batman's earliest tales and visually allude to the cover of *Detective Comics* #27, the 1939 comic that debuted Batman. Looking at the visual reference to Batman's first appearance, Gordon muses, "Heh. Look at this one. First time they met. Now what year was that?" (Moore 1988a: n. pag.). When paired with the visual cues to Batman's various iterations, this dialogue articulates the murky connection the present moment of the narrative has to Batman's then-half-century publication history; moreover, Commissioner Gordon's rumination on the past occurs right as the exceedingly cruel and savage Joker of the late-1980s barges in and paralyzes Barbara.

Here the violence of the present is allegorically invading and incapacitating memories of the past. Of course, these visual references to

Batman's publication history could be dismissed as mere clever in-jokes, or ways to symbolically connote "pastness" in the minds of an informed audience. Yet, little in a comic written by Alan Moore is incidental, and, at the time of writing *The Killing Joke*, Moore was attuned to the general views on continuity held by the dedicated readers of superhero comics. In his proposal for *Twilight of the Superheroes*, Moore notes the "current seeming obsession with a strict formal continuity" (Moore 1988c: n. pag.); the use of "obsession" and "strict formal" indicates the seriousness with which Moore believes his readers take issues of continuity. This comment suggests Moore's recognition of the continuity contradictions produced by *Joke*'s visual nods to Batman's pre-*Crisis* past and the disruptiveness of those paradoxes for some readers.

In addition to visual cues to the Silver Age that fold pre-*Crisis* story elements into a stylistically modern and otherwise apparently post-*Crisis* continuity, flashbacks to Joker's origin feature anachronisms like bowler hats and fedoras redolent of the early 1940s, the time of the first Batman stories. When Batman is glimpsed in flashback, Bolland draws his cowl's hornlike "ears" to evoke their original curved design. Such imagery dovetails with *Joke*'s version of Joker's origin, which is a loose adaptation of 1951's "The Man Behind the Red Hood!" Images and narrative bits from across Batman's history negated by *Crisis* therefore linger in, and haunt, *The Killing Joke*.

Although *Joke* makes visual references to the earliest years of Batman's history as a character and franchise, the flashbacks collapse the distance between past and present. Flashbacks as a literary device, generally, bring past incidents to bear on present circumstances, and Moore and Bolland underscore this narrative function by bridging the main narrative to flashbacks via symmetrical panel compositions. When the narrative moves between present and past, the arrangement of figures in the transitional panels mirror each other, emphasizing the organic links across the two periods. At times, this technique bridges scenes taking place in the present: mirrored panel compositions also indicate the interconnected lives of the principal characters.

Complicating these collapsed distinctions between characters and chronologies, however, is the ambiguity infused into *The Killing Joke*. Near the end of the comic, the Joker speculates that Batman must have experienced some traumatic event as motivation for his crime-fighting. According to Joker, "Something like that happened to me, you know. I . . . I'm not exactly sure what it was. Sometimes I remember it one way, sometimes another . . . if I'm going to have a past, I prefer it be multiple choice! Ha ha ha!" (Moore 1988a: n. pag.). In this one line, Moore calls into question all the preceding flashback material, undermining the validity of the portions of narrative construed as memories despite those scenes' thematic significance and contributions to Joker's character development.

The ending of *Killing Joke*, too, is deeply ambiguous. After Batman narrowly defeats Joker in combat, as police cars near, the two men share a hearty laugh over a joke told by the villain. Apart from the questionable appropriateness of Batman apparently bonding with a man who has shot, assaulted, and terrorized friends and allies, this finale has sparked competing interpretations from critics and fans. One popular reading contends that the comic's final pages are meant to suggest Batman's murder of Joker. After all, as the showdown between the two commences, captions reproduce Batman's speech from *Joke*'s opening pages in which he declares the inevitability of a fatal outcome to their intertwined lives. The repetition of those words in this climactic moment retroactively turns their original usage into foreshadowing. Once the fight winds down, Batman offers Joker a chance at rehabilitation: "Maybe I can help. We could work together. . . . We don't have to kill each other" (Moore 1988a: n. pag.). Joker considers, but after a pause laments, "No. I'm sorry, but . . . No. It's too late for that. Far too late" (Moore 1988a: n. pag). Joker's resignation segues into the jest that ends the book, one about two men in an insane asylum. This joke, in which two men try to escape their institution but one is too far detached from reality to make good on the breakout, seems to serve as an analogy for Batman and Joker: both mad, but only one of them inescapably so.

As Batman and Joker laugh together, Bolland's gridded panels move away from the two silhouetted figures, pulling back and down to end with a worm's-eye view of muddy puddles of rain. This sequence of panels moves from a profiled full-body shot of Batman and Joker, with the former's arm clasped to the clavicle of the latter, apparently as physical response to laughter. By the midpoint of the nine-panel page, the receding images of Batman and Joker share space with two sound effects: their manic "hahaha" laughter plus the "weeeeee" scream of an oncoming police car's siren. By the seventh panel in this sequence, only the siren continues; in the eighth panel, no sound effects remain. Notably, at this point in his career, one of Moore's formal innovations was to "dispense with thought bubbles and sound effect captions" (Chapman 2011: 228). Sound effects as devices, Moore reckoned, were distracting and unnecessary. Their noticeable inclusion here suggests purpose, namely to signal that the abrupt end to Joker's laughter is the result of choking, making Batman's outreached arm in panel five a lethal gesture. Thus, the comic's title is literalized.

Such a reading of *Killing Joke* is compelling, supported by a set of coherent textual clues; in contrast, rebuttals to the "killing joke" interpretation turn on the Batman character's established refusal to kill. To read the ending as Batman's murder of Joker, this counterargument alleges, betrays a characterological aspect that holds across most canonical and prominent depictions. Yet both interpretations—Batman kills because textual clues suggest so versus Batman does not kill because his character has an established ban on taking any life—misrecognize a literary ambiguity that is deployed precisely for the generative possibilities of indeterminacy. *The Killing Joke* both thematizes and is structured around uncertainty. A joke, after all, is not a puzzle to be solved, but rather a verbal construction built around the strategic withholding or misdirection of information; likewise, the meaning of *The Killing Joke* inheres in its refusal to reconcile its parts. The comic's impact derives from the reader's inability to harmonize its visual cues or its internal narrative alignments: *The Killing Joke* may or may not be set in post-*Crisis* canonical continuity; it may or may not present the "true" origin for the Joker; Batman may or may not execute the Joker.

Accepting these ambiguities and contradictions in turn allows *The Killing Joke*'s congruity with *Whatever Happened to the Man of Tomorrow?* to become apparent. Both comics give visual and narrative references to superhero comics' Silver Age past, a history made noncanonical by a contemporary series, *Crisis on Infinite Earths*, and blend them with modern, revisionist storytelling styles. These engagements with comic book histories reflect Moore's reservations about the type of continuity resets performed first and relatively decisively by *Crisis*. Moore in fact discloses several of these concerns in his proposal for *Twilight of the Superheroes*. In the pitch, Moore describes *Crisis* as "excellent" and says its "motive was pure and the aim true" (Moore 1988c: n. pag.); however, he recognizes, "In the wake of the time-altering at the end of the *Crisis* we are left with a universe where the entire past continuity of DC, for the most part, simply never happened. . . . [B]y far the larger part of DC's continuity will simply have to be scrapped and consigned to one of Orwell's memory holes along with a large amount of characters who, more than simply being dead, are now unpeople" (Moore 1988c: n. pag.). The reservations Moore expresses here points to an investment in the integrity of fictional characters that he foregrounds later in his even more intertextual comics.

The broader point made in the *Twilight* proposal, though, is that when established narratives histories are invalidated—an editorial move that also implicitly invalidates the creative labor responsible for producing that history—serialized comics lose the crucial ability to engage productively with their pasts, both narrative and genre pasts. If *Whatever Happened to the Man of Tomorrow?* functions as commentary on a transition from one historical moment for the superhero genre to the next, *The Killing Joke* refuses to be placeable within a distinct continuity. *Joke* thus theorizes how serialized storytelling revitalizes itself through dynamic engagement with its own narrative and publication histories, a point extended in later comics like *Supreme* and *Tom Strong*.

Watchmen

Watchmen, a twelve-issue series published by DC Comics from mid-1986 to late-1987, is the most mature realization of the revisionism that defines Moore's 1980s comics. Although it is not, chronologically, the last of Moore's superhero comics for DC in the 1980s, the perspectives and techniques Moore brought to bear on the superhero genre throughout the decade all coalesce in *Watchmen*, making it the most successful, creatively and commercially, of his superhero comics.

In 1983, DC purchased ownership rights to many of the creative assets of Charlton Comics. Lance Parkin recounts that Moore thought the Charlton heroes would work well for a story "that applied real-world logic to superheroes" (2013: 166), akin to his approach to *Miracleman*. Moore brought the idea to artist Dave Gibbons, previously one of Moore's collaborators at *2000 A.D.*, and the two of them "started referring to the idea as *The Charlton Project*" (Parkin 2013: 166). But executive editor Dick Giordiano realized that *The Charlton Project* would limit DC's future options with the assets, so he mandated Moore and Gibbons instead use original characters.

Inventing new characters, albeit ones modeled on Charlton's properties, enabled Moore and Gibbons to make their figures represent common variations on the basic superhero archetype. Rorschach, a noir figure with trench coat and overheated narration, takes direct inspiration from *The Question*, a Charlton hero created by Steve Ditko; in the context of *Watchmen*, he represents the urban vigilante superhero type more generally, too. Notably, Moore injects into Rorschach the right-wing sensibilities of another Ditko creation, Mr. A, a character that ventriloquized Ditko's own libertarianism. Exaggerating these politics, Rorschach is a harsh reactionary and paranoid conspiracist, possessing an ideologue's discipline and presumed moral clarity. Consequently, like Moore's Miracleman, Rorschach discloses a fascistic undercurrent to the very idea of a superhero—a troubling intimation that extends throughout the series to become a major theme.

Other protagonists also have Charlton models yet function as representative figures. Nite-Owl, patterned on Charlton's Blue Beetle, is the scientist adventurer-hero, one whose weapons and gizmos are designed to reflect his heroic identity's avian motif. Silk Spectre, a composite from Charlton's Nightshade and Quality Comics' Phantom Lady, functions as the femme fatale, but her reluctance to embrace that persona discloses *Watchmen*'s critique of superhero comics' misogynist history, one in which being a "superheroine" is itself counted as a novelty. Some of the resentment felt by Silk Spectre, real name Laurie Juspeczyk ("stage-named" Jupiter), stems from her mother, Sally, who originated the Silk Spectre identity in the 1940s and pressures Laurie to carry on her role. Nite-Owl, or Dan Dreiberg, is also a second-generation hero, but he reveres his predecessor and father-figure, Hollis Mason. Laurie and Dan bond over their experiences as legacy heroes.

Three other Charlton-inspired characters round out *Watchmen*'s core ensemble: The Comedian, Ozymandias, and Dr. Manhattan, based on, respectively, the characters Peacemaker, Thunderbolt, and Captain Atom. Edward Blake, codenamed the Comedian, straddles a line between anti-hero and nationalistic hero, an appropriate amalgamation for *Watchmen*'s post-Vietnam context. Adrian Veidt, or Ozymandias, represents the "peak human," who may not have superpowers per se but is perfected in his abilities, physical and intellectual. He is also, like several popular superheroes, an obscenely wealthy business tycoon. Lastly, the narrative includes one actual superhuman: Jon Osterman, nuclear physicist, becomes the aloof, godlike being codenamed Dr. Manhattan after an accident in his lab's experimental Intrinsic Field Subtractor. The transformation goes beyond Jon's eerie, glowing, blue physical appearance, since the exposure to radiation gives him quantum perceptions and reality-bending powers. Collectively, these characters not only substitute for their Charlton counterparts, but also signify character types and tropes in the genre.

At its most basic, *Watchmen* is a murder mystery. The plot begins with Edward Blake, thrown from his high-rise apartment. Rorschach investigates the death, discovering that Blake was the government-sponsored crime-fighter known as the Comedian. Suspecting a killer targeting masked vigilantes, Rorschach reaches out to other superheroes, most of whom have been inactive since the Keene Act, a law that outlawed costumed adventuring. As the series goes on, more heroes are assailed, until Rorschach, Nite-Owl, Silk Spectre, and Dr. Manhattan learn that the mastermind is one of their own, Ozymandias, whose plan culminates with a simulated alien invasion of New York City. This hoax kills millions but so terrifies the world that antagonistic governments across the globe broker peace agreements in order to unite against this fake extraterrestrial threat. Ozymandias seems to usher in world peace, even if it is founded on a lie that costs countless lives.

This plot overview, however, does no justice to the complexity of the series. For instance, although the main narrative spans a relatively short period of time—from October until December, 1985—a series of intricately designed flashbacks expands the scope of the story, linking incidents from the past, mostly from the 1940s and 1960s, with the 1985 present of the primary narrative. The presence of superheroes during this roughly forty-year period changes how history unfolds compared to the reader's real-world referent. In this alternate history Dr. Manhattan empowers the United States to win the Vietnam War, US president Richard Nixon never resigns, and people drive electric cars created by Dr. Manhattan and Ozymandias. The world is changed culturally, too: since costumed heroes here exist in real life, superhero comic books themselves were only a fad. Although many of the details of this alternate history are largely incidental to the plot, they signal key thematic questions animating *Watchmen*: what sort of people would actually become masked vigilantes, and what effects would they have on the world in which they inhabit and intervene?

Because it pursues these questions, a common plaudit for *Watchmen* is its "realism." DC Comics' blurb on *Watchmen* for their webpage notes that the comic "has been universally acclaimed for its psychological depth and realism." Andrew Hoberek comments that *Watchmen* is "famous for bringing a darker, putatively more realistic tone to the superhero genre" (2014: n. pag.). And in a contemporaneous review from *The Chicago Tribune*, Larry Kart uses the odd locution "real-life superheroes" to describe *Watchmen*'s characters. Yet, despite its subversions, *Watchmen*'s fidelity to its genre "inevitably short-circuits any attempt to treat superheroes 'realistically'" (Parkin 2013: 194). Adherence to genre expectations negates realism, at least realism understood as believability or plausibility.

Watchmen belies a "realistic" depiction of superheroes within its first few pages. At the start of the first issue—or, when published as one volume, first chapter—Rorschach investigates the murder of the Comedian, thrown from his New York City apartment. Rorschach gains access to this high-rise crime scene by firing a grappling gun into the broken apartment window, and then scaling the building. The immense height of this climb is established in a panel on the first page that gives a birds-eye view from the apartment itself: a detective investigating the case looks at the dizzying drop to the street below and mutters, "That's quite a drop" (Moore 1987d: n. pag.). Stretching credibility, however, Rorschach pulls himself up a rope to ascend this skyscraper.

Notably, the single panel economically depicting Rorschach's climb—reducing what would be a grueling physical feat into a fleeting moment—is drawn in a way that evokes a recurring sight gag from the campy *Batman* television series from the late 1960s. The panel is a wide-shot, and depicts Rorschach climbing the building by planting his feet on the exterior wall for balance, keeping his body virtually perpendicular to it, and pulling himself up the rope one hand in front of the other. This rendering calls to mind *Batman* stars Adam West and Burt Ward using ropes to "climb up" walls, an optical illusion created by having the camera turned on its side. *Batman's* visual effect is deliberately transparent, drawing attention to its own artificiality for a visual gag—a joke whose target is the absurdity of the comic book superhero trope it translates, unconvincingly, to television. The first issue's opening with Rorschach therefore faithfully reproduces a patently unbelievable genre convention, yet, by visually cuing the popular and culturally influential *Batman* show, the scene also registers the irony that pervades *Watchmen*.

Other moments signal *Watchmen's* defiance of "realism" in its treatment of superheroes. Nite-Owl maintains an arsenal of self-designed advanced weaponry, including an airship, in an underground bunker; Ozymandias has such precise reflexes that he can catch a fired bullet in his hands; and a scientific mishap turns Jon Osterman into a superhuman, not killing him. At times, *Watchmen* gestures at stricter realism—the superhero Dollar Bill is shot by bank robbers after his cape is stuck in a revolving door, highlighting the impracticality of that costuming accoutrement—but *Watchmen* mostly preserves genre tropes and conventions in order to ponder their implications.

Meditating on these tropes yields a commentary on the superhero figure and genre. Consider Rorschach: a reactionary, if not outright fascistic, vigilante. *Watchmen* opens with Rorschach's journal, excerpts of which function as captions throughout the series. These entries denounce "communists" and "liberals and intellectuals" (Moore 1987d: n. pag.), giving the journal the tone of a screed from a right-wing crank; yet, the entries also articulate a clear moral code. In an overt instance, Rorschach's diary declares, "there is good and there is evil, and evil must be punished" (Moore 1987d: n. pag.). By attaching the prototypical "good-versus-evil" perspective of superhero narratives to a figure who displays extremist politics, tendencies toward brutal violence, and psychotic outbursts, *Watchmen* parodies its genre's traditional moral framework and questions its latent authoritarianism. Moore and Gibbons, however, ironize Rorschach's Manichean values by naming him after psychology's famously subjective personality test, an identity evoked in the inkblot-adorned mask covering his face.

Superheroes' fascistic underpinnings, however, are not isolated in the figure of Rorschach. *Watchmen* rejects any reductive political alignments for its characters. The apolitical and amoral Comedian, for instance, delights in his physical dominations of others. Ozymandias is politically liberal, but he exalts tyrants from antiquity and commits mass murder to "conquer the world," in a sense. In an interview with a leftwing magazine included in issue #11, Ozymandias admits that Rorschach (like other costumed heroes) is right wing, with a blinkered view of the world; however, he finds Rorschach's perspective to be merely "an intellectual limitation" and that Rorschach is a "man of great integrity." Ozymandias' respect for Rorschach suggests a certain continuity across the two characters, despite their political differences, a dynamic that extends to Comedian, since the narrative implies that Ozymandias' plan is inspired by Comedian's cynicism toward heroism.

Watchmen, then, finds authoritarian and fascistic streaks running throughout the superhero figure itself, despite surface distinctions between the heroes' political orientations and affects. The ideological violence of the superhero cuts across other forms of difference. Moore and Gibbons reject simplistic political schematizations: no one is fully noble, characters occupy contradictory political positions, and even unsavory characters like Rorschach are humanized and given redeeming traits.

This approach to the characters carries over from protagonists to minor characters. Consider Captain Metropolis, a hero from the first wave of masked adventurers. In a flashback scene set in 1966, an aging Captain Metropolis—a White and blonde-haired ex-soldier cut from the mold of nationalistic heroes like Captain America—attempts to recruit superheroes, most of them new and younger, into a team called the Crimebusters. The meeting disintegrates after the Comedian ridicules the Crimebusters' enterprise, insisting on the futility of costumed crime-fighting. In a key moment, Comedian burns an easel set up by Captain Metropolis that displays various ills for his proposed team to solve: "Riots," "Drugs," "Promiscuity," Anti-war demos," and "Black unrest." This subtle detail, never explicitly addressed within the narrative, discloses Captain Metropolis' reactionary politics: the iconic superhero sets his agenda against civil rights activism, sexual revolution, and counterculture. Though Captain Metropolis comes across as an earnest and upright do-gooder, lurking beneath this presentation are racist and reactionary values.

Yet, perhaps thwarting expectations, Captain Metropolis is also a closeted homosexual man. Captain Metropolis' homosexuality is not a major plot point, but it is intertwined with many key thematic threads running throughout *Watchmen*. The snippets of information about Metropolis' sexual identity gesture toward the rounded, full characterizations granted for even the narrative's minor players. On this note, Moore mentions in a 1988 interview, "I wanted to approximate real life as much as possible, and that meant giving each of the characters a sexual identity, a political identity, and most components one would usually associate with personality" (Sharrett 2012: 50). *Watchmen* captures the paradoxes and contradictions of individuals with multifaceted senses of self, complexities that have been historically absent in comic book superhero characterization.

The character's gayness, however, is not only about superheroes containing multitudes; Captain Metropolis' homosexuality, and superhero sexuality in *Watchmen* generally, goes hand-in-hand with the book's meta-textual analysis of the superhero figure. To this point, Captain Metropolis should be read as a parodic superhero caricature, one who cues laughable superhero clichés. For example, in issue #9's paratext—a text that operates with and alongside the main text; in *Watchmen*'s case, illustrated prose pieces included at the end of each chapter—we see some personal effects from Sally Jupiter, the original Silk Spectre who served with Captain Metropolis in the 1940s superhero team, The Minutemen. One document is Captain Metropolis' personal invitation to join his nascent crime-fighting squad. This letter includes phrases like "stamping out crime and injustice wheresoever it should rear its ugly head" and "war on infamy"; Sally responds in her marginalia: "Jesus Christ! Are you kidding!" (Moore 1987d: n. pag.) Sally's comment articulates the incredulity of modern readers toward the superhero clichés that the purple prose of Metropolis' letter emulates.

If Rorschach, Comedian, and Ozymandias bring the violent, authoritarian, and even fascistic subtexts of the genre to the surface by pushing their respective character types to their darkest limits, Captain Metropolis performs a complementary move, showing that reactionary currents are also compatible with the genre's clichés and routinely mocked history. To return to issue #9's paratext, the exact line marked by Silk Spectre for ridicule is its closing, "Your costumed Comrade in the campaign against crime" (Moore 1987d: n. pag.); this alliterative sentiment registers the hackneyed dialogue of early superhero comics, also of the sort archly parodied by the *Batman* TV show. In this way, Captain Metropolis is a decidedly camp figure: his homosexuality and his naïve sincerity play on the dual meanings of "camp," kitsch as well as queer strategic affectation.

Watchmen thus confronts the gay subtext that has long figured in the superhero tradition. Notably, Captain Metropolis' romantic partner is Hooded Justice, who in the broader narrative of *Watchmen* is identified as the first costumed superhero. If the bright-hued, civic-minded Captain Metropolis calls Superman to mind, then the mysterious, shrouded Hooded Justice signals Batman. Superman and Batman, the original and most enduring superheroes, are reimagined via Captain Metropolis and Hooded Justice as a gay couple. The stalwarts of the genre are wedded together, described as acting "like an old married couple" (Moore 1987d: n. pag.), suggesting that the superhero's template is queer. Yet, Captain Metropolis' conservatism plus references to his lover Hooded Justice's own comments sympathizing with Nazis unite superheroes' dual strands of queer kitsch and pulp heroism, and suggest they are equally compatible with reactionary politics.

Watchmen's core contention for its genre, then, is that while the superhero may seem like a simplistic but heroic ideal, or at the very least a benignly silly pop culture figure, it in fact has serious political dimensions. The politics of individual superheroes may vary, but the politics of the superhero *as a type* are authoritarian. Though the progressive Ozymandias does bring world peace, his achievement requires deception and mass murder and it is coded as a form of conquest. Bradford Wright avers, "Moore's central thesis was rather simple. *The Watchmen* [sic] was Moore's obituary for the concept of heroes in general and superheroes in particular" (2001: 272). Dan Mazur and Alexander Danner likewise argue that *Watchmen* intends to be its "genre's epitaph" (2014: 176).

The core of this eulogy to superheroes is *Watchmen*'s insistence that models of heroism and morality that define superhero comics are relics of a naïve past. Moore's verdict on comics nostalgia is typified in Rorschach, whose strict black-and-white worldview parodies the simplistic good-versus-evil conflicts associated with superhero comics. If the series projects wary admiration for the steadfastness with which Rorschach holds to his convictions, Dr. Manhattan nonetheless must kill Rorschach to protect the benevolent lie manufactured by Ozymandias—a secret Rorschach's values bar him from upholding. The clear-cut moral divisions of the superhero genre are incompatible with the complicated and ambiguous ethical dilemmas of *Watchmen*'s narrative.

Watchmen's political interrogation of superheroes coexists with an examination of comics itself—the form in which the superhero genre first flourished. Matthew Levy and Heather Mathews remark that "*Watchmen* is a comic about comics" (2362013: para. 5), and Moore has noted that *Watchmen*'s true impact is its display of the comics form's potential for creative expression. Moore says that ultimately "what *Watchmen* was about was its own structure" (Millidge 2011: 131). *Watchmen*'s intricate structure showcases comics' affordances for storytelling and meaning-making.

To this end, *Watchmen* employs one of Moore's trademark techniques: ironic counterpoint. An example is *Watchmen*'s comic-within-a-comic, a horror-pirate comic entitled *The Black Freighter*, read by a peripheral character throughout the series. At times, *The Black Freighter* merges with the main narrative, so its panels alternate with panels depicting events in the primary narrative. Across this juxtaposition, caption boxes aligned with the two counterpoised narratives overlap, which is to say a caption for the main narrative will overlay a panel from *Black Freighter* and vice versa. Such mixing-and-matching offers the *Black Freighter*'s tale of madness, doom and self-destructive violence as an interpretive guiderail for reading the primary narrative it interrupts.

In addition to ironic counterpoint, visual repetitions yield motifs that generate and build on key themes. Variations on the inkblot splatter of Rorschach's mask, for example, reinforce *Watchmen*'s emphasis on subjectivity and clashing perspectives. Joe George notes the inkblot shape often takes the form of "two people embracing, often in silhouette," dovetailing with an underappreciated "emphasis on empathy and connection" (2017: n. pag.). Repetitions of images also structure panel transitions. Movements across panels regularly use parallel compositions to suggest thematic continuity or offer insight into characters. During the Comedian's funeral in issue #2, a set of four panels zooms into an image of Adrian Veidt, rendering him larger in each successive panel. The fourth panel is a close-up, but he appears younger and is adorned with his superhero mask; that panel segues into a flashback scene of the ill-fated Crimebusters meeting. At the scene's end, similar paralleling within panel compositions returns the narrative to Blake's funeral.

This specific use of panel transitions, then, indicates that the flashback moment is on the mind of Veidt during the funeral. Even if this information is only barely registered, it nudges the reader to pay special attention to the dynamics between Ozymandias and Comedian in the flashback itself, a directive cue that takes on greater significance by the end of the series when we learn that the flashback depicts the genesis of Ozymandias' twisted conspiracy to create world peace. The transitions from panel to panel in *Watchmen*, then, bear directly on the narrative. They also chime with the series' broader interest in the complex relationships between past and present.

Watchmen is also famous for its densely packed panels, housing bits of information that develop meanings. In some cases, such details speak to characterization. Hollis Mason, the first Nite-Owl and Dan Dreiberg's mentor, is in 1985 an aged ex-superhero who runs an auto shop. A sign outside his garage, foregrounded in an issue #1 panel with Dan's shadow in the background, proclaims, "Obsolete Models A Specialty!" (Moore 1987d: n. pag.). This detail encourages readers to see Mason, and by extension the idea of superheroes, as old-fashioned and useless.

An extraordinarily dense panel occurs near the end of issue #12. The panel is a wide-shot of Ozymandias in his Antarctic fortress, surrounded by banks of television screens broadcasting that his fabricated alien attack is prompting an end to geopolitical hostilities. In this moment of glory, Ozymandias raises his arms and yells, "I did it!" (Moore 1987d: n. pag.). Ozymandias' figure is centered and framed in a circle of yellow light: in this moment he is literally in a spotlight, basking in his triumphant performance. The lighting, however, casts a slight shadow over his face, signaling the dark aspects to this celebration. Ozymandias' figure is seen from a side-view, so one of his outstretched arms is foreshortened. When viewed in the semicircle of spotlight that frames the panel, Ozymandias' upraised arms resemble a clock's hour- and minute-hands at just before midnight; thus, his figure joins a visual motif that runs throughout the series, that of a "doomsday clock" countdown.

Other visual details reveal Ozymandias' character. Hanging on the wall behind him is a large painting of Alexander the Great, one of Ozymandias' idols and inspirations. The specific moment portrayed in the painting is Alexander's solution to the Gordian knot, a supposedly unbreakable binding. Rather than attempting to untie the knot, in this tale, Alexander slices it with his sword; the story thus serves as a parable for creative problem-solving that speaks to Ozymandias' ingenious plot. Also, the placement of Ozymandias' arms in relation to the painting intersects his wrists with images of Alexander's sword and a pole. His outstretched arms appear impaled, so Ozymandias' body evokes the iconography of Christ's crucifixion, cuing Ozymandias' self-perception as a Messiah figure. For Ozymandias' conspiracy, as in the Crucifixion story, humanity's salvation is achieved through bodily pain and sacrifice. Lastly, on the far-left side of the panel are towers of TV screens. The visual similarity between this grid of screens and a comics page subtly reminds that within *Watchmen* it is the comics form that depicts and reports the world.

A key technique in *Watchmen* that Moore extends in later comics is his and Gibbons' experiments with page layouts. *Watchmen* adheres to a rigid nine-panel grid template. Within this framework, however, Gibbons displays an array of different page layouts, dividing the page into horizontal and vertical thirds, then varying the numbers and sizes of panels. Such compositional regularity is leveraged toward innovative storytelling effects. See, for example, issue #5, titled "Fearful Symmetry," arguably the most acclaimed individual chapter of *Watchmen*. The page compositions for this issue, as its title's allusion to the William Blake poem "The Tyger" suggests, are symmetrical: the panel layout on the first page mirrors the layout of the final page, the second and penultimate pages, and so on, with the middle two pages of the issue appearing as mirrored, side-by-side compositions. This design resonates with the issue's focus on Rorschach, whose name and mask refer to the symmetrical inkblots of the psychological test he takes for a name.

Visual symmetry bookends the entire series, in fact, for the first issue's first panel and the last issue's final panel both spotlight a yellow smiley-face image smeared with red. This blood-stained smiley-face is also the cover image for issue #1 and has become closely associated with the series. The smiley-face button is the Comedian's ironic logo, and the first time we see the face in *Watchmen* it is streaked with his blood, a symbol of his murder. The smiley-face image reappears constantly throughout the series, often in subtle ways. At the end of issue #9 a wide-shot of the landscape of Mars shows tracks and ridges made forming a smiley-face pattern on the Martian surface, and in issue #12 a circular doorway into Ozymandias' Antarctic palace is illuminated by yellow lighting and framed with snow, icicles, and smoke in a way that evokes the smiley-face.

Several effects are at play with *Watchmen*'s uses of the smiley-face image. Scott McCloud's theorization of comics form, *Understanding Comics*, contends that a basic smiley-face is cartooning's most fundamental icon. The simple lines reduce a human visage to the greatest level of abstraction, but this lack of detail allows for the greatest degree of reader identification. The three-lined smiley-face, for McCloud, exemplifies comics and cartoons' power to compel recognition from readers, and is the keystone for the ways that comics make meaning (1993: 29–31). *Watchmen*'s use of this icon, then, anticipates McCloud and grounds the series' implicit arguments about the necessity of imagination and creative invention in the specific form of comics.

The smiley-face is not only an essential image of comics art, but also a signifier for bygone innocence. Moore observes that, according to some (unsourced) scientific studies, "a yellow circle with two black dots for eyes and a black smile drawn in was the simplest design that will elicit a response from a newborn baby. So in some ways, you could say that image is the ultimate scientifically tested image of innocence" (Khoury 2008: 117). Moore also notes that the marketing image "came about during the '60s" (Khoury 2008: 117): the iconic smiley-face image was reportedly created in 1963 and associated with kitschy merchandise bearing the slogan, "Have a nice day." Splattering blood on this image visualizes a critique of nostalgic impulses that distort the past as a "simpler" time.

Such functions of the smiley-face motif join wider thematic meditations on time, memory, and history. Riffing on the series' title, watches and watchmaking are also motifs, with the elegant precision of timepieces signaling the book's careful organization. This preoccupation signals Moore's broader creative interest in temporality and history. In *Watchmen*, this fascination with time dovetails with Moore's investments in affordances of the comics medium. According to Moore, the book's experiments with comics form and its dense structure were "suggesting new ways in which to view reality" (Millidge 2011: 131). The series asks how we see the world within comics and how comics allow us to see the world. These engagements tend to center on Dr. Manhattan.

The only character in the world of *Watchmen* with actual superhuman powers and abilities is Dr. Manhattan. Once a scientist named Jon Osterman, he is transformed by an accident in a technologically advanced test chamber containing radiation. The US government realizes his value as a Cold War asset, so he is enlisted and codenamed Dr. Manhattan for its ominous insinuations of The Manhattan Project's creation of an atomic bomb. In a paratext that accompanies issue #4, Dr. Manhattan is described as "a form of electromagnetic pattern resembling consciousness" (Moore 1987d: n. pag.) that created "an approximation of the body it had lost." The powers that come from this metamorphosis are virtually infinite: "this new and wholly original entity achieved a complete mastery of all matter; able to shape reality by the manipulation of its basic building blocks" (Moore 1987d: n. pag.). Dr. Manhattan perceives all events as they happen and all possible events as they can happen, in a singularity.

Dr. Manhattan's quantum perceptions make him a figure for analogizing the effects of the comics form and the experience of interfacing with comics. McCloud's *Understanding Comics* notes how "in comics, the past is more than just memories for the audience and the future is more than just possibilities! Both past and future are real and visible all around us! Wherever your eyes are focused, that's now. But at the same time your eyes take in the surrounding landscape of past and future!" (1993: 104). Comics' temporal landscapes, which give the reader the ability to perceive narrative past, present, and future in one glance, mirror Dr. Manhattan's perceptions. David Barnes writes, "For Moore our lives are not unlike the form and structure of a comic book page" (2009: 58), which Manhattan allows us to recognize. Adnan Mahmutović likewise argues that *Watchmen*, especially through Dr. Manhattan, shows how "comics can exhibit a certain kind of complexity that helps us look at space, time, history, identity, morality, particularity, and universality in different ways" (2018: 273). *Watchmen* meditates on various complex perceptions of time, experience, and history, and uses the comics form as analogy.

Such formal experimentation, thematic complexity, and metafictional depth were groundbreaking, and the impact of *Watchmen* is hard to overstate. In 2005, for example, *Time* created a list of the 100 best English-language novels since 1923 (reflecting the duration of *Time*'s publication). Designated a "graphic novel," *Watchmen* was the only comics text to rank. This recognition has received considerable attention, given *Time*'s status as outlet for mainstream opinion. *Watchmen*'s inclusion symbolizes comics' entrance into a mainstream literary culture.

In a similar vein, *Watchmen* is the recipient of considerable critical attention. Sara J. Van Ness' *Watchmen as Literature* (2010) and Hoberek's *Considering Watchmen* (2014) are scholarly monographs dedicated to *Watchmen*. Alongside these books are scores of peer-reviewed scholarly articles, not to mention the vast amount of ink spilled on *Watchmen* in general-reader venues like *New York Times Book Review* and *The Village*

Voice as well as the comics press. As all of this critical attention suggests, *Watchmen* has long been considered a first-rank entrant into the comics canon. Mazur and Danner put *Watchmen* squarely in "the canon of important superhero literature" (2014: 176) and Wright refers to it as "the magnum opus of super-hero comic books." *Watchmen*, with Art Spiegelman's *Maus* and Frank Miller's *Dark Knight Returns*, "established a beachhead for 'graphic novels' in the book trade" (Hatfield 2005: 30). These books were at the forefront of a surge of interest in comics and "brought an unprecedented degree of critical attention to the medium" (Chapman 2011: 232). But where does *Watchmen* currently stand in the comics field?

Watchmen's position in the comics canon, perhaps for the first time since its publication, seems questionable. Critics have for some time lamented what has come to be seen as an unfortunate, if inadvertent, legacy: if *Watchmen* demonstrated that "superhero comics could be far more complex" than assumed, many of its descendants "simply aped the darker tone and violent content, but without the more layered narrative, complex characterizations and social commentary" (Mazur and Danner 2014: 178). This critique is so pervasive it is now axiomatic.

More than ever, though, *Watchmen* itself as a text is being reconsidered. Of course, as with all classics, there have always been *Watchmen* dissenters: Moore's rival comics writer Grant Morrison has criticized *Watchmen* for its conspicuous design: "*Watchmen*, you can't turn the page without [Moore] saying "Look at me, look at me, look at me" (Pulliam-Moore 2018: n. pag.). Similar sentiments are now also registering in scholarship on comics. Although Bart Beaty and Benjamin Woo acknowledge that "*Watchmen* remains a milestone achievement" (2016: 58), they suggest that much of *Watchmen*'s prominence in the field is due to its propensity to "flatter those readers who have mastered the medium's formal codes and can notice them" (2016: 58). Put differently, *Watchmen* rose to "the apex of the canon" by "mobilizing fannish knowledge toward sophisticated, artful ends" (2016: 60). According to Beaty and Woo, *Watchmen*'s rootedness in obscure superhero history means that its prestige inside the comics field privileges "the hardcore comic book fan" (2016: 60), which in turn relegates its status outside the comics field to "small fish in the big, literary field" (2016: 64). Nevertheless, in terms of its popular cultural visibility *Watchmen* in fact persists as a juggernaut.

Indeed, *Watchmen* is now the cornerstone of a whole mini-franchise for DC Comics. Firmly against the wishes of Moore, *Watchmen* no longer exists as an autonomous work of comics art. Starting in 2012, DC began publishing a raft of miniseries under the banner title *Before Watchmen*.

These comics revisited *Watchmen*'s characters for "prequel" tales that elaborated the backstories for major and minor characters. October 2020 saw the release of *Rorschach* #1, a twelve-issue series by writer Tom King and artist Jorge Fornés, set in the continuity of Moore and Gibbons's *Watchmen*. *Rorschach* comes on the heels of *Doomsday Clock*, a twelve-issue series launched by writer Geoff Johns and artist Gary Frank in 2017. *Doomsday Clock* controversially integrated *Watchmen* into the larger tapestry of DC's mainstream fictional universe. Beyond co-opting Moore and Gibbons' characters, in *Doomsday Clock*, Johns and Frank purposely ape *Watchmen*'s pacing, composition, and even its cover designs and advertising campaign. This mimicry is also found earlier in Grant Morrison and Frank Quitely's *Pax Americana* #1, an issue of Morrison's 2014 *Multiversity* series. Although *Pax Americana* does not directly adapt *Watchmen*, it features the properties DC acquired from Charlton that inspired *Watchmen*'s characters and its narrative and visual design position it as a rewriting, and rebuke, to *Watchmen*. Outside comics, director Zack Snyder's *Watchmen* film adaption was released in 2009. And an acclaimed 2019 *Watchmen* television series developed for HBO "remixes," in showrunner Damon Lindelof's terms, the comic into a story about American racism.

The mere existence of these auxiliary texts resituates *Watchmen* in a comics canon and tradition. *Watchmen* can of course still be read as an isolated text akin to a novel, but it now must also be understood in dialogue with its prequels, sequels, adaptations, and spin-offs (not to mention imitators, parodies, and pastiches). Ironically, recognizing that *Watchmen* exists in a constellation of texts making up a corporate franchise may refresh, rather than diminish, the original series.

After all, *Watchmen*'s significance is tied to timing: its arrival coincided with the boom of interest in graphic novels. That phenomenon marked "a critical mass of comics written for adults and a publication format that could reach new audiences outside the usual comics stores and spinner racks" (Singer 2019: 54). Comics scholars, however, are increasingly seeing this revolution for its distortions. Beaty and Woo observe that "the very term 'graphic novel' is intended to ennoble the comic book by stealing fire from the better-established art form" (2016: 5). The graphic novel boom feeds into a wider tendency to talk about *Watchmen* in terms of the novel form. This insistent habit persists; Mazur and Danner write, "By creating an ambitious and fully self-contained story, with all the narrative and thematic intricacies of a literary novel, [Moore] proved that the genre was capable of unexpected complexity" (2014: 177). Such sentiments are common. Moore himself, moreover, fuels this fire: as Hoberek notes, Moore regularly "insists on describing his work in literary terms" (2014: n. pag.). Comparisons to the novel form are not totally unfounded, but they are still in the end a "category mistake" (Hoberek 2014: n. pag.) that can muddle key distinctions.

Charles Hatfield warns that "there is much about comics, historically and aesthetically, that may be lost in the drive to confer legitimacy on the graphic novel" (*Alternative* 2005: 153). For instance, reading *Watchmen* as graphic novel, not a serialized miniseries, can obscure the narrative elements that "cannily exploit the 'wait time'" between issues, one example of how the "serial packaging of a long-form comic lends certain structural and design elements that can be used to reinforce the shape and continuity of an overarching story" (2005: 155). Along such lines, reading *Watchmen* against and with its derivations can be regenerative, revising how the comic is perceived and appreciated.

Watchmen's sequels and spin-offs may help recuperate aspects of the series obscured or neglected due to its reputation as an exemplary and autonomous "graphic novel." Consider that *Watchmen* itself is comprised of a principle comics narrative in dialogue with supplemental paratexts done in styles found in other sites of cultural production: memoir, reportage, the sciences and social sciences, and so on. *Watchmen's* text itself thus compels readers to consider how texts from different media and genres discourse with each other. Furthermore, if the fleet of *Watchmen* spin-offs are taken as crassly exploitative endeavors, *Watchmen* reminds us that crass exploitation is deeply ensconced in comics' history. Such exploitation exists at the level of contracts and norms of corporate publishing—the forces that drove Moore away from the mainstream comics industry.

But the series' awareness of comics' history of exploitation goes beyond its easy corporate targets. In issue #2, Laurie finds an old "Tijuana bible" featuring her mother, Sally, the original Silk Spectre. A Tijuana bible, as Sally explain it, is "a little eight-page porno comic they did in the '30s and '40s . . . They did 'em about newspaper funnies characters like Blondie, even real people like Mae West" (Moore 1987d: n. pag.). Historically, these disreputable underground comics were unlicensed and circulated via a black market. Laurie finds the objectively objectifying comic book vile, but Sally finds it flattering and notes its value as a collector's item. The Tijuana bible returns at series' end, when we learn that Dan Dreiberg once owned a copy, since he was a "fan" of the first Silk Spectre.

Tijuana bibles crassly appropriate and exploit profitable characters like Blondie. As with corporate publishers who license the properties that they own, Tijuana bibles take another's creation and denigrate it for financial gain, an act that reshapes how the original creation is viewed. Yet, the Tijuana bible also exists within comics' subversive, iconoclastic, and dissident histories. *Watchmen* recognizes how creative pilfering and exploitation seem to be entrenched, if not intrinsic, parts of the comics tradition. While Moore and Gibbons' landmark series can be compartmentalized and appreciated on its merits, the sequels and other extra-textual developments surrounding *Watchmen* can potentially make visible the ways that *Watchmen* contemplates and allegorizes key questions of creative ownership and open-ended serialized narratives, medium-specific concerns that are often occluded when it is treated as a singular work. Ironically, Time Warner's exploitation of *Watchmen*—turning it into a "brand" and wringing profits from it—may inadvertently refresh the series by putting its critical reflections on such practices into relief.

CHAPTER 3
KEY TEXTS PART TWO

Key Texts Part Two continues Part One's account of Alan Moore's major comics, starting with work done after *Watchmen* and ending with his apparent retirement from comics in 2019.

Horrors of History

The onset of the 1980s saw Moore's breakthrough in mainstream comics, but by the decade's end he was breaking out of it. After roughly five years publishing at DC Comics, Moore's frustrations over a lack of creative control led him to cut ties with the company. Leaving DC, Moore told *The Comics Journal* in 1987, "was simply a matter of me quitting the company when I no longer felt that I could abide by their practices" (Groth 2012: n. pag.). In the wake of this decision, Moore initiated several idiosyncratic projects outside mainstream channels. The period 1988–93 saw a genuine creative explosion for Moore, though his attempts to work outside comics' publishing establishment, combined with turbulence in his personal life, meant that the projects from this period were subject to delays, extended gaps between serialized installments, and outright cancelations.

Moore's raft of comics from this period is eclectic. These comics move away from popular genres, and amount to what Moore calls a "major personal cycle" (qtd. Parkin 2013: 251). Along with their personal dimensions, Moore's comics from this time represent a turn to historical narratives. These historical comics, notably, keep an eye on the present moment of the turn of the millennium: they use representations of history to diagnose the late-twentieth century. Tellingly, these narratives orient around crimes and traumas.

From Hell

Shortly after *Watchmen*, in 1989, Moore launched a new serialized comics project: *From Hell*, an expansive historical fiction done with the acclaimed

Scottish cartoonist Eddie Campbell. *From Hell* debuted in the second issue of *Taboo*, cover dated 1989. *Taboo* was a black-and-white, independent comics anthology founded by one of Moore's artistic collaborators on *Saga of the Swamp Thing*, Stephen Bissette. The first six installments of *From Hell* appeared in the pages of *Taboo*, issues #2–7, over a span of three years. When scheduling and management problems took their toll on *Taboo*, later episodes came in occasional instances published by Kitchen Sink Press.

From Hell is a historical fiction centered on the notorious serial killer Jack the Ripper, who in 1888 murdered at least five women in London's Whitechapel district. Yet, according to Moore, *From Hell* was initially not about the Ripper at all. In a 2001 interview, Moore explains that, as far as he remembers, "the original idea was . . . to do a comic strip about a murder" (Robinson 2012: 107). He adds, "I thought a murder seemed like a complex and interesting human event which thankfully doesn't happen to many of us. But when murders do happen, they are so intense that it's the human condition in some sort of extreme" (Robinson 2012: 107). Fictionalized murder, then, offers an opportunity to explore human experience in concentrated form. As Moore imagined the thematic possibilities of murder, he was bombarded with headlines about the Ripper: it was 1988, the centenary of the murders, so Jack the Ripper seemed ubiquitous. The anniversary hoopla compelled Moore to realize that Jack the Ripper was the perfect vehicle for his idea about an exploration of murder, for in the Ripper case the murders are both real and symbolically freighted.

To do justice to this project, Moore did substantial research. A chief source was Steven Knight's *Jack the Ripper: The Final Solution* (1974), which provides the comic's basic narrative architecture. Moore's preparation, though, went beyond that one book. An appendix featuring annotations, which runs over forty pages in the *From Hell* collected edition, testifies to his exhaustive research. Yet, *Hell* is far more than a composite of prior representations and accounts.

In fact, Moore makes a conscious effort to avoid the conventions of so-called Ripperology, which often lean into the case's lurid details. According to Moore, when representations of the Ripper draw on the conventions and aesthetics of the horror genre, as they so often do, an audience is allowed a vicarious thrill that diminishes the reality of the horror and dishonors the suffering of the Ripper's victims (Robinson 2012: 100–1). *From Hell* therefore aims to humanize the Ripper's victims, and it depicts the Ripper's murders in grisly but detached detail. Another way Moore sidesteps glamorized Ripper tropes is to decenter the Ripper himself. *From Hell* discloses a motive and identity for the Ripper in its second chapter; it is thus not a "who dun' it?" that places the Ripper at its narrative core, a move that risks granting mystique to the murderer. Instead, *From Hell* names the Ripper from the start. The comic also puts his crimes in the context of a conspiracy, thereby casting him as a participant in a network, not a singular and exceptional historical actor.

In *From Hell*, Jack the Ripper is Sir William Gull, a physician appointed in 1871 to be a Physician-in-Ordinary to Queen Victoria. Ripperology research has long postulated Gull as Jack the Ripper, claims animated by the apparent medical knowledge displayed by the killer's vivisections of his victims. Such accounts allege that Gull killed as part of a conspiracy meant to hide the royal heir Prince Albert Victor's sexual relationships with working-class women, one of which produced a child. Chapter Two's introduction of Gull moves rapidly through his biography, jumping from his childhood to his time in medical school, rise within his profession, initiation into an occult version of the Masonic Freemasons, and then his first act of murder under order from the Crown. *From Hell* thus tells the basic story of the Ripper in its second chapter. Dispensing this information early on signals that as *From Hell* goes on it will move beyond core facts of the case.

Notably, when Moore and Campbell first present us with Gull in Chapter Two, they employ a first-person point-of-view storytelling device that bestows the reader with his perspective. Much of the chapter is told from Gull's point of view, with the contents of panels framed as if it were being viewed from his eyes. This device conflates reader's and Ripper's perspectives. Intercut with these panels, however, are more conventional third-person-perspective panel constructions. The reader thus alternates between identification with Gull and ostensibly objective observation. These juxtapositions make the reader complicit in the narrative's horror: by putting the reader in the position of the killer, but then retracting for a putatively neutral perspective, the chapter suggests that the formation of Jack the Ripper is a social, collaborative enterprise in which the reader is an active participant. Pointedly, at chapter's end, the first-person perspective device moves from Gull to a victim, Anne Crook, as he kills her. Even as *From Hell* asks readers to see themselves inside the Ripper role, then, it also denies facilitating the vicarious thrill of violence: at the moment of murder, *From Hell* instead has the reader assume the subjectivity of one of the Ripper's victims.

Chapter Two's movements across perspectives speak to a pattern that holds for the rest of the narrative. *From Hell* interweaves the stories of Gull and his fellow conspirators with the daily lives and experiences of the Ripper's victims and the investigators pursuing the Ripper. These intersecting narratives feature minute period details and historical figures, creating a portrait of late-Victorian London both panoramic and granular. But, *From Hell* is not a historical fiction per se; instead, it is an interrogation of the Ripper's social meaning. Consider Appendix II, a comics supplement that blends an overview of Ripperology, a gloss on the main narrative, and background on *From Hell's* production. In it, Moore dismisses "the idea of a solution, any solution" to the murders as "inane" (Moore 2006a: Appendix II, 16). Appendix II continues: "Five murdered paupers, one anonymous assailant. This reality is dwarfed by the vast theme-park we've built around it. Truth is, this has never been about the murders, nor the killer nor his victims. It's about us" (Moore 2006a: Appendix II, 22). *From Hell* attends to the discursive construction of Jack the Ripper, as an idea, and that idea's lineages and legacies.

To be sure, a focus on symbolic resonances—to the degree that the factuality of *From Hell's* account of the murders is nearly irrelevant altogether—sits uneasily with Moore and Campbell's commitment to deglamorizing the murders and recovering the dignity of the victims. The Ripper is treated as a transcendent symbol: to cite Appendix II once more, "Jack mirrors our hysterias. Faceless, he is the receptacle for each new social panic" (Moore 2006a: Appendix II, 22). Positioning the Ripper this way creates tensions across the Ripper as historical reality and as source of mythopoeia. If *From Hell* sees Jack the Ripper chiefly as a transhistorical cultural idea, what then is its historical vision? How does it comprehend history?

From Hell's historical perspective, first, is entwined with Moore's interest in magic and the occult. Moore's researches into magic began as preparation for *From Hell*, since the story involves ceremonial magicians and occult conspiracies, and leads to his own identification as a magician a few years later. This investment in magic relates to *Hell's* sense of history, for Moore declares, "a major theme [of *From Hell*] would be the examination of history in a different light—history in an occult light, using the word 'occult' in its purest sense, to mean hidden" (*Feature* 1997: 12). Magic acts as metaphor for histories that shape us even if they are invisible to us.

This idea is strikingly visualized in Chapter Four, when Gull takes his carriage driver and unwitting accomplice John Netley on a tour of London landmarks that, Gull alleges, have been charged with magical power by Freemasons throughout history. At the tour's end, Netley traces these sites on a map and together they form a Satanic pentagram drawn atop London, which symbolizes Masonic power coursing through the city's figurative veins. Of this scene, Moore clarifies:

> There is no secret society or conspiracy of Freemasons that actually put these sights [sic] into a pentacle shape, *but*, those points can be linked up in a pentacle and that means that those ideas, the ideas that those ideas represent can be linked up into a pattern as can events in history, like the events of the Ripper murders. (*Feature* 1997: 7)

From Hell's postulation of occult energies pulsating through London models how historical narratives assert meanings rather than simply assemble and describe sequences of causal events.

These narratives delimit interpretations of history, and interpretations of history shape identities—individual and collective. History is a narrative project, and prevailing narratives construct us. If historical narratives shape consciousness, then occult or hidden histories can recalibrate consciousness. Enacting changes to consciousness is also remit of art, hence Moore's declarations that *From Hell* led him to believe "that there is no difference between history and fiction" (*Feature* 1997: 8), an equivalence that rests on the ways in which history and fiction alike construct narratives. Moore thus triangulates history with magic and art; the Critical Questions chapter will turn to the commonalities Moore finds between art and magic more fully.

In the end, *From Hell* as a historical fiction is less about reconstructing the Victorian past and more about how narratives of that past create our present selves. Annalisa Di Liddo notes that Moore's representations of the Victorian era in *From Hell* and elsewhere suggest he views "that time as a pivotal moment in the development of English identity" (2009: 111). Elizabeth Ho clarifies this point: it is not the Victorian period itself that animates *From Hell*; rather, the comic "looks back to the Thatcher administration and forward to that of New Labor and simultaneously traces the anxieties and confusion over the breakdown of traditional notions of Englishness" (2006: 102). Per Ho, "Moore's graphic novel is an intervention . . . in what seems to be an uninterrupted and at times uncritical expression of Englishness" (2006: 108). *From Hell* locates, in England's Victorian past and especially in the Ripper murders, a turning point for the historical development of English identity. This excavation of Englishness is leveraged toward commentary on late-twentieth-century Britain.

Key here is the question of power. *From Hell* speculates, after all, that the Ripper killings took place specifically as a way for England's ruling class to preserve its legitimacy. When Queen Victoria expresses the need to hide Prince Albert Victor's surreptitious marriage and "illegitimate" child from the public, she tells Gull, "if this scandal is not to rock the throne she must be silenced" (Moore 2006a: Chapter Two, 28). The essential motivation for the Ripper murders is preservation of the ruling order, dictated by a monarch who is the living embodiment of the body politic. As for the powerless subjects, when four of the women who will be murdered by the Ripper realize they can use their knowledge of the prince's transgressions to their advantage, they hatch a blackmail plot inside a pub pointedly named The Britannia (Moore 2006a: Chapter 3, 11). Within the culturally relevant site of the pub, by virtue of its name coded as microcosm for Britain and by extension British identity, these four working-class women attempt to overthrow the traditional hierarchy. The silencing and desecrations of their bodies by the Ripper on behalf of the Crown therefore represents the cruel means by which the ruling order wields its cultural power and hold on national identity.

From Hell posits that the Ripper's violent reassertions of power shape the incoming twentieth century, making the Ripper murders of 1888 a fount for the conditions and experiences of that century. According to Moore, the Ripper "is more or less acting as a midwife in the gory birth of the Twentieth Century" (qtd. Millidge 2011: 179). Indeed, as the occultist Gull carries out his ritualized murders he has visions of future worlds. In Chapter Eight, after brutally killing a victim, Campbell depicts Gull in a full-page image standing above the corpse with outstretched arms: before him is a modern skyscraper, rendered in photorealistic detail (Figure 3.1). After snapping back to the Victorian present, Gull's accomplice notes that he lost sight of Gull briefly, and asks, "Where did you go?" Gull responds, "Not far" (Moore 2006a: Chapter Eight, 40). Besides allowing for the possibility that Gull physically went to the future, this exchange implies that little distance exists between Victorian and modern Britain. Gull's visions persist with later murders and they mesmerize him.

These visions of a twentieth-century future culminate with Gull's undignified death in a decrepit Victorian asylum in 1896. In his final moments, Gull's consciousness travels throughout space and time in a final prophetic reverie. The course of his mind's movements seems to

Figure 3.1 William Gull appearing before a modern skyscraper in *From Hell*. Art by Eddie Campbell. *From Hell* © Alan Moore and Eddie Campbell. Courtesy of Top Shelf Productions. Used with permission.

be guided by other legendary English serial killers, past and present, from the London Monster of the late seventeenth century to the Halifax Slasher of 1938. These spiritually related murderers and their impacts on social orders, cultural development, and collective psyches become the guideposts for English history: "An invisible curve, rising through the centuries" (Moore 2006: Chapter 14, page 14). The Ripper—and his ancestors and descendants, all of whom in fact constitute one essence—form "an architecture" for history (Moore 2006, Chapter 14, page 14). As he nears death, Gull communes with this spirit of history; once he dies, his soul leaves the physical plane altogether, ascending into the ethereal substance of history itself.

Jack the Ripper, then, is positioned as outside of history while also immanent within it. As Moore writes in the Appendix II, "Jack is a superposition" (Moore 2006a: Appendix II, 16). Nevertheless, Jack is still an intervention in history with profound and cascading effects, a point driven home in the framing prologue and epilogue. These scenes take place in 1923 and feature Inspector Abberline, the investigator in charge of the Ripper case, and Mr. Lees, a spiritualist who assists with the investigation. In the bookending episodes, Abberline and Lees look back on the Ripper case but also express anxieties about the current state of the world. Lees has the final word in the comic, telling Abberline that his psychic premonitions lead him to think "there's going to be another war" (Moore 2006a: Epilogue, 10). Juxtaposing Lees and Abberline's ruminations on the destructive new century with reflections on the Ripper case imply a causal relationship. Indeed, Abberline's rueful line to close the prologue, as he and Lees enter his home, is that his "fancy new address" is "the house that Jack bought" (Moore 2006a: Prologue, 8). The Ripper constructed the modern world in which these aged men now uncertainly inhabit.

From Hell here again historicizes the present. Contemporary Britain, causally and spiritually, is descended from the late-Victorian moment of the Ripper. *From Hell* makes "explicit use of Jack the Ripper to comment on the present's relationship to the past" (Ho 2006: 100). The comic's turn to the Victorian past stems from a sense that the era provides insight into the millennial moment of *From Hell*'s composition; as we shall see, Moore's other historically minded comics from this time are likewise attuned to the historically contingent circumstances and conditions of late-twentieth-century Britain.

This notion is driven home in "I Keep Coming Back," a 1996 short comic done with Argentinian artist Oscar Zárate for *It's Dark in London*, an anthology of British comics supported by the London Arts Board. Moore has acknowledged that "I Keep Coming Back" functions as an unofficial coda to *From Hell* (Sobel 2016a: 109). "I Keep Coming Back" recounts Moore's experience doing an interview for a documentary on London fiction, filmed in the Whitechapel district; in it, Moore reflects on the unsettling effects of dedicating a decade of his life to the Ripper. Narration explains how the camera crew films Moore outside a pub, with the intention of using editing effects to "recreate a drawing from my book, dissolving from the fiction into me, in real life" (Moore 2016f: 100). The double meaning of this line—reinforced by the next caption, "Dissolving / From the fiction / Into me"—registers how Moore's imaginative investigation of murder blurred lines between himself and his subject. This transfer extends to physical spaces. In the comic's closing panels, Moore's narration muses, "Do these buildings keep the coded centuries? . . . The cobbles coax our steps" (Moore 2016f: 108). Taking "I Keep Coming Back" as an extension of *From Hell* reiterates the unnerving possibility that the violence of the Ripper not only inhabits but propels the present. This notion about history, that it and especially its traumas invent us, animates Moore's comics during the immediate post-*Watchmen* period.

A Small Killing

"I Keep Coming Back" is in fact Moore's second comics project with Oscar Zárate: they previously collaborated on *A Small Killing*. That graphic novella follows a middle-aged advertiser named Timothy Hole (pronounced "Holly"), who lands a campaign to market a diet soda brand in post-Glasnost Russia. Before making his business trip, Hole travels from his current residence in New York City to his home country, England. This return home prompts a flood of memories for Hole, painful recollections compounded by unsettling dreams and frightening visions. To convey the protagonist's disturbed state of mind, Zárate's art contrasts bright pastels with browns and pale yellows done in watercolor, creating an unreal atmosphere. At times, jarring changes in visual style make the narrative's hallucinatory aspects more overt. For example, when the narrative turns to a dream sequence, the art switches to smudgy pencil line work to register the shift in perception. Across its permutations in visual style, Zárate's art carries a dreamlike bent, complementing Hole's slippery grasp of reality—a breakdown focalized around a ghostly boy following him everywhere.

This spectral child haunts Hole after he lands in London and later returns to his hometown, Sheffield. At the same time, Hole's delirium intensifies, and the number and frequency of flashbacks increase. As Hole's mental state destabilizes, we see him "obsess over the lingering ghosts of his past indiscretions, his memories taunting him with guilt over his failed marriage, his lack of loyalty to the boss who gave him his first break, and his avoidance of responsibility for a girlfriend's unplanned pregnancy" (Millidge 2011: 156). These various betrayals resonate with Hole's substitution of yuppie careerism for his youthful countercultural idealism, as well as his discomfort with his working-class roots. The phantasmal child signifies the lingering ghosts of Hole's past.

Such an association is driven home near the end of the graphic novella when we learn that the wraithlike child haunting Hole is a vision of Hole himself as a child. This ghost symbolizes Hole's confrontation with what is figured as his personal original sin: as a boy, Hole captured several insects in a jar and then buried that jar in his yard. This ostensibly minor, juvenile indiscretion is made pivotal. In his recollection of this act of cruelty, Hole recounts, "I buried them alive, like little Eichmann" (Moore 2011i: n. pag.). Hole's term "little Eichmann," nodding to the infamous Nazi bureaucrat Adolf Eichmann, is an idiom used for people whose actions seem minor or value-neutral but are in fact complicit with a corrupt, harmful system. Moore has said that he and Zárate meant Hole to "represent the sum and synthesis of the culture that surrounded us in those times, the end of the eighties" (Rodriguez 2011: n. pag.). Reading Hole as a representative figure means that the "little Eichmann" expression signals the pitiless values of the period, values entwined with the post-Cold War expansion of global capital. Indeed, the title *A Small Killing* itself has a dual meaning, referring to Hole's torture of insects but also being slang for capitalist profit.

A Small Killing opens in New York City—America's financial capital—in the years 1985–9. The latter year marks the fall of the Berlin Wall, leading to the reunification of the liberal democracy West Germany and communist East Germany. That year has thus become a symbol for the end of the post-Second World War Cold War era, a period structured around two global superpowers, the United States and the Soviet Union. In this early post-Cold War context, the American conservative political commentator Charles Krauthammer wrote of a "unipolar moment" in which the "center of world power is the unchallenged superpower, the United States, attended by its Western allies" (1990: n. pag.). The historical backdrop for *A Small Killing*, then, is the USSR's collapse as global superpower, symbolized by its policy of Glasnost, translated as "openness" or "transparency". Some ad copy that Hole workshops with colleagues even riffs on the word Glasnost, suggesting that this policy was seen by sectors in the West as an opening for commercialization.

Hole as a representative figure gives an ambivalent impression of this historical transition occurring in the late-twentieth century. Zárate says, "There were parallel forces struggling with one another. But one manipulated the other and eventually subdued everyone. It is the United States, the new empire" (Rodriguez 2011: n. pag.). In this light, we see Hole as an Englishman and global citizen subsumed into American hegemony. The painful memories haunting Hole therefore allegorize a collective reckoning: per Moore, "there is a parallelism between the acts of a person and the acts of a whole culture. . . . All of them block their past, deny the nasty parts of their story, the buried crimes, the forgotten sins, the archived atrocities" (Rodriguez 2011: n. pag.). The narrative's swings from past to present, and art evoking delirium and horror, capture Hole's denial of his past and allegorize how an unchallenged American empire, represented by Hole's advertising firm, has commandeered his (and Britain's) values and identity.

The path toward this Americanized identity is construed as a carnival of horrors and perfidies. Key betrayals from Hole's life are presented as grotesquerie: for instance, after pressuring his paramour to terminate a pregnancy, she sends him the fetus in a test tube. And in the most visually arresting example, the insects that Hole trapped as a boy spring from the jar in which he buried them as luminous, giant monsters. Hole's terrifying, uncanny encounters with his life's mistakes allegorize a need for England to reckon with its ignoble past, which, as his residence and career remind, are inextricable from US dominance. In this sense, *A Small Killing* meditates on modern empire's burdens upon individual and national identities. Not unlike *From Hell*, *A Small Killing* projects individual acts of violence and interpersonal cruelties onto a national body.

At the same time that *Killing* comments on its historical moment, it is also one of Moore's most personal comics. Zárate initially shared with Moore an idea for a story about a man being haunted by a boy, a premise Moore connected to a dream that he once had as a teenager in which he met his child self. Moore also notes that Zárate "decided to use aspects of Northampton to portray Sheffield" because he, Zárate, realized that Moore "could write better about a place to which [he] was linked with an emotional contact" (Rodriguez 2011: n. pag.). Hole thus seems patterned on Moore. After all, he is an English creative worker—advertising, like comics, is commercial art—who finds himself far removed from his countercultural roots, a professional climber within a crass American industry. Despite his ostensible success, however, he is experiencing debilitating ennui.

Throughout the comic, we see Hole traveling by car, plane, train, bicycle, and on foot; all these forms of locomotion take him, slowly, back to his hometown. Hole escapes, by hook or by crook, from the enervating environment in which his profession has taken him back to his geographic, familial, and spiritual roots. Amid the hallucinatory climax, Hole apologizes to his ghostly younger self; in the morning after, he seems refreshed. The final page shows Hole strolling down a romanticized English village lane, the sun rising brightly on the horizon, with all the forms of travel he once used as methods of escape in motion depicted somewhere in the scene. This full-page final image is combined with a rhapsodic caption, "There's a new yolk in the blown egg. There's a new pulse in the scraped womb. Everything is pregnant" (Moore 2011i: n. pag.), evoking rebirth and promise. This finale resonates with Moore's experiences at this point in his career: Hole's lucrative but hollow work in advertising can be aligned with Moore's mainstream success, and Hole's new day recalls Moore's abandonment of corporate comics for a return to roots in independent publishing.

A Small Killing therefore tells a story both deeply personal and distantly historical. Hole's acts of cruelty and betrayals of his values allegorize England's national experience in the face of a dominant American empire. At the same time, Hole is one of Moore's most autobiographical protagonists, whose artistic compromises for financial gain seem to narrate Moore's own creative redefinition during the late 1980s and early 1990s. Hole's eventual exorcizing of his demons, putting him on a path to redemption, suggests Moore's convictions that better futures are possible.

Big Numbers

Shortly before *A Small Killing* saw print in 1991, Moore embarked upon an ambitious project with artist Bill Sienkiewicz. *Big Numbers*, as a comics project, is a classic tale of "what could have been." Only two issues of this unusual comic were published, in part because Sienkiewicz became overwhelmed by the script's demands and could not maintain a pace on the art that was financially sustainable. *Big Numbers* was abandoned and will likely never be finished.

Big Numbers is a social drama with a large ensemble cast, set in an English village, called Hampton, clearly patterned on Moore's hometown of Northampton. A protagonist, insofar as one exists, is Christine Gathercole, a writer returning to Hampton after ten years away. Like *A Small Killing*'s Timothy Hole, then, she is a creative worker drawn back to the provincial English village from which she came—chiming with Moore's own creative re-centering at this point in his career. Through Christine we see the economic damage and social tumult wrought by Margaret Thatcher's decade in power: Hampton's industrial economic backbone is broken, people scrape together an existence on social security benefit, and communal bonds seem shattered. Several characters suffer from debilitating, often dangerous, forms of mental illness, conditions that are a metaphor for the community's more broadly felt senses of dislocation and detachment from a stable, shared reality.

Meanwhile, in Los Angeles, an American corporation selects Hampton as the location for a massive, gaudy new shopping center. As a result, Hampton becomes a site for the convergence of Thatcherism's disruption of England's local industries with the intrusion of US transnational capitalism. According to Moore's outline for the series, vignettes featuring over forty characters would slowly establish links and patterns uniting Hampton's populace while the slow construction of the shopping mall would be "a powerful symbol of the shit that is coming down" (Millidge 2011: 164) around them. The mall would therefore serve as a locus for Hampton residents' suffering, as well as an organizational storytelling device that systematizes seemingly disparate lives into one entity.

With *Big Numbers*, Moore committed to innovation. He recalls in 2008 that he and Sienkiewicz wanted the comic "to have constantly experimental and progressive storytelling techniques that hadn't been seen before" (Khoury 2008: 149). One way in which we see such formal experimentation is in the comic's representations of time. How time operates within and across comics panels is a topic for Scott McCloud's groundbreaking theoretical study, *Understanding Comics* (1993). McCloud argues that in comics "time can be controlled through the content of panels, the number of panels, and closure between panels" as well as "the panel shape" (McCloud 1993: 101). *Big Numbers* issue #2 indicates Moore's own growing interest in the ways time can be rendered and manipulated on the comics page. A remarkable page depicts a couple, Colin and Hilary, as they bicker over breakfast; their children sit with them, distracted and preoccupied. The entire page is devoted to this scene, divided into a grid of twelve evenly sized rectangular panels (Moore 1990c: 7).

While the actions and dialogue in the panels convey a clear sequence when read standardly from left to right, the panel backgrounds' render progressive images of the kitchen's interior. When the scene is apprehended as an entire page, however, the reader can see a complete overhead shot of the setting, continuous but for the slight dividing lines of panel gutters. Viewed as one image, the characters' discrete placements in the panels give an illusion of their smooth movement, across and down, the depicted kitchen space. This push to visualize time on the comics page in different and multiple ways comports with Moore's broader ambition that *Big Numbers* use comics to express his "view of how reality hangs together" (Khoury 2008: 153) in complex configurations.

Big Numbers also discloses Moore's incipient interest in place. The importance of place in *Big Numbers* registers from the start: the first panel shows a timetable for trains running through middle England. From this image follows a largely wordless montage of England's rail network, ending with Christine's arrival by train at the Hampton station. These scenes of central England are later contextualized when a character named Brian, teacher and local historian, lectures on the history of Hampton and its county, Hamptonshire. Brian drives home the relevance of his lesson by declaring, "It's important to have a sense of where we're living, of when we're living, a sense of history's patterns . . . of time's passing . . . I say, if we don't pay attention to the place where we are, well . . . then we might as well not be here" (Moore 1990b: 29). Notably, as this monologue plays out, first in dialogue balloons and then captions, the contents of the panels shift from images of Brian and the historical figures or events he references to his students departing his classroom and school. During this transition, Sienkiewicz's art goes from pristine and detailed to scratchy and smudged. These visuals cue a historical movement toward uncertainty: the slow vanishing of the community's young people, rendered indistinctly by the blurry art, visually enacts the warning made by Brian's speech.

Lost connections to a place and its history recur in the completed issues. In issue #2, Brian pontificates on history over breakfast with his wife, Victoria. She ignores him, however, given her preoccupation with the needs of daily life, a dynamic that signals disconnection between knowledge of the past and attunement to the present. Brian's discourse on Hampton tells a tale of conflict, conquest, and displacement. In his account, "Hampton's first citizens were mammoths . . . until Paleolithic man. He could use weapons." Next comes Neolithic tribes, superseded by a Celtic clan, then the Britons, followed by the Romans, and so on. This sequence, as he puts it, "'slike a mathematical progression." Notably, he speculates that, for the Britons, "Roman technology must have seemed like Martian's invading!" (Moore 1990c: 22–3). This observational aside is recalled at the end of the issue when Christine stumbles upon the groundbreaking for Hampton's new shopping mall. Panels on the final page track a construction worker who casually tosses the wrapper for his candy bar snack. In the final row of panels, we see that the candy is in fact a Mars bar; Sienkiewicz's art then moves in closer on the wrapper to end on close-up images of its manufacturing address in the US. The Mars reference recalls Brian's comment about Roman technology, situating American mass production and transnational industry within Brian's story of historical civilizational successions.

Furthermore, the pointed choice of Mars candy bar—at a construction site featuring a giant hole buried into the English countryside—alludes to H. G. Wells' classic science fiction novel, *The War of the Worlds* (1898). This allusion drives home the idea that the American presence is not some benign next step in a natural historical process, but rather an instance of alien invasion and conquest. Indeed, in the middle of issue #1, we see a model of the mall as it will be constructed, and it is a bizarre and asymmetrical assemblage of triangular buildings with a dome and giant tower—a design that seems at home in some fantastic extraterrestrial landscape. The encroachment of American transnational capitalism into England is thereby coded as an aggressive alien attack.

Yet, it is an alien invasion that has been primed by domestic conditions, and in fact many of Hampton's villagers enthusiastically welcome the mall. For example, in the aforementioned groundbreaking scene at the end of issue #2, a Hampton local reacts to seeing the construction site with almost religious ecstasy. Upon realizing that the mall is being built, first his eyes widen and jaw opens, and then he thrusts his arms into the air and exclaims, "At last. At last!" (Moore 1990c: 40). In the third issue, never published but now available to read online, a small business owner explains why he welcomes the American shopping complex: "Worry me? Ha ha! No, doesn't worry me. I mean competition, it's what free enterprise is about. It's a fair system here: you work, you're rewarded" (Moore 2009c: n. pag.). Despite such assurances, Moore's outline for the series indicates that this shopkeeper is anxious but unable to admit it to himself, given his evangelical devotion to Thatcherite economic pieties.

The policies and values of Thatcherism have thus left Hampton both vulnerable to and desperate for US-style transnational capitalism. Had the series continued the mall would, in Moore's words, "completely alter [Hampton] forever . . . [and] the community that had been there for hundreds of years suddenly starts to fall apart under new and unfamiliar strains" (Khoury 2008: 153). These strains occur at multiple levels: "the threat to the life of Hampton's community comes not only from commercial globalization. The social changes under way also involve jobs and the welfare state" (Di Liddo 2009: 123), namely Thatcherism's end to full employment and cuts to social provision.

Big Numbers presents an English community complicit with the external forces that threaten it. In issue #2, we see Delia Judge, English wife of Stephen Judge, the American architect of the shopping mall. The Judge family will relocate to England while Stephen oversees the construction project. When their daughter, Tiffany, expresses some uncertainty about the quality of a British education, Delia jests, "At the very least, it gave me sufficient intelligence to emigrate" (Moore 1990c: 34). In Moore's notes for issue #3, he writes that when Delia arrives back in England she realizes that "she has been away too long, and that England is as foreign as America now" (Millidge 2011: 172). Delia might therefore be seen as vanguard for the broader processes of disruption, Americanization, and alienation that the mall's construction in Hampton will bring in force—rendering Hampton's former world extinct.

Brought to Light

Moore's collaboration with artist Bill Sienkiewicz for *Big Numbers* is slightly predated by "Shadowplay: The Secret Team," a comic made for a slim anthology, *Brought to Light: A Graphic Docudrama*. *Brought to Light*'s three entries condemn US foreign policy, particularly in Central America. As the book's cover copy breathlessly declares, its contents expose "30 years of drug smuggling, arms deals and covert operations that robbed America and betrayed the Constitution." Like *Big Numbers*, "Shadowplay" attends to crimes of recent history in terms of political changes.

Brought to Light was published through Eclipse Comics by the Christic Institute, a leftwing public interest law firm founded in 1980 and dedicated to social reform. The project partnered Moore with Sienkiewicz, setting up their later collaboration on *Big Numbers*. *Brought to Light* appeared in 1989, amid Christic's federal lawsuit *Avirgan v. Hull*, which alleged assassinations and other illegal actions were committed by the Central Intelligence Agency (CIA). In a sense, *Brought to Life* is an attempt to mobilize public support for Christic's ultimately failed lawsuit.

To help Moore prepare, the Christic Institute provided him with research and case files. The historical account of the CIA that emerges from Moore's immersion in this material leans on horror tropes. As Moore recalls, "It was exhilarating compiling all that information, making it fit and then finding a way to convey it to the readership in an interesting and entertaining way. At the same time, it was harrowing. I mean, I've written a lot of horror comics, but Oliver North is a much more horrifying being than any of those" (qtd. in Millidge 2011: 154–5). Such horror is reflected in the comic's aggressive tone and disquieting imagery. In an introduction to "Shadowplay," Daniel Sheehan—General Counsel for the Christic Institute—writes that "Shadowplay" offers "a subjective, surreal and artistic interpretation" of the Christic Institute's legal case against the CIA and that, because the "conduct of the defendants is shocking and violent" the comic "is, correspondingly, shocking and violent" (1989: n. pag.). The portrait that emerges in the comic is of an undemocratic, corrupt, and criminal shadow government within and across American institutions.

Speaking this counter-narrative to heroic American myths about its altruism and innocence is an anthropomorphic bald eagle. Rendered as a boorish traveling salesman, getting drunk at a dingy bar, he is an obvious symbol for a debauched America. Breaking the fourth wall for a direct address to the reader, the narrator announces, "I'm watcha' call a representative. I represent The Company" (Moore 1989b: 3). The salesman eagle's use of "The Company" plays on a familiar nickname for the CIA. Moreover, when explaining the CIA's post-Second World War global interventions, he remarks, "See, business-wise, we recognized our real competitors" (Moore 1989b: 5). This language of commerce, markets, and enterprise persists throughout the comic, suggesting US foreign policy's underpinnings in the crassest capitalistic opportunism.

A second important motif is introduced early: puppetry. The eagle narrator's introduction of himself involves a two-panel sequence in which the avian spook manipulates its appendages to cast on the wall a shadow puppet of a vicious bear. This symbol of communist Russia suggests the exaggerated and illusory nature of any so-called Red menace. Furthermore, the bear shadow puppet begins a visual motif, imagery that casts the CIA as manipulative puppet-master.

Despite this disquieting portrait, the comic maintains a sense of possible redemption for the United States. The comic's narrative is bookended by full-page images of the Statue of Liberty, though in the first instance the statue holds a suitcase full of money and burning dynamite instead of a tablet and a torch. The closing illustration gives a realistic if still impressionistic rendering, but perceptible in the hazy foreground is an outreached hand, futilely grasping at the statue. Both images share the caption, "This is not a dream." This framing device casts the intervening historical account of the US government's dirty dealings as both harsh reality—not a dream—and, due to the caption's juxtaposition with the Statue of Liberty, a betrayal of the so-called American Dream.

In the first framing image, that of the debauched Statue of Liberty, captions read, "This is not your home. It is instead as if someone had traced the shadow of America. . . . No, this is not America: it has a different tradebase and economy . . . a different government" (Moore 1989b: 1–2). The puppeteering CIA, then, is differentiated from an abstracted idea of America: while the shadow government may be a ventriloquist for America, it is not America itself. This idea is driven home at comic's end, when the eagle narrator attempts to buy silence: in the surrealistic finale, the eagle opens a suitcase gushing forth blood, and offers, "All we're askin' is your indifference. Just turn away. Pretend it ain't happenin'. . . . Well? C'mon . . . whaddya say? Can we do business?" (Moore 1989b: 28). The final, bookending image of a barely visible hand reaching for a more accurately rendered Statue of Liberty therefore implies that were individuals to reject the CIA's bargain and refuse to turn away from the truth of the conspiracy, a truer representation of America might possibly be in reach. Like *A Small Killing*'s finale, the ending of "Shadowplay" suggests at least the possibility for salvation.

"Shadowplay," like much of Moore's work from this period, offers a dense historical narrative that draws connections between the past and the conditions of the present moment. Collectively, Moore's comics from the early post-*Watchmen* moment aim to craft explanations for the material and psychic experiences of the late twentieth century. Moore infuses within these historical narratives the imagery and tropes of horror, registering the despair and confusion of the millennial historical moment. And yet, they also demonstrate a utopian sense that some atonement for the horrors of past and present may open up possibilities for brighter, even redemptive futures.

Re-imagining Superheroes

After five years in independent comics and alternative publishing, in 1993 Moore makes a mainstream comeback with a batch of new superhero comics. This return to popular genres in the early 1990s is often cast as compensatory: Eric Berlatsky says that indie projects like *Big Numbers* and *From Hell* are Moore's "real work" of the time, and his superhero comics redux are merely a means "to finance his longer, more complicated projects" (2012b: ix). Even if we accept this view, Moore's superhero second act injects an intense focus on creator rights into his revisionist project.

1963

Five years after swearing off superheroes, Moore was contacted by comics creators Steve Bissette and Rick Veitch about doing a superhero comic for a new publisher, Image Comics. The invitation yielded *1963*, a miniseries that parodies superhero comics from the 1960s, especially those from Marvel Comics. This pastiche of older comics is a rejoinder to the 1990s' dominant genre trends of darker narratives and antiheroes—trends associated with Moore's own revisionist work. While on the one hand *1963* expresses ambivalence about Moore's prior superhero comics, on the other hand it discloses Moore's increasingly hardline positions on comics creators' rights that will guide his future engagements with superheroes and related popular genres.

Moore's publisher for *1963*, Image Comics, is implicated in both matters of aesthetics and creator rights. Image was founded by seven artists, including Todd MacFarlane, Jim Lee, and Rob Liefeld, whose work at Marvel made them industry stars. However, these artists began to feel underappreciated and exploited, so they made a highly publicized collective exit from Marvel. Upon departure, they criticized the working conditions at Marvel, focusing on the denials of artistic freedom and proper remuneration. In this way, these artists echoed complaints made by Moore and other independent-minded auteurs. Image Comics' commitment to creative control and full ownership rights for its talent hence appealed to Moore.

The lighthearted and self-consciously kitschy *1963* seems not only worlds apart from the dark, "adult" takes on the genre that made Moore famous, but also at odds with the Image style so popular at the time. In contrast to the character designs and page layouts associated with Image in its early days—respectively, characterized by their excessive musculature and extravagant double-page spreads—*1963* mimics the look of Marvel Comics from its 1960s heyday. Moore's artistic partners, Bissette and Veitch on pencil art, with other collaborators like Dave Gibbons and Jon Totleben doing ink jobs, evoke if not imitate the styles of artists whose work defined early Marvel Comics. Visually, *1963* starkly contrasted with prevailing aesthetics of 1990s superhero comics.

These visual differences extend to the materiality of the series. Image, as a company, led the way on improvements in paper quality, using sturdy and glossy pages that gave more heft to comics' otherwise flimsy pamphlet form. Importantly, upgraded paper stock also maximized the vibrancy of new digital coloring techniques that Image was pioneering, which speaks to the ways that Image's innovations were often guided by its founders' priorities as artists first and foremost. Similarly, Image relocated its internal advertisements to the back matter of an issue, meaning those ads would not limit artists' pacing and other visual choices. But *1963* was printed on cheaper newsprint, so the comic literally feels older than other comics produced in the 1990s. Ian Hague argues that newsprint carries with it a scent that registers an older stage of comics publishing: "the power of smell contributes to what we might call a manufactured nostalgia that permeates *1963*" (2014: 128). In its aesthetics and materiality, *1963* recalls sensations of an older comics experience.

Narratively, each of *1963*'s six issues takes the appearance and title of a different faux comics series, patterned on popular 1960s Marvel franchises like *The Fantastic Four* and *The Mighty Thor*. This format gives it the appearance of an anthology, but each issue involves its characters investigating a mysterious energy wave, foreshadowing narrative convergence. *1963* #6, meant to be the penultimate issue, finally reveals the identity of a mysterious figure appearing sporadically in the series: he is Shaft, leader of Image's flagship team of antiheroes, Youngblood. This revelation ends with Shaft declaring, "This is where things start to get interesting" (Moore 1993f: n. pag.)—which perhaps functions as promise to readers weary of amusing but seemingly pointless pastiches. *1963*'s characters were meant to meet in a finale, presented as a lengthier *Annual*, which would feature its mock 1960s characters confronting Image's 1990s superheroes. However, the series finale was delayed when its intended artist, Jim Lee, took a sabbatical from art. Subsequent editorial chaos at Image, Moore's changing priorities, and strained relationships among collaborators left *1963*'s final issue abandoned altogether. Like *Big Numbers*, *1963* surely will never be completed.

Comments from Moore and others involved with *1963* suggest that the finale would have contrasted Image's stable of hardened antiheroes against the comparatively happy-go-lucky Marvel analogues to critique the current state of the genre. Moore recalls that in an early talk with Bissette and Veitch, he suggested, "If we do six issues of Marvel Comics pastiches from the early 1960s, we can probably make some sort of point about how different the values in comics are now compared to then" (Khoury 2008: 171). Assuming *1963* was in fact working toward a condemnation of the vogue for dark, hard-boiled, and often lethal heroes—a superhero model that thrived at Image—Moore's name on the series would serve, at least implicitly, as confession of complicity: *Watchmen's* shadow hangs over *1963's* dim assessment of 1990s superhero comics.

Yet, a sense of connection works against this contrast. Moore's Marvel analogues meet their Image counterparts by traveling across parallel worlds. However, by naming the series *1963*, exactly thirty years prior to the year of the series' publication, Moore implicitly crafts a historical narrative about the genre. This perspective emphasizes evolution rather than a break. To this point, Andrew Hoberek notes that *Watchmen's* "darker, putatively more realistic tone" was in fact "not an unprecedented breakthrough so much as an extension of earlier movements in this direction. The Marvel Comics titles that Stan Lee produced with the artists Jack Kirby and Steve Ditko in the early sixties, such as *Fantastic Four* and *Spider-Man*, featured heroes who were vexed about their powers and missions" (2014: n. pag.). Marvel paved the way to *Watchmen* and, in turn, Image.

By positing Marvel's tetchy, maverick heroes from the 1960s as ancestors to Image's antiheroes, *1963* "implicitly draws a parallels between Marvel in 1963 and the Image Comics of 30 years later" (Beaty and Woo 2016: 82). Such links are reinforced by *1963's* foregrounding of comics' visual energy. While Moore has made disparaging remarks about Image's subordination of substance and narrative coherence to showy art, *1963* suggests that the revered Marvel Comics titles of the 1960s had a similar imbalance. Moore even changed his writing method for *1963*, abandoning full-scripts to do a "kind of '60s Marvel style" (Khoury 2008: 171) approach, one in which the writer supplies the artist with a brief treatment of the issue's plot, but only adds captions and dialogue after artwork is completed. And *1963's* artists pay homage to the innovations of early Marvel artists: the final page of *Mystery Incorporated* uses photographic op-art for its background, a technique favored by Jack Kirby. These emphases suggest that the magic of the 1960s-era Marvel Comics that *1963* honors derives from its frenetic and outlandish art—not unlike Image Comics.

Yet, if *1963* posits that Image's rebellious superheroes and flashy art descend from classic Marvel Comics, the comic also suggests a critical distinction between the two companies, namely Image's ethos of creative freedom and its practice of creator ownership. Here, one must recognize that *1963* features two narrative levels. One level, of course, consists of the stories of the various Marvel analogues. However, a second, meta-narrative develops across the paratextual parodies of comics' supplemental content like letters pages and editorial pages. The meta-narrative gives glimpses into a fictional company, apparently called Sixty-Three, behind the narrative content.

This narrative level confuses the already fuzzy historicity of the main narrative. A faux ad for a Chicago-area comics shop, featuring a crystal ball with "1993" materializing within it, blares the copy, "In the future there will be stores that sell nothing but comic books!" (Moore 1993a: n. pag.). Other ads parody the Cold War anti-communism prevalent at early 1960s Marvel. In these instances, the paratextual narrative seems set in the past, yet elsewhere—e.g. references to the rock band Bikini Kill and habits of modern comics collectors—it suggests contemporaneity. An editorial in issue #3 mentions Sixty-Three's "RETRO-format" of printing: "RETRO-format stands for Really Easy To Reproduce Old-format" and it includes printing techniques like "color reproduction where you can ACTUALLY SEE all the little dots, a definite delight denied to you by the majority of modern magazines!" (Moore 1993c: n. pag.). Here, "retro" and the reference to advanced coloring techniques found in "modern magazines" imply that "Sixty-Three" exists in an alternate 1990s.

Notably, the meta-narrative's mixture of nostalgic past with alternate present turns *1963*'s pastiche of Marvel from affectionate parody to pointed critique. *1963* adopts Silver Age Marvel's use of boisterous nicknames for creators' names in credits boxes: Moore is "Affable Al" Moore. In the meta-narrative, Affable Al becomes a character in his own right, the voice behind responses to reader letters and a column in the editorial page. Moore apes Marvel writer-editor and figurehead Stan Lee with Affable Al, writing with Lee's hyperbole, tendency toward silly puns, and blend of self-aggrandizement with self-effacement. "Al's Amphitheater" is based on "Stan's Soapbox," with Al ending each column with "Excalibur," a nonsensical play on Lee's sign-off, "Excelsior!"

As *1963* goes on, the Lee parody grows harsher. In issue #4, Al delves into his biography: a tongue-in-cheek account of his road to success in the comic book business—"one long hard slog, all the way across town to the offices of Modern Magazines Ltd. and then up three flights of stairs to Uncle Morrie's office" (Moore 1993d: n. pag.)—discloses the alleged nepotism behind Lee's career. *1963* also suggests that Lee exploited the labor of his more talented colleagues. In issue #4's column, Affable Al recounts "working with all-time greats like Ed 'The Emperor' Evans," a nickname suggestive of Lee's primary artistic partner, Jack "King" Kirby. Al recalls giving Ed "a manuscript that said, 'Maybe something about a space monster. Big fight. Good guys win'" and then Ed would "take it away and tidy up a few loose ends like character concept, plot, panel breakdowns and suggested dialogue" (Moore 1993d: n. pag.). The next Al's Amphitheater, in issue #5 (Moore 1993e), includes a throwaway reference to a book, *Origins of Sixty-Three Part Two: How I Created Everything All By Myself And Why I Am Great* by A. A. Moore, alluding to *Origins of Marvel Comics* (1974) and *Son of Origins of Marvel Comics* (1975). Those two volumes were among several paperbacks that collected pivotal stories from Marvel's history; however, misleadingly, Lee alone receives authorial credit within the book series.

Moore's unmistakable accusations against Lee via "Affable Al" mark a hardening of his views on Lee. While Moore's 1983 essay on Lee is subtitled "An Affectionate Character Assassination," its assessment of Lee is mostly favorable. Despite calling Lee a "flawed genius" (Moore 2012a: n. pag.), Moore praises the innovations of Lee's writing and holds more criticism for Lee's imitators. But *1963*'s Affable Al anticipates Moore's later public denunciations of Lee as a swindler who stole credit and financial rewards for characters and stories for which his artistic partners were overwhelmingly responsible. This implicit argument as it appears in *1963* extends beyond Lee as an individual, rebuking the corporate comics industry that Lee's Marvel has long dominated. To this point, the editorial page in *1963* reworks Marvel's folksy nickname for its offices, "The Bullpen," into the barbed "Sixty-Three Sweatshop." Such cutting jabs at Marvel create tension between primary- and meta-narratives, for the former is a celebration of Marvel's Silver Age model for superhero storytelling, but the latter functions as a blistering critique of the exploitative working conditions under which those stories were produced.

Despite its seeming discomfort with the style of superhero narrative published by Image, then, *1963* champions the creator-owned publishing model that Image represents. In what became its final issue, *1963*'s hero team the Tomorrow Syndicate travel through space and time, moving across parallel worlds. Near the end of their journey, the Tomorrow Syndicate speeds through the interdimensional space that separates parallel worlds toward The Aleph, "a point from which all other points are visible" (Moore 1993f: n. pag.). The double-page spread depicting this climax features an assortment of jagged "windows to other universes," (Moore 1993f: n. pag.) within which are renderings of prominent creator-owned comics characters. They include, among others: Dave Sim's Cerebus, Frank Miller's Marv from

Sin City, Bob Burden's The Flaming Carrot, along with the protagonists from creator-owned titles by Moore's *1963* collaborators, Rick Veitch's *The Maximortal* and Steve Bissette's *Tyrant*. The Aleph's interdimensional array situates *1963* and in turn Image within a network of independent creators and publishers that constitutes a counter-model to the corporate publishing model of DC and Marvel.

1963's final appraisal of the Image paradigm is encapsulated in dialogue from Tomorrow Syndicate member Ultimate Special Agent. Upon arriving in the parallel world inhabited by Image's heroes, a grimy urban landscape, U.S.A. exclaims, "Everything looks so harsh and vivid!" (Moore 1993f: n. pag.). In this line, the judgmental connotation of "harsh" is offset by the positive connotations of "vivid": the world these comics project is grim and gritty, but at least it amounts to a distinct creative vision.

Supreme

1963's meditation on superhero comics' history has a companion in another Image series: *Supreme*. The character Supreme debuted in Rob Liefeld's *Youngblood* before getting a solo title in late 1992; Moore took over writing chores for the flailing superhero title starting with issue #41, dated August 1996. In both visual design and powers, Supreme is patterned on Superman—the similarity of the characters' names telegraphs the relationship—but, keeping in line with the era's sensibilities, Supreme was originally characterized as an unrelenting, aloof, brutal, and even lethal anti-hero. By the time that Moore took over, however, the novelty of hard-edged heroes was gone, so Moore had a mandate to revamp the character from the ground up. Coinciding with this creative shake-up were business rearrangements: after hiring Moore, Liefeld removed his studio, Extreme Studios, from the Image consortium. *Supreme* relocated to Liefeld's new company, Awesome Entertainment.

Moore's *Supreme* transformed a directionless series into an examination of comics' history. As Orion Ussner Kidder writes, "From practically the first panel, [Moore's *Supreme*] launches into a highly self-reflexive analysis of the superhero as a generic type that developed over the course of decades" (2010: 82). Bart Beaty and Benjamin Woo write that Moore's "run on Rob Liefeld's *Supreme* became a comic about Superman and the history of American comics" (2016: 59); likewise, Geoff Klock argues that *Supreme* recognizes "that superhero comic books are invigorated by interaction with their history" (Klock 2003: 191). In *Supreme*, Moore returns to superhero revisionism but, ironically, he redirects its critiques to rebut genre trends that his earlier revisionism yielded.

The narrative device that facilitates Moore's historicizing project in *Supreme* is The Supremacy, an ethereal realm that Moore introduces in his debut on the title. At the start of Moore's first issue, Supreme returns to Earth after world-hopping adventures from the preceding issues. Upon approaching Earth, he is shocked to see a strange flickering phenomenon affect all matter. When Supreme alights in an urban center, he declares, "The entire city shifts and flickers between different versions of itself! The population are like shimmering statues, trapped 'twixt who they are and who they might have been!" (Moore 2002c: n. pag.). Amid his confusion, Supreme is confronted and subdued by four superpowered figures, all wearing costumes similar to his own. These counterparts have diverse embodiments: for example, one is a Black woman, and another is an anthropomorphized mouse à la the cartoon hero Mighty Mouse. This cadre whisks Supreme to a realm found "nowhere in space-time," an expanse "formerly known as Limbo" (Moore 2002c: n. pag.). Within this void is the Supremacy, a glittering and monumental kingdom populated by countless versions of Supreme.

The varieties of Supreme in the Supremacy reflect variations on the superhero figure over time. Characterizations and designs mostly cue memorable eras, renderings, or stories from *Superman*, since that character is Supreme's template. For instance, "Original Supreme" has a streamlined visual design and limited power set that, along with his designation as the first Supreme, make him an analogue for Jerry Siegel and Joe Shuster's original portrayal of Superman. "His Majesty Supreme the Fifth," or the "Supreme Supreme," is said to hail from "the 1960's Silver Dynasty," thereby aligning him with the "Silver Age" era of *Superman* from Moore's childhood, which he considers the character's and franchise's apex. Along with the Supremes, the Supremacy also houses the supporting characters, artifacts, and locales from the fictional histories of Supreme, most of which also allude to different moments in Superman's publication history. Additionally, the Supremacy hosts the "future-variants," "secondary Supremes," and "imaginary versions" of the primary character that seem to accompany every major iteration of Superman and, more generally, are common to superhero narratives. Indeed, *Supreme* itself had introduced spin-offs Lady Supreme and Kid Supreme, plus innumerable alternate realities, before Moore's run.

His Majesty Supreme aptly describes the Supremacy as a "Valhalla" for Supremes: it is in fact a sort of afterlife. His Majesty Supreme explains that the Supremacy is a heavenly space for Supremes and their affiliates "who'd been displaced in the unfathomable periodic changes in space-time we call Revisions" (Moore 2002c: n. pag.). The current Supreme learns that he is merely the latest avatar of Supreme, prepared by the universe for the upcoming Revision to reality; however, he is unique in that he came into being, and gains access to the Supremacy, before experiencing his Revised world. All other Supremes only encounter the Supremacy and learn its secrets after they have been blinked from existence by a Revision. Therefore, when Supreme departs the Supremacy at the end of issue #41, entering into a totally reshaped reality and history, he knows existence has been reset and that the memories crystallizing in his mind are in fact being actively invented as an effect of the Revision. Although the cosmological mechanics involved in the Revision are not entirely coherent, the series hinges on this narrative contrivance that allows Supreme to recognize the experience of the Revision as its effects settle upon him. Supreme's meta-awareness of the Revision as he confronts and internalizes his new history facilitates *Supreme*'s meditation on comics history itself.

Post-Revision, Supreme learns that he is now the heroic alter ego of Ethan Crane, a comic book artist. Crane draws *Omniman*, a series whose titular hero resembles Supreme and Superman. Supreme faces dire threats as Supreme plus workplace and romantic conflicts as Crane, all the while learning about his new existence. Details about his new past come in flashbacks, drawn by Rick Veitch in the styles of older comics: these flashbacks give a fresh backstory and an impression of a publication history that extends back decades. The crux of the series is the dynamic between Supreme's new, revised status quo and the flashback pastiches of key moments in comics history.

This dynamic plays out at the level of narrative: the plot of Moore's first twelve issues, collectively known as "The Story of the Year," centers on the return of Supreme's mad scientist nemesis, Darius Dax, a villain patterned on Superman's archenemy Lex Luthor. The seeds of Dax's attempted revenge in the present are found in the flashback episodes; likewise, Dax's defeat hinges on the returns of Supreme's allies, who also appear in flashbacks. As if to drive home this reciprocal relationship between past and present, the finale of "The Story of the Year" creates a time paradox in which Dax, sent back in time, becomes the catalyst for Supreme's acquisition of superpowers in the first place. Supreme's present actively creates its own past to open up the future.

Simply at the level of narrative, then, *Supreme* suggests that superhero comics draw energy and meaning from purposeful engagements with their history. Unfortunately, *Supreme* suggests, modern superhero storytelling is set on denying its own history. In Moore's 1987 proposal for *Twilight of the Superheroes*, he admits ambivalence over the continuity reset of DC's *Crisis on Infinite Earths*. Moore writes, "In the wake of the time-altering at the end of the *Crisis* we are left with a universe where the entire past continuity of DC, for the most part, simply never happened" (Moore 1988c: n. pag.). At the time Moore drafted that proposal, he had just written *Whatever Happened to the Man of Tomorrow?* as a farewell to Superman's pre-*Crisis* continuity: as "Key Texts Part One" shows, *Whatever Happened* is an elegy for the characters, storytelling styles, and tropes disappeared from *Superman* comics after the reset inaugurated by *Crisis on Infinite Earths*.

Notably, the plot of *Whatever Happened* revolves around the slow elimination of characters and elements from Superman's life. The terminated characters and elements in Moore's plot, from Supergirl and Krypto the Super-dog to multicolored Kryptonite, are the same ones that DC was retroactively removing from Superman's freshly wiped continuity. The removals were done to make Superman more accessible and current, yet for Moore this *tabula rasa* post-*Crisis* Superman was "changed into something more synthetic and less appealing. So I decided that I'd rather liked the old Superman, that I'd rather enjoyed that rich mythology and continuity, all those kind of stupid but enduring elements, you know?" (Khoury 2008: 174). *Supreme* revives these elements: in a narrative reversal of *Whatever Happened*, *Supreme* resurrects Suprema and Radar, analogues of Supergirl and Krypto, thereby reinserting the histories that the continuity reset of *Crisis* sought to erase. Against claims that resets give clean slates for franchises to be made relevant, *Supreme* counters by saying that engaging, not denying, comics' histories revitalizes and propels the genre.

Adding to *Supreme*'s meta qualities, by naming the inciting incident that facilitates this recaptured history "The Revision," Moore seems to be pointing toward his own reputation as a writer of revisionist superhero narratives. Yet, despite *Supreme*'s apparent rejections and reversals of the revisionist method popularized by Moore himself, *Supreme* does not in fact depart from Moore's revisionist strategies; rather, it repurposes them for a new comics landscape. *Supreme* reverses some of Moore's revisionist aims, but it does not fundamentally change his revisionist model.

If Moore's prior revisionist representations of the superhero draw out the unpleasant ideological implications and underpinnings of the genre's comparatively naïve origins, *Supreme* begins with a post-revisionist superhero and grafts onto it the putatively naïve trappings of earlier superhero comics. As Moore writes in a preface to the collected edition *Supreme: The Return*, he tries "to infuse this new '90s model type with all the imaginative power of the superheros [*sic*] of the previous 50 years. To give it that sort of humor and grace and see if we can come up with some composite that's viable for the next century" (Moore 2003d: n. pag.). Moore's earlier, and darker, revisionist superhero comics like *Miracleman, Watchmen*, and *Batman: The Killing Joke* all similarly dialogue with their respective narrative and publication histories. For instance, *Miracleman* never jettisons or erases the earlier, Mick Anglo iteration of the character; its rewriting of the character's past preserves the existence of those narratives, but simply reframes them as simulations within a new narrative that serves to comment upon those older stories. While the effect is an ideological critique of the genre, it makes its critique by contending with the history.

In this way, *Supreme* is a clarification of Moore's revisionist project. *Supreme*'s embrace of the silliest elements from 1960s *Superman* reveals that Moore's revisionism is not about tone nor any so-called realism or graphicness of its representations. *Supreme* is not written for a younger audience akin to the one who once read the whimsical and inventive, if also ephemeral and childish, comics that *Supreme* reverentially evokes. Indeed, the sophistication and thematic elements of Moore's *Supreme* make its target audience likely overlap considerably—in terms of demographics and reader interests—with readers of *Watchmen*. Rather than content or tone, *Supreme* reminds readers, Moore's revisionism centers on critically engaging the histories of the medium and genre.

To the extent that *Supreme* marks a shift in Moore's revisionism, it is in its assertiveness on creator rights. *Supreme*, like *1963*, comes down firmly on the side of individual comics creators' distinct artistic voices, which, in Moore's view, are hampered by the commercial demands and factory-like working conditions for most mainstream US comics. In *Supreme*, this critique registers in subplots involving Supreme's secret identity, Ethan Crane, a comic book artist. Ethan's romantic relationship with Diana Dane, the writer paired with him for *Omniman*, develops around their shared interest in bringing some craft and credibility to their assignment. Their ambitions are stymied by their sleazy editor, Lucas Tate, whose constant shouting about deadlines indicates his prioritization of quantity over quality, as well as Moore's self-parody, Bill Friday, an egotistical writer of pretentious and sensationalist superhero comics. Ethan and Diana attempt to bring artistry and personal expression to their comic book, despite their unconducive working environment.

Relatedly, in a late issue during Moore's run, entitled "New Jack City," Supreme explores an otherworldly "Psychoverse" in which he encounters a procession of outrageous characters, all of which recall the creations of legendary comics artist Jack Kirby, nicknamed "King" Kirby. Recall that *1963*'s meta-narrative implies that Marvel's creative explosion during the 1960s was largely Kirby's doing. The overseer of the Psychoverse is "King," a floating, cosmic head smoking a cigar—an image that not only visually resembles Kirby but is also Kirby-esque in its absurdity. King tells Supreme of an "idea space," a magical realm of ideas that can be "farmed" (Moore 2003d: n. pag.) to feed creativity. This issue, then, not only pays tribute to Kirby as an innovator, but also registers Moore's growing interest in collective imaginations and the relations between fiction and reality, a dynamic he will revisit in later comics.

Moore's '90s Superheroes

1963 and *Supreme* generally stand as Moore's best-received superhero work with Image (though most of *Supreme* was done for an Image splinter company, Awesome Entertainment). But those two titles represent only a portion of Moore's superhero output for Image's studios during the 1990s. Moore wrote several issues of Image founder Todd McFarlane's series, *Spawn*, plus some spin-off miniseries such as *Spawn: Blood Feud*. Throughout the 1990s, Moore would also pen several comics for Wildstorm, the studio of another Image founder, Jim Lee, including its flagship title *WildC.A.T.s* as well as its ancillary and spin-off books. And Moore was heavily involved with Liefeld's Awesome line of comics beyond *Supreme*, revamping *Youngblood* and penning *Judgment Day*, a miniseries meant to be a prelude for a Moore-driven overhaul of the entire line.

In these comics, Moore adheres to the house style of 1990s Image, from an emphasis on eye-popping art to their vulgar representations of violence and sexuality (especially female sexuality). Moore now explains that much of his Image work was an experiment with a form of storytelling at odds with his own sensibilities: according to him, he saw industry trends epitomized by Image as a creative challenge (Khoury 2008: 171). He now rates those Image experiments as failures.

The stipulated failure of Moore's experiment discloses a tension between two, perhaps irreconcilable, models for comics value. In their study of the competing regimes of prestige within the comics field, Beaty and Woo devote a chapter to the poetics of *Supreme* creator Rob Liefeld. They assess his style as "the reduction ad absurdum of a dynamic visual style" and add that with this style "Liefeld was simply working the same aesthetic vein as many of his contemporaries" (2016: 79). Liefeld, then, is representative of a wider 1990s model of comics value, one that finds "no necessary contradiction between art and commerce" (2016: 84) and consequently remains widely dismissed "by critics and academics steeped in regimes of value that privilege literariness, seriousness, or difficulty" (2016: 84). This critical regime hostile to Liefeld operates with the values and sensibilities of a different model for value and prestige identified by Beaty and Woo, one that champions "the quality popular comic book" popularized by "Moore and his British Invasion cohorts" (2016: 63). Moore's inability to accommodate his craft to the frameworks prevailing at Image discloses a clash between two models, one commercially visual and the other aspiringly literary, which are fundamentally contrary.

Still, individually, Moore's Image comics offer glimpses of his trademark techniques and sensibilities. Moore's work on *Spawn* brings levity and self-deprecation that punctured the ponderous tone of the series, a tone that elsewhere—given McFarlane's limitations as a writer—comes off as inflated self-importance. Humor is also found in the *Violator* miniseries, which costars a satirical figure, The Admonisher, who is directly mocking Marvel's popular anti-hero The Punisher. The absurd Admonisher deflates the model of anti-hero Punisher represents—brooding, grimacing, cruel, and lethal—which, of course, is the model that prevailed at Image and the pages of *Spawn*. Tim Callahan in fact reads *Violator* as a superhero parody comic connecting it to "the juvenile delinquent kind of humor Moore honed back in his *D.R. & Quinch* days" (2012f: n. pag.). In *WildC.A.T.s*, Moore brings his interest in conspiracy to the series, in turn narratively reshaping how readers understand the franchise's characters, their relationships, and their mission. His *Judgment Day* miniseries at Awesome extends the critique of excessively dark superhero narratives and grim antiheroes also found in *Supreme*.

Overall, Moore's output at Image and Awesome is hit or miss. Scattered throughout it are gems like the short comics story for *Wildstorm Spotlight*, "Majestic: The Big Chill," featuring the superhero Mr. Majestic, as well as the miniseries *Deathblow By Blow*, a clever and ironic postapocalyptic narrative in the vein of Moore's "Future Shocks" stories for *2000 A.D.* At other times, Moore's attempts to bring craft and intelligence to the currents of mainstream superhero comics fall flat. For instance, the crossover miniseries *Violator vs. Badrock*, which paired characters from McFarlane's and Liefeld's respective studios within Image, as well as the *Voodoo* miniseries at Wildstorm, indulge more than subvert the mindless violence and crass, exploitative sexuality so pervasive in 1990s superhero narratives. Still, the slyness of Moore's Image work, especially *WildC.A.T.s.*, anticipates a millennial wave of post-Dark Age superhero titles done in an overtly ironic, self-parodic, and self-reflexive style—these later comics include *Stormwatch*, *The Authority*, and *The Ultimates*, series written by fellow British Invasion writers Warren Ellis, Garth Ennis, and Mark Millar. If Moore's smattering of superhero comics for Image done in a so-called 90s style occupy an odd place in his comics corpus, they nonetheless drove wider comics trends.

Cultural Commons

On November 18, 1993, his fortieth birthday, Alan Moore declared that he is a ceremonial magician. This unusual assertion represents a turning point in Moore's creative growth. Per Moore, he began his "explorations of occult material, but with a creative end in mind" in order "to make progress as an artist" (*Feature* 1997: 14). Magic guides Moore's creative development directly and indirectly. A pivotal outgrowth of Moore's magical researches is "Ideaspace," Moore's model of intertextual cultural production. Ideaspace refers to dynamics across individual and cultural imaginations, creative production and material conditions—relations explored in Moore's comics.

"In Pictopia"

Over time, Moore's developing interest in magic gives him a framework for formalizing his nascent theories on language and consciousness, including his formulation of Ideaspace—an ethereal but accessible wellspring of stories, signs, and ideas. Yet, the fundamentals of Ideaspace register in his comics before he acquired the occult vocabulary to express them. A key example here is the short story "In Pictopia," first published in *Anything Goes!* #2 in 1986. "In Pictopia" not only previews Moore's post-*Watchmen* ambivalence with revisionist superhero narratives, but it also offers an early example of Ideaspace's intertextual model of collective cultural production.

Pictopia, originally called "Fictopia" by Moore but renamed by artist Don Simpson to suggest comics' visual character, is an imaginary polis populated by analogues of characters and character types from varied comics genres. Buildings' windows and graffiti give their exteriors the appearance of comics pages' panel frames and text. Our narrator is Nocturo the Necromancer, patterned on the newspaper strip character Mandrake the Magician, created by Lee Falk in 1934. Nocturo is a tour guide through the districts of Pictopia, the states of which reveal the city's social hierarchies. For example, in a "ghetto on the edge of town" (Moore 2016g: 26) called Funnytown, anthropomorphic animals live in squalor. Nocturo expresses admiration for these citizens, describing their liveliness and talent—"they made just walking around seem like poetry" for "every movement expressed so much"—which meta-textually refers to the funny animal genre's vibrancy and the economical artistry of its creators. However, these characters were pushed to the city's outskirts when "there wasn't any work for them" (Moore 2016g: 26). Nocturo even senses the area itself "is getting smaller" (Moore 2016g: 26). The inequality mapped onto Pictopia allegorizes a comics world where once-prominent genres are marginalized to the edge of extinction. Driving home this idea, the story concludes with Funnytown bulldozed to the ground.

Superheroes are the social group at the top of Pictopia's hierarchy, a position first registered in Nocturo's laments that "only superheroes can afford to live in color" (Moore 2016g: 25). Despite their social power, superheroes are hardly flourishing. Nocturo passes by a gang of young superheroes beating a "dog man" from Funnytown, knowing that—in the spirit of resilient cartoon icons like Wile E. Coyote or Tom Cat from *Tom and Jerry*—he will bounce back from the damage and thus be able to sustain more abuse. The cruelty of this gang reflects the decadence of the city's superhero caste. Superheroes, at the zenith of power and prestige in Pictopia, are becoming increasingly nasty. This transformation takes literal form with Nocturo's one superhero friend, the pliable Flexible Flynn, an elastic hero who appears to be based on Jack Cole's zany character from 1941, Plastic Man. By the end of the story, however, he encounters Flynn socializing with the newer superheroes at a bar. In this moment, Flynn gives his old friend Nocturo the cold shoulder. Nocturo, shocked, comments on his friend's new appearance: "The costume was similar, but with slight modifications. The visor looked more sinister, somehow. And his face, his build, they were more ... well, more realistic. It wasn't Flynn, I thought quite lucidly, 'This is Flynn's replacement'" (Moore 2016g: 32). The allegory of "In Pictopia" parallels the degenerative effects of superhero revisionism with the ghettoization of comics' other genres: in both cases, older, seemingly outdated traditions and histories are erased.

Many commentators, like Marc Sobel and Tim Callahan, detect consistencies across "In Pictopia" and the superhero revisionism that Moore was doing at that time. Callahan writes, "Like *Marvelman* and *Watchmen* . . . this thirteen page short takes the traditions of superhero comics and upends them" (2012a: n. pag.). At the same time that "In Pictopia" performs revisionism, it conveys ambivalence about the direction and tone of superhero comics amid the revisionist turn, concerns that anticipate *1963* and *Supreme*, Moore's semi-repudiations of *Watchmen*'s legacies.

While true that "In Pictopia" comments on perhaps regrettable trends and tendencies in superhero comics from the mid-1980s, at an even more fundamental level it offers a blueprint for Moore's views on cultural production. Sobel perceives this connection, writing, "The creative paradise at the heart of this story represents one of the earliest examples of 'Ideaspace,' a concept that would grow into a predominant theme in Moore's later body of work" (2016b: 38). Although Ideaspace's logics certainly have deep roots in Moore's comics work, "In Pictopia" is perhaps the first realized depiction of Ideaspace as an inhabitable plane, setting up several future variations.

Lost Girls

Moore and artist Melinda Gebbie's *Lost Girls* began serialization in 1991, but the creators soon decided to halt future installments in order to instead publish their project, when finished, as a complete graphic novel, which was eventually released in 2006. Initial work on *Lost Girls*, however, coincides with Moore's work on *From Hell*, including his research on magic for that project. Eric Berlatsky contends that though *Lost Girls* and *From Hell* predate Moore's "conversion" to magic, "both reflect his increasing attachment to magic and Ideaspace" (2014: 1652). Magic eventually gave Moore a framework for formalizing theories on language and consciousness that he initiates in his comics after *Watchmen* period. A key concept here for Moore is Ideaspace: a neo-Platonic realm of stories, signs, and ideas from which innovators tap. *Lost Girls*' premise chimes with Ideaspace: its protagonists migrate from the "Ideaspace" of children's literature into Moore and Gebbie's shared narrative for them.

Such deployment of Ideaspace's logics is inextricable from *Lost Girls*' genre: pornography. Moore and Gebbie appropriate characters from children's literature, but those personages—Alice from Lewis Carroll's *Alice's Adventures in Wonderland* (1865), Dorothy from L. Frank Baum's *The Wonderful Wizard of Oz* (1900), and Wendy from J. M. Barrie's *Peter Pan* (1904)—are depicted in graphic sexual activities. Through these scenes, the comic pitches pornography as a space to explore sexual fantasies. Pornography, like Ideaspace, is a liberating imaginative fantasia.

Lost Girls is set in an Austrian mountain resort in 1913, on the eve of the First World War. Since this setting is years after the publication dates of its children's literature source texts, the borrowed characters are aged accordingly: Alice is an elderly, grey-haired aristocrat called Lady Fairchild, Dorothy is a twenty-something American abroad, and Wendy is in her thirties and in an unsatisfying marriage with an older man named Harold Potter. While staying at the lavish hotel, the women encounter each other by chance; as they develop friendships, they share their sexual histories. The women's personal memories of their formative intimate experiences are in fact their famous source narratives, reinterpreted as tales of sexual awakening. Gebbie's art recalls the lavish illustrations of late-Victorian children's fiction, but defamiliarized by its pornographic content.

To be sure, *Lost Girls'* pornographic label is accurate: it depicts countless, graphically rendered sex acts. Moore has suggested that part of the rationale behind the project was to normalize representations of sex. The label "pornography" itself, moreover, is for Moore an unpretentious, less classist, and simply more honest term for art "mostly about sex . . . [and] designed to make people feel horny" (Khoury 2008: 210). Eschewing the more culturally legitimate "erotica" for "pornography" stakes a claim for the social value of disreputable and debauched art.

If embracing pornography in its crudest and most taboo manifestations contests traditional cultural hierarchies, *Lost Girls* complicates this move by simultaneously striking a highbrow posture. *Lost Girls* is an ostentatiously literate work, filled with nods to avant-garde artistic movements and forms of elite European high culture. This pornographic comic, ironically, celebrates modernist cultures of experimental expression and playfulness. Visually, Gebbie's delicate figures and soft watercolors contrast with the raunchy content. Such moves challenge cultural hierarchies, but arguably in a counterproductive way. Hans Maes defines pornography by "low aesthetic standards" (2011: 63); thus, he contends, "in contrast to cliché instances of pornography, *Lost Girls* is not one-dimensional, unimaginative, or anti-intellectual. In that respect, one could say that the pornographic work of Alan Moore and Melinda Gebbie is decidedly unpornographic" (2011: 62). Moore and Gebbie's overtures for pornography's legitimacy paradoxically diminish *Lost Girls'* ability to perform as let alone *be* pornography, thereby undermining the graphic novel's ability to realize pornography's purportedly subversive potential.

Regardless, as an exercise in comics art, *Lost Girls* displays comics storytelling techniques that Moore pioneered in his revisionist superhero comics. For instance, at the end of Book One's third chapter, a two-page sequence depicts Wendy and her husband having a lifeless conversation while performing some routine tasks before bed. During this mundane exchange, which showcases the platonic character of their marriage, their shadows suggestively misrepresent their activities as sexual ones: when projected on the wall as shadows, actions like bending over, arching back, and holding a phallic-shaped rolled letter appear as sexual positions and maneuvers. The visual double entendre—also alluding to the living shadow in *Peter Pan*—conveys the couple's unfulfilled sex lives. Here we see Moore's trademark technique of ironic juxtaposition, or the clever contrasting of text and visuals, used for a shorthand expression of a loveless marriage's phantom pleasures.

Keeping with the ways that *Lost Girls* is in tune with Moore's earlier work is the comic's ideological view of sex. Charles Hatfield writes, "Speculative and erotic ruminations on sex have run like a quartz vein in Moore's work from early on" (2007: para. 1). *Miracleman* posits the creative potential of superhero sex; *V for Vendetta* maps political positions onto non-normative sexual bodies; Moore's 1985 back-up story for Howard Chaykin's satire *American Flagg* analogizes sexual gratifications from pornography with consumerist desires for gratification spurred by commercial advertising; *Watchmen* aligns superhero identities with sexual fetishisms, queerness, and impotence; and *Saga of the Swamp Thing* examines the ecstatic, mind-expanding possibilities for human and flora intercourse. In short, sexuality "is not a new concern for Moore, but rather a constant" (Hatfield 2007: para. 4), one that continues past *Lost Girls* in many later comics as well as *25,000 Years of Erotic Freedom* (2009a), Moore's illustrated treatise on the histories of erotica.

Lost Girls uses sexual fantasy—the stuff of pornography—to explore relations between desire, imagination, and actuality. Hatfield concludes that *Lost Girls* "is a paean, not to embodied sexuality, but to the imagination" (2007: para. 15). This tribute is articulated by the character Monsieur Rougeur, owner of the Austrian resort where most of *Lost Girls* is set. Rougeur is impresario for the sexual exploits of his guests, and he directly comments on the sexual activity around him, contextualizing it and outright explaining its meaning. Early in Book Three, Rougeur warns that "a cold wind is blowing through Europe"—referring to the imminent outbreak of the First World War—so in defiance of war's encroachment he insists that his hotel's residents "make each other warm, as people do" (Moore 2006b: Chapter 21, page 8). Following this announcement, he leads his guests in a massive orgy. By including in his declaration instigating this bacchanalian revelry that sex is what "people do," Rougeur adds a touch of banality to sex—it is merely a routine part of everyday life—but when performed in the face of war's carnage, unbridled fornication becomes a radical protest.

Rougeur, at times, serves as Moore's proxy within the narrative. Annalisa Di Liddo, to this point, identifies Rougeur as Moore's narrative "alter ego" (2009: 161). Moore's voice behind Rougeur seems apparent in Chapter 22, which depicts the hotel orgy itself, as Rougeur pontificates on sexual fantasy and pornography. Amid the orgy, Rougeur tells of a "very wicked" narrative from his prized book of scandalous tales. This book is a device used to divulge a pornographic artistic tradition. Rougeur's selection for this occasion is attributed to the French poet Pierre Louÿs with illustrations by the Austrian artist Franz von Bayros, both actual figures associated with the Decadent artistic movement. Rougeur mentions that the art was commissioned first, and that "Monsieur Louÿs added his writings later" (Moore 2006b: Chapter 22, page 2), a creative process that might align it with comics. Indeed, the illustrations and text of this story run alongside the orgy and Rougeur's recitation of the tale, performing a contrapuntal storytelling function: the story itself tells of an adolescent boy who has sex with his parents and prepubescent sister, thus depicting both incest and pedophilia.

Lost Girls contends with such reprehensible material by stressing distinctions between fantasy and reality: "Incest, *c'est vrai*, it is a crime, but this? This is the *idea* of incest, no? . . . You see, if this were real, it would be horrible. Children raped by their trusted parents. Horrible. But they are *fictions*. They are uncontaminated by effect and consequence. Why, they are almost *innocent*" (Moore 2006b: Chapter 22, pages 4–5). In this schema, fictional representations are effectively above reproach because of the distance between representation and actuality. As Rougeur pithily summarizes, "Fiction and fact: only madmen and magistrates cannot discriminate between them" (Moore 2006b: Chapter 22, page 4). The scene drives home this distinction by having Rougeur engage in sex with a pubescent girl at the very time that he ruminates on the difference between imagined and real hebephilia: "I, of course, am *real*, and since Helena, who I just fucked, is only thirteen, I am very *guilty*" (Moore 2006b: Chapter 22, page 5). Rougeur, of course, is not real, a fact that compels readers to recognize his commentary on fictionality as a lens through which they read and receive *Lost Girls*. For Rougeur, pornographic fantasies are special sites for mental, imaginative exploration that can lead to recognition of aspects or versions of ourselves kept repressed, sublimated, or otherwise denied to ourselves.

If pornography is a private space, sex is social. *Lost Girls* emphasizes sexual activities that underscore this point: group sex, multiple partners, even the bonding that comes from sharing details of one's sexual history. But here we shift from pornography's fantasia to the actuality of sex, which in turn must contend with the types of consequences for sexual activity from which pornography, according to Rougeur, is exempt. This slippage between pornographic imagination and lived sexual experience undercuts Rougeur's separation between "fact and fiction." *Lost Girls* posits real and imaginary as binary opposites, hence Marc Singer's observation that it discloses hypocrisy: Moore is "happy to claim fiction's most beneficial effects, but he is all too willing to disavow its reprehensible ones" (2019: 104). *Lost Girls* is an ingenious intervention in literary and popular cultures, reframing its source texts' meanings and relevancies, but Singer's critique of hypocrisy and what is either Moore's naiveté or rhetorical sleight of hand about representations' capacity to make meaningful impacts in the world point to perhaps fundamental flaws in *Lost Girls*' design.

League of Extraordinary Gentlemen

Lost Girls' engagements with literary and popular cultures are taken further in *League of Extraordinary Gentlemen*, a series co-created with artist Kevin O'Neill and that debuted in 1999; Moore says *Lost Girls* "actually gave birth to *The League of Extraordinary Gentlemen*" (Khoury 2008: 209). Eventually comprising four serialized volumes, a sourcebook, and a trilogy of spin-off graphic novels published across twenty years, *League* is one of Moore's most expansive comics projects. Initially, the comic was an exercise in genre-blending and intertextual play: in its first two volumes, *League* pulls characters from Victorian literature into an action-oriented thriller. Over time, however, *League*'s narrative—and base of source texts—expands beyond the Victorian era, and the story transforms into a site for Moore's condemnations of what he sees as the poverty of contemporary culture, criticisms drawn in part from his bitterness with the comic book industry.

Volumes I and II first appeared as two six-issue serialized miniseries. The first volume recounts the Victorian League's formation and first mission. Led by Mina Murray from Bram Stoker's *Dracula*, the team includes Captain Nemo from Jules Verne's seafaring novels, Dr. Jekyll and Mr. Hyde, Allan Quatermain from Rider Haggard's imperialist adventure novels, and other classic characters. MI6 agent Campion Bond, whose surname suggests a famous fictional spy as his descendant, recruits this ragtag group. Across their missions, the League encounters countless figures from nineteenth-century literature. Allusions scattered throughout Volume I reveal that British Intelligence has formed iterations of the League over the centuries, previewing the series' inclusion of characters from pre-Victorian (and as a spy named Bond implies, post-Victorian) eras.

Volumes I and II of *League* are fairly straightforward adventure narratives. The first series centers on a criminal conspiracy to attack London and Volume II retells the alien invasion plot from Wells' *War of the Worlds*. Within their potboiler narratives, Volumes I and II offer incisive interrogations of their source texts and the modern inheritances of Victorian culture broadly. For instance, Mina Murray, mostly depicted as passive victim in Stoker's book, is transformed into a decisive if nonetheless traumatized leader; in a similar vein, Captain Nemo's Indian heritage and anti-imperialist attitudes, present in Verne's work but diminished in later popular adaptations, are recuperated. *League* celebrates the vibrancy of Victorian literature and draws out its contemporary relevance, which often requires confronting its racist, imperialist, and sexist elements and legacies.

League's first two volumes include paratexts that expand and enrich the primary narratives. Fake advertisements akin to those in *1963* parody the style of Victorian penny dreadfuls, boys' weeklies, and other pulp genres. These materials reinforce *League*'s grounding in British historical print cultures: the faux advertisements function as reminders that Victorian literary production was marked by many of the same commercial forces found in mass culture comic book production. This commonality reinforces *League*'s application of superhero comics' visual motifs and narrative tropes, such as the idea of a "shared universe" and crossover team-up device, to Victorian literature.

Additional paratexts serve narrative ends. In *League*'s first two volumes, paratexts include serialized prose narratives appearing as back-up features in individual issues. Volume I has an Allan Quatermain tale, written in the pulpy style of the character's creator Rider Haggard, in which the colonial hero meets Wells' enigmatic Time Traveler from *The Time Machine* (1895). The back-up feature for Volume II is an almanac detailing strange geographies and landscapes, all of which come from Victorian fantasy narratives. These two paratexts also include vital plot information. Volume II's almanac recounts Murray and Quatermain's discovery of a magical source of eternal life in Africa, thus explaining their youthfulness for *League* volumes set in the twentieth century.

In these later volumes, which bring the timeline to the present, the series moves from an implicit meditation on cultural production and the creative consciousness to an overt commentary. The perspective of this commentary is cynical. In an interview about *League*'s third volume, a trilogy of graphic novels collectively entitled *Century*, Moore explains that "the prevailing thing about [*Century*] seems to be a critique of culture" (Banerjee 2011: n. pag.). *Century* moves from 1910 to 1969 before ending in 2009. Of course, as Moore and O'Neill draw on more modern characters they face restrictions of active copyright protections against their uses of those characters, in contrast to the Victorian characters that are in the public domain and thus available for free use. *League*'s later installments, then, increasingly use analogues for popular characters, or leave characters unnamed but use narrative and visual hints to suggest their identity. This latter strategy can be seen in *Century: 2009*'s depiction of a nameless English boy sorcerer with a scar on his forehead. A legal need to sidestep outright appropriation of characters itself becomes a target of critique in the series.

The critique of culture made across *League*'s volumes is at bottom a critique of access to culture, with "access" here theorized in terms of copyright and other legal protections of intellectual property. This aspect of *League*'s critical allegory of cultural development registers in the Blazing World, an interdimensional space reached via a portal in the Arctic, based on the utopian kingdom of the same name created by seventeenth-century English fantasy writer Margaret Cavendish. The Blazing World is first mentioned in Volume II's travelogue paratext, but its debut within the main comics narrative occurs in the graphic novel "sourcebook" *Black Dossier*.

Populating this bizarre magical plane are representations of characters and concepts from throughout history and across cultures. These icons, when inhabiting the Blazing World, are immortal and free. Like similar ethereal zones found elsewhere in Moore's comics, the Blazing World is a narrative version of Moore's concept of Ideaspace. In these magical realms, fictions and ideas exist in their truest, most essential forms: they are pure thought-forms, liberated from constrictions of material or temporal existences. Within the context of *League of Extraordinary Gentlemen* and its critique of culture, then, the figures populating the Blazing World can be read allegorically as a public sphere, a space for fictions freed from the constraints of the physical world.

The cosmic commons of the Blazing World speaks to Moore's commitment to the inherent integrity of fictions and ideas as well as their legitimate claims to material effects. To this point, one of the most prominent residents of the Blazing World is Prospero, based on the sorcerer character of the same name from Shakespeare's *The Tempest*. In *League*'s continuity, Prospero formed the first League in England during the early seventeenth century; moreover, he still surreptitiously directs League groups who are officially under orders from the English government. Prospero is the one who assigns Murray's League its mission to obtain the titular *Black Dossier*.

Black Dossier's ending has Prospero gratefully accepting the titular dossier from his agents before launching into a fiery, poetic monologue—directed at the reader—in which he pontificates on the essences of the characters living in the Blazing World. This speech makes a case for the primacy of fictions over corporeal beings, positing that ideas are not conjured from materiality by a human creator; rather, fictions animate humanity. According to Prospero, "If we mere insubstantial fancies be, how more so thee, who from us substance stole? Not thou alone, but all humanity doth in its progress fable emulate. . . . The fantasies thou've fashioned fashion thee" (Moore 2008: n. pag.). The Blazing World offers refuge for fictions; in that zone, they are "unshackled from mundane authorities" and "made safe from bowdlerizer's quill, or fad, or fact" (Moore 2008: n. pag.). Prospero articulates the notion, one running throughout the *League* series, that ideas materialized in cultural products have ontological credibility and substance.

Prospero's denunciation of the violence committed against fictions by the material realm functions as a broadside against a comics industry whose legal and management practices, such as corporate authorship, he resents. *League*'s allegorical commentary on copyright "reads as a polemic against the economic injustices and cultural devastations caused by copyright regimes that produce *de facto* perpetual protection terms and enshrine corporate authorship as the dominant, even sole, model for collaborative cultural production" (Ayres 2016: 146). The ratcheting stridency of *League*'s allegory aligns with Moore's acerbic public comments about his negative experiences with, and the broader ethical and creative failures of, a corporate US comics industry.

Later installments of *League* expand its narrative world and reiterate its critique of copyright. A trilogy of spin-off graphic novels known collectively as *The Nemo Trilogy—Heart of Ice* (Moore 2013), *The Roses of Berlin* (Moore 2014c), and *River of Ghosts* (Moore 2015b)—focuses on Janni Nemo, a character created by Moore and O'Neill for *League*'s third volume, *Century*.

The Nemo Trilogy spans the globe and decades, even introducing a new Nemo generation, as it follows Janni's attempts to uphold her father's legacy as renegade captain of the Nautilus. Nemo's encounters with clones created by Nazi eugenics programs and androids mass-produced by American industry extend "a theme begun in *Black Dossier* and elaborated at length in *Century*—namely, Moore's belief in the decline of popular culture and modern society more generally" (Singer 2019: 107). The "disposable imitations" (Singer 2019: 107) that populate *League*'s later volumes index the cultural deterioration by maximalist copyright regimes and corporate control over cultural production.

A final volume, *League: Tempest*, appeared in 2019. The time-hopping plot of *Tempest* involves Satin Astro, a superhero from the thirtieth-century, going back in time to stop a catastrophe that leads to her dystopian society. Satin Astro mobilizes heroes who come to learn that the impending crisis is the handiwork of *League*'s leader Prospero, whose machinations over the centuries have made the League unwitting collaborators in his plot. Prospero's tempest is a storm of fictions let loose from the Blazing World to run amok in a physical realm that exists to tame them. Prospero explains at issue #4's end, "Civilisation's end shall fit its crime. The fantasies it banished and repressed returned. . . . The unforgiving fictions are unleashed, figment and fable dire, from every land" (Moore 2020: n. pag.). Despite the efforts of Mina Murray, Satin Astro, and their comrades, Prospero's scheme cannot be foiled and Earth is devoured by the storm of fictions; a contingent of the Murray group, however, flees in a new Nautilus equipped for space travel. *Tempest* ends with its immortal heroes living happily in space in 2164, as invasion fleets pummel Earth (Figure 3.2).

Though *Tempest*'s narrated escape into space has an upbeat tone, it despairingly implies culture as we know it is doomed. Brian Nicholson argues that *Tempest* is

> Moore reconsidering the role of the fantastic in human life. Before, he viewed it as an inspiration that brought out our better selves. Science fiction inspired great achievements, while witches and fairies were meant to remind us of our ties to the natural world through the folklore of the past. Now superheroes dominate the culture, our times are at their bleakest, and things need to be reconsidered. (2019: n. pag.)

One apparent reconsideration is the value of comics as a medium: *Tempest* is not only the last installment in *The League of Extraordinary Gentlemen* series, but also allegedly the last comic book that Moore will ever write. With its finale, Moore claims he is retired from comics and will for now concentrate his creative energies elsewhere, from prose fiction to film. *Tempest* represents a reversal from the first volume of *League* published twenty years prior. Over the course of its sprawling narrative, *League* goes from playfully remixing superheroes and celebrating the vibrancy of cultural production and exchange to indicting superheroes as a major culprit in a process of cultural decline now so far gone that its damage may be irreparable.

America's Best Comics

From 1999 to early 2006, Moore was the creative mastermind behind America's Best Comics, an imprint published by Jim Lee's Wildstorm Comics. But, soon after making the ABC deal, Lee sold Wildstorm to DC Comics. Since Moore gave ownership rights to Wildstorm—done to ensure larger upfront compensations to his collaborators—DC now owns most ABC properties. Despite these aggravations, compounded by DC's persistent editorial interferences, in his ABC line Moore produced a diverse raft of books that collectively posit an alternative history for the superhero genre and comics publishing generally. ABC is another revisionist project, examining comics history and speculating on the medium's unmet possibilities and unrealized futures.

Tom Strong

Tom Strong presents a hero who recalls the comic book superhero's antecedents in pulp fiction adventure narratives while still drawing on superhero tropes and conventions. The character was co-created by Chris Sprouse, Moore's primary but not exclusive artistic collaborator on the series. Sprouse's crisp, clean-line art style gives Tom Strong a classic superhero visual design: the character's barrel chest and square jaw resemble iconic images of Superman by longtime Man of Steel artists Curt Swan and Wayne Boring. At the same time, Tom Strong's origins are reminiscent of superheroes' genre-adjacent predecessors like Tarzan, The Phantom, and Doc Savage. This blending of the superhero with related tropes and archetypes is the overriding conceit for the series.

Figure 3.2 The conclusion of *League of Extraordinary Gentlemen: Tempest* #6, the comic book that marks the end of Moore's comics career. Art by Kevin O'Neill. *The League of Extraordinary Gentlemen.* © Alan Moore and Kevin O'Neill. Courtesy of Top Shelf Productions. Used with permission.

Tom Strong's origin begins in 1899. His parents were American scientists who shipwrecked on a mysterious Caribbean island called Attabar Teru. Raised on the secluded island in a high-pressure chamber, according to a strict diet and rigorous education, Tom was his parents' way to test humanity's evolutionary potential. After an earthquake kills his parents and destroys his chamber, adolescent Tom is adopted by Chief Omatu, leader of a nearby tribe of Attabar Teru's indigenous Ozu people. Tom Strong's biological parents' experiments gave him super-strength and superior intellect, and his adoptive parents' provision of Goloka root, a remarkable plant native to Attabar Teru, gives Tom an extended lifespan and "higher cognitive awareness" (Moore 1999c: n. pag.). In 1921, Tom Strong departs for Millennium City, a fictional American metropolis, where he establishes himself as a scientist-adventurer and quickly becomes a celebrated popular hero. He later returns to his island home to marry Dhalua, his childhood friend and daughter of Chief Omatu. Shortly after marriage, the happy couple has a daughter, Tesla. Rounding out the main cast is King Solomon, an anthropomorphic ape, and Pneuman, a robotic manservant. King Solomon's name alludes to *King Solomon's Mines*, exemplar of the Victorian imperialist adventure novel, and Pneuman's retro-futuristic design shades *Tom Strong*'s aesthetics into steampunk territory. *Tom Strong* thus gestures toward different pulpy genres while remaining grounded in the visual and narrative conventions of superheroes.

The series' main narrative is set in 1999 and tracks chronologically with its publication schedule into the early twenty-first century. Yet, Moore uses narrative devices like flashbacks and time-travel to bounce around the character's timeline. Scattered throughout these movements across time are references to adventures, characters, and events, which gives the impression of a hundred-year life story for the character and, by extension, publication history for the comic book. Adding to this effect are changes in the comic's visual and narrative styles, done to evoke bygone genres and storytelling modes. Moore employed this technique in *Supreme*, and *Tom Strong* uses it, like that earlier series, to examine comics history—specifically, US comics' diverse lineages.

Tom Strong retains the pulp fiction elements of his origin even as his adventures follow the scripts and styles associated with superhero narratives. In effect, *Tom Strong* revisits antecedents for the superhero genre, and then projects how comics history may have looked had the pulp fiction model remained dominant. Yet, rather than speculating some wholly original story of genre development, *Tom Strong* maps the actual genre trajectory for superheroes onto a character who is askance from superheroes. Indeed, Tom Strong calls himself a "science-hero," a designation that evokes "superhero" but also calls to mind the kin genre of science fiction. As a result, *Tom Strong* is a funhouse mirror reflection of American comic book history, one in which the superhero figure develops in such a way that hews far more closely to the genre's pulp fiction antecedents and influences. Moore's superhero revisionism thus here gets another manifestation.

In this spirit, *Tom Strong* is attuned to superheroes' relations with other genres and traditions. Karin Kukkonen notes how "[Tom] Strong is incarnated as a hero in the various popular-culture styles of the twentieth century, including those associated with its pulp fiction and superhero comics. Chronicling the history of these various styles and the heroes who figure in them, Moore portrays Tom as repeatedly encountering other versions of himself" (2013: 41). Among Tom Strong's friends and allies are Tom "Doc" Strange from Terra Obscura, a bizarre duplicate Earth that exists on the other side of the galaxy, and an anthropomorphic rabbit, Warren Strong, from a dimension that follows the logics of funny animal cartoons and comics. In stories centered on Tom Strong's daughter Tesla—who is chronologically in her sixties, but, thanks to the Goloko root's de-aging effects, has the characterization and appearance of a young adult—we meet countless versions of Tesla and Tom Strong, including a cowboy, a spaceman, and a master thief. The many angles from which the series refracts its hero echo the key takeaway from the narrative's skewed take on superheroes: genre development, like all historical events, is contingent and revisable. *Tom Strong* rethinks the superhero figure by rearticulating it in other genre dialects.

Complementing such moves is Tom Strong's characterization itself. While Tom Strong is imprinted with qualities standard in heroic fiction, a consistent and striking trait is his compassion. A motif that develops throughout the series is Tom Strong's diplomacy with his enemies, to the point that many rehabilitate and become allies. *Tom Strong* #2 has our hero "defeat" Modular Man, an artificial intelligence antagonist, by gifting Venus for Modular Man to inhabit and terraform. This generosity toward villains is taken to its limit in "How Tom Stone Got Started," running from issues #20–22. Notably, Moore left the flagship *Tom Strong* title after this tale—only returning to write the series finale—suggesting that this storyline can be taken as Moore's capstone for the character. In it, a change to the timeline produces significant ripple effects: Tom Strong's father Sinclair is killed at sea, so his mother Susan is shipwrecked on Attabar Teru with their West Indian sailor, Tomas—a character who is the casualty in the baseline chronology. When we see Tomas' death in issue #1, the implication is that Susan had tender feelings for him; in this alternate timeline, she acts upon those feelings, marries Tomas, and together they have a son, Tom Stone. The character development of this biracial hero, Tom Stone, parallels that of Tom Strong, albeit with occasional significant differences usually attributable to his race. After he arrives on the scene in Millennium City, for instance, a newspaper headline tellingly reports, "Negro Foils Robbery."

The comparative suspicion Tom Stone feels in Millennium City leads Tom Strong's enemy Paul Saveen to see Tom Stone as kindred spirit. Whereas Saveen and Tom Strong become foes right away, Saveen approaches Tom Stone in a spirit of friendship: he tells Tom Stone, "I'm like you. I'm underappreciated" (Moore 2003e: n. pag.). Tom Stone admits that "the city as a whole seems to have its prejudices" and Saveen empathizes: Saveen is "illegitimate" and as a result, he says, "it doesn't matter if I'm a scientific genius. I'm still excluded" (Moore 2003e: n. pag.). The two men bond and become crime-fighting comrades. Tom Stone marries a white woman, Greta; Paul marries Dhalua; and they are all happy.

Although friendships fracture after Tom Stone and Dhalua begin an affair, the story reimagines the archetypical hero–villain relationship. We see that Saveen's antipathy toward Tom Strong is rooted in Tom Strong's adoration from Millennium City. But, when the hero is a comparatively less privileged figure—in this case, one marginalized by his racial identity—Saveen identifies with him and is given the opportunity for his own heroism to emerge. The alternate history allows Saveen's latent goodness to appear. Here, then, we see *Tom Strong* the series displaying the generosity and compassion that Tom Strong the character consistently shows toward his opponents. Unlike most superheroes and other, similar heroic figures, Tom Strong is more interested in rehabilitating his enemies than punishing them.

"How Tom Stone Got Started" also clearly brings questions of race to the surface, concerns that run implicitly through the series as a whole. Although Tom Stone faces racism and assorted soft bigotries upon his arrival in Millennium City, in the primary timeline we see relatively little indication of racist public backlash against Tom Strong's interracial marriage nor direct racism experienced by Dhalua upon her arrival in America in the 1930s. Nevertheless, Tom Strong's origin has patently colonialist overtones: as a white child raised by the Ozu tribe on Attabar Teru he effectively becomes a version of the racist "White Savior" trope.

And in issue #4, we see Tom Strong's Second World War-era conflict with Ingrid Weiss, a Nazi super-soldier. Weiss identifies with Tom Strong, since both of them were bred under strict eugenicist principles, but she sees him as a "race traitor" for marrying a Black woman (Moore 1999e: n. pag.). Such racially inflected conflicts foreground how the genres and character types informing *Tom Strong* are imbricated with colonialist tropes and white supremacist assumptions. *Tom Strong* admits these inheritances but strives to subvert and rewrite them.

Tom Strong proved popular enough to yield more than one spin-off series and miniseries. An anthology series, *Tom Strong's Terrific Tales*, featured stories by Moore as well as notable creators like Steve Moore (no relation), Jaime Hernandez, Arthur Adams, Peter Bagge, Michael Kaluta, Sergio Aragones, among others; it ran for twelve issues. Moore and Peter Hogan co-wrote two six-issue *Terra Obscura* miniseries spotlighting Tom Strange and his home world's heroes. The superheroes of *Terra Obscura* are in fact old, forgotten comic book characters published by the defunct Nedor Comics; having lapsed into the public domain, Moore was able to use them outright. *Terra Obscura* thus stands as complement to Moore's concurrent comics project centered on public domain heroes, *League of Extraordinary Gentlemen*, as well as being an act of world-building for the *Tom Strong* constellation of books and a rousing yarn in its own right. On a related note, around this time Moore was also involved with another revival of forgotten heroes: he drafted the plot for *Albion*, a six-issue miniseries published by Wildstorm that resurrected old British superheroes owned by IPC Media. *Albion* was scripted by Moore's daughter, Leah Moore, and featured covers by Dave Gibbons.

After Moore left ABC, Hogan and Tom Strong co-creator Chris Sprouse did two miniseries. More recently, Tom Strong appeared in DC's recent superhero series *The Terrifics*, possibly foreshadowing integration into DC's line. A character designed to reflect possibilities for comics genre and storytelling if untethered to superheroes now may be absorbed by that dominant genre.

Tomorrow Stories

Tomorrow Stories revives the comic book anthology: each issue usually includes four strips, all written by Moore, running about eight pages apiece. The initial four strips were *Jack B. Quick* with artist Kevin Nowlan, *The First American* with artist Jim Baikie, *Cobweb* with artist Melinda Gebbie, and *Greyshirt* with artist Rick Veitch. Halfway through *Tomorrow Stories'* twelve-issue run, however, *Splash Brannigan* with artist Hilary Barta debuts as an occasional replacement for *Jack B. Quick*. At a basic level, *Tomorrow Stories* is a reminder of the vibrancy of the short story form for a comics scene that has largely abandoned it for long-form narratives.

As an anthology of short tales, *Tomorrow Stories* is a return not only to US comics' publication formats, since anthologies were once an industry standard, but also to the early days of Moore's comics career when he cut his teeth on short stories for British anthologies. Relatedly, like other ABC titles, *Tomorrow Stories* breathes life into older comics genres—especially humor.

Case in point is Moore and Nowlan's *Jack B. Quick*, which centers on the titular whiz-kid farm boy from Queerwater Creek, United States. Jack directs his scientific genius and technical proficiency toward rural problem-solving, yet he inevitably causes more hijinks than solutions. In his debut strip, Jack attempts to help a beloved cow suffering from "bovine night-fits." Jack promptly jury-rigs a "quantum vacuum cleaner" to exploit "a loophole in Einstein's theory of relativity that might save Bessie!" His device creates a miniature sun that keeps Bessie in perpetual daylight, so "the madness that comes with nightfall need never descend upon Bessie again!" (Moore 1999f: n. pag.). However, Jack's small sun soon spawns small planets, creating a small solar system, until eventually the sun's life cycle ends and contracts into a black hole—which then engulfs Bessie into its gravitational pull.

Jack B. Quick's absurdity recalls Moore and Steve Parkhouse's *Bojeffries* strips: while the latter focuses on English identity and contexts and the former is set in rural America, both draw on surrealist humor to capture the peculiarities of a particular way of life. In a prose essay for *Tomorrow Stories* #1, Moore writes, with only some irony, "*Jack B. Quick* is not surrealism, it's a gritty, documentary portrait of bucolic living." *Jack B. Quick*'s use of O. Henry-style twist endings, moreover, recall Moore's short strips for *2000 A.D.*, and its anarchic spirit seems descended from *D.R. and Quinch*. This lineage matters. In contrast to Annalisa Di Liddo's claim that the *Tomorrow Stories* strips are minor works and mainly formal exercises (2009: 61), the series' short, funny strips join an emphasis on parody running throughout Moore's body of work.

To this point, Moore's reputation as a writer of thematically serious, even ponderous, comics belies his sense of humor and investment in humor comics. In fact, even as he was leading the charge toward hard-edged superhero revisionism with his *Warrior* comics, he was also parodying it. Case in point:

the short 1983 gag strip "Grit!" for Marvel UK's *The Daredevils* featuring "Dourdevil," a spoof on Frank Miller's violent revamp of Marvel's hero Daredevil (Moore 1983a). Yet, in the same magazine just a few issues before the "Grit!" parody, Moore endorsed Miller's work on *Daredevil* in a glowing review essay entitled "The Importance of Being Frank" (Moore 1983b). Moore's revisionist comics are thus coextensive with his humor comics: Moore has noted how his classic revisionist comics, namely *Miracleman* and *Watchmen*, are indebted to the caricatural style of legendary humor cartoonist Harvey Kurtzman, especially Kurtzman's work at *Mad* magazine.

Moore cites the influence of Kurtzman and *Mad* on other *Tomorrow Stories* strips, too. *First American*, done with his *Skizz* collaborator Jim Baikie, is a parody of patriotic American superheroes like Captain America and Fighting American, done with "a bit of Harvey Kurtzman and his satirical bite" (Khoury 2008: 185). The strip pokes fun at genre clichés and the more embarrassing and debauched aspects of American culture; in the context of the early twenty-first century, *First American*'s bite comes from its incisive satire of American chauvinism and militarism. In a similar vein, Moore claims his strip with Hilary Barta, *Splash Brannigan*—about a manic, loudmouth, living ink blot—brings together his love for Jack Cole's spastic superhero Plastic Man (a hero alluded to in "In Pictopia") with classic "*Mad* super-hero parodies" (Khoury 2008: 186). Moore considers *Splash Brannigan* a "cocktail" with "many different ingredients" (Khoury 2008: 186), a description that also applies to his strip with Melinda Gebbie, *Cobweb*. While humor is rarer in the pulpy *Cobweb*, the strip at times reinvents itself for comedic ends. In *Tomorrow Stories* #4, for instance, Gebbie's art imitates Marjorie Henderson Buell's *Little Lulu* for a parody called *Li'l Cobweb*. For typical *Cobweb* episodes, however, Gebbie uses gauzy painted art and surrealist techniques like collage to create *Cobweb*'s pulpy, dreamlike, and erotic atmosphere. *Cobweb*'s noir overtones—Cobweb is an heiress who moonlights as an adventurer costumed in domino mask and translucent negligee—act as homage to a subgenre of midcentury lesbian pulp fiction, books that can carry quasi-feminist subtexts.

The eroticism and sex-positive feminist ethos behind *Cobweb*, moreover, link it to *Lost Girls*—unsurprising, given Gebbie's substantial contributions to that comics project. Indeed, much criticism on *Lost Girls* could apply equally to *Cobweb*: Rebecca Wanzo and Anna Kérchy, respectively, put *Lost Girls* in a sex-positive feminist comix lineage in which Gebbie herself has been a major figure. Wanzo argues *Lost Girls* "is reminiscent of some feminist comix cartoonists [like Gebbie] who intentionally depicted the taboo or obscene to address sexual and gender inequalities" (2008: 351). *Cobweb*, likewise, teases lesbian and incestuous sexual relationships to give its protagonist a transgressive, subversive power. Moore has indicated that much of *Lost Girls* is "Melinda's vision" (Khoury 2008: 209), and, given the resonances between the two comics, one might surmise the same for *Cobweb*. Indeed, all of *Tomorrow Stories* bear the strong signatures of their respective artistic co-creators. Moore frequently stresses the contributions of his collaborators, and tailors his projects to the strengths and interests of his artists, but his artists' creative presences are pronounced in *Tomorrow Stories*—perhaps to sharpen distinctions between the four different stories appearing in a single issue. Driving this point home are credit attributions on *Tomorrow Stories'* covers: while the possessive form of Moore's name is in the series' main title, in blurbs for individual stories the artists receive sole billing: "*Jack B. Quick* by Kevin Nowlan," "*Cobweb* by Melinda Gebbie," and so on.

Moore's artist for *Tomorrow Stories'* other feature, *Greyshirt*, is his longtime collaborator and veteran writer-artist, Rick Veitch. Greyshirt is patterned after *The Spirit*, a crime series by Will Eisner, legendary comics writer-artist. Recalling the Spirit's origin as a detective falsely believed dead, Greyshirt is Franky Lafeyette, son of a crime lord, who after being betrayed and left for dead stalks criminals in retro-futuristic Indigo City. This metropolis evokes *Spirit*'s Central City, itself inspired by the vibrant multiethnic neighborhoods of New York City in the early twentieth century.

Greyshirt is in fact Moore's second tribute to Eisner's work on *The Spirit*. In 1998, Moore wrote three stories for *The Spirit: The New Adventures*, an anthology comic published by Kitchen Sink Press. *Watchmen* co-creator Dave Gibbons drew Moore's first three *Spirit* stories, which comprised the entirety of the anthology's first issue; Moore returned to the comic for its third issue, joined by Spanish artist Daniel Torres. Tim Callahan, who places these *Spirit* tales "among Alan Moore's most overlooked work," notes, "In most of the fondly remembered [Eisner] Spirit stories, the title character played a mere supporting role, and the story itself—or the storytelling— shone brightly in the spotlight" (2012c: n. pag.). Following Eisner's lead, Moore's *Spirit* stories "revel in the playfulness of their form" (2012c: n. pag.). On this note, "Last Night I Dreamed of Dr. Cobra" (Moore 2016h) is set in a future in which Central City uses "Logotechture" for buildings constructed in the form of words. Logotechture nods to Eisner's trademark integration of the *Spirit* logo into background art. This gimmick is pretext for a tour of Central City, with Torres' detailed renderings of crowded alleyways and dizzying cityscapes. Such visual play with urban environments is revisited in *Greyshirt*. Moore notes that "it was great to have . . . a character that could explore some of those Will Eisner alleyways and cul-de-sacs" (Khoury 2008: 185). In addition to its urban milieu and hero's characterization, *Spirit's* influence on *Greyshirt* registers in the comic's formal experimentation.

Greyshirt's play with the comics form is exemplified in "How Things Work Out," the lead feature in *Tomorrow Stories* #2. In a 2001 interview, Moore describes this story's unique design:

> We had an apartment building, the same building, upon every page. There are four horizontal panels on each page. Then, to add another element, we made it so that the top panels are all taking place in 1999, the second panel down on each page is taking place in 1979, the panel beneath that takes place in 1959, and on the bottom panel of each page, you're seeing the bottom of the building as it was in 1939, when it was a fairly new building. We're able to tell, by some quite complicated story gymnastics, quite an interesting little story that is told over nearly sixty years of this building's life, with characters getting older depending upon which panel and which time period they're in. (Robinson 2012: 102)

Notably, in his description, Moore refers to the "building's life," suggesting that the focus of *Greyshirt* is the urban landscape itself. At any rate, in its eight pages, "How Things Work Out" highlights the storytelling affordances of comics. The strip can be read in multiple ways: read page-by-page, the story offers snapshots in its characters' lives from across decades, but if only one panel tier per page is read, a linear narrative set in a specific year plays out. When read page-by-page, moreover, visual symmetries in panel compositions create thematic resonances across the narrative's temporal jumps (Moore 1999g).

"How Things Work Out" speaks to *Tomorrow Stories* as a whole: its characters facilitate experiments with form and explorations of novel ideas. To take the short, episodic nature of individual strips as ephemerality misjudges the series' interrogations of comics form and history.

Top 10

Top 10 adapts narrative structures of American television police programs like *Hill Street Blues* and *NYPD Blue*. The twist is that in *Top 10* everyone—

cops, criminals, citizens—has superpowers. *Top 10*'s co-creator is artist Gene Ha, who did pencil and ink artwork over layouts by Zander Cannon. Ha's detailed craftsmanship suits the comic's ensemble cast and crowd scenes. His art for *Top 10* includes intricately rendered architecture and backgrounds, and it is cluttered with gags and sly references to characters from comics, film, and other media. As Geoff Klock writes, *Top Ten* is "an erratic but encyclopedic collection of allusions to various aspects of superhero tradition brought to the most quotidian level" (2003: 115). *Top 10* therefore shares the dizzying intertextual visual density of *League of Extraordinary Gentlemen*.

Moore saw in the storytelling practices of American police TV shows an alternative model for balancing the ensemble cast of a superhero team book. To avoid a series that was "exactly like an ordinary super-hero book, but with sort of a vague cop conceit grafted on" (Khoury 2008: 182), Moore realized that his superheroes could be cops only if *everyone* had superpowers. If "everyone was a super-character of some sort, then it would become completely normal and mundane and boring" (Khoury 2008: 182). This premise justified super-cops and, hence, the lifting of TV police procedurals' narrative structures. Police TV shows' main affordance for *Top 10* is an ensemble cast that decenters the narrative from any particular character. While *Top 10* #1 follows Robyn Slinger, aka Toybox, on her first day of the job at Precinct 10—making her a point-of-view character for the reader—that debut issue also launches several other plots, all of which crosscut each other and get equal time over the duration of the series. Ultimately, Toybox's initiation into the police force and her rocky relationship with her unwelcoming partner Jeff Smax stand as one storyline equal among others.

Top 10 grounds its large ensemble in a sharply realized setting, one that not only helps define the characters and their relations but also serves as an organizing principle for the narrative. In *Top 10*, the fantastical city of Neopolis is a vibrant, chaotic, and multilayered urban playground populated by diverse superpowered humans and humanoids, as well as nonhuman citizens like robots, monsters, anthropomorphic animals, and more. Tim Callahan notes that while the dozen or so major characters in *Top 10* are important, at bottom the "world of Neopolis is the story" (2012e: n. pag.). To this point, as the series moves through its twelve-issue run, illuminating details about the history of the city emerge alongside information about its districts, denizens, and dynamics.

Moore and Ha develop the texture of Neopolis in a 2005 prequel graphic novel, *Top 10: The Forty-Niners*, which depicts the city's founding. The city was established, according to *Top 10*'s backstory, in 1949 as response to the proliferation of super-beings across the United States. Neopolis thus became the designated home for this unruly and expanding population. As the city and its superpowered citizenry grew over the decades, law enforcement by standard methods became untenable, so Neopolis gave its jurisdiction to a multidimensional peacekeeping force. Within this array of alternate earths, Precinct 10 (nicknamed "Top 10") is Neopolis' outpost. Significantly, Neopolis' historical basis as repository for super-beings unwanted in other major American cities—making it a dumping ground of sorts—points to one of its more interesting thematic strands. *Top 10* takes the superhero figure as a displaced meditation on marginalized identities linked to non-normative embodiments, subjectivities, and experiences. Neopolis' founding sprung from prejudice toward superhumans, and within Neopolis we see biases, bigotries, and hierarchies. Since superhumans are the demographic majority, superhero-adjacent figures like robots and monsters face the systemic disadvantages and interpersonal hostilities of minoritized populations. In this way, Neopolis recalls the stratified city districts of "In Pictopia."

Otherwise heroic and likeable figures in the cast are not exempted from such dynamics. Pete "Shock-Headed Peter" Cheney is a goofy-looking and naïve officer from Precinct 10, a colleague generally respected by his peers, but nevertheless he is also cruelly bigoted toward robots. Shock-Headed Peter refers to robots as "clickers," construed as an offensive epithet. Other moments indicate similar forms of prejudice. In issue #3, an anthropomorphic shark named Larry "Frenzy" Fischmann—a lawyer, naturally—takes umbrage at a snide comment about his "predatory species" by yelling back, "Of course we've evolved! That is one of many uninformed misconceptions people have about sharks" (Moore 1999j: n. pag.). The humor here is evident, but such examples of bigotry against nonhuman characters and characters that stray, generically, far from the superhero template accumulate over the duration of the series.

The allegorical treatment of characters with nonhuman embodiments as racial or ethnic minorities dovetails with questions of sexuality. Issue #3 includes a conversation between Kemlo "Hyperdog" Caesar and Sung "Girl One" Li about sex. Hyperdog, a super-intelligent Doberman with a robotic humanoid exoskeleton, tells Girl One that he is "only attracted to other dogs"

(Moore 1999j: n. pag.). Nevertheless, later in the series Hyperdog begins a relationship with Neural 'Nette, a human woman. The two fall in love and eventually marry despite their species difference. *Top 10* thus displaces the fluidity of sexual identity, as well as a queer disjuncture between physical embodiment and social expectations for appropriate sexual desire, onto the types of fantastical and even outrageous physical bodies at home in superhero, fantasy, horror, and science fiction genres.

These moments chime with mimetic representations of sexual and gender difference. *Top 10* has several gay characters, including the precinct's Captain Steve "Jetlad" Traynor and Officer Jacqueline "Jack Phantom" Kowalski. In issue #2, Smax bluntly asks Toybox, "You another of these dyke feminists?" Toybox responds, "I'm not homosexual. To be perfectly honest, right now I'm not anything-sexual" (Moore 1999i: n. pag.). Evan Torner argues that Toybox's asexuality reflects a motif in Moore's comics that "foreground[s] asexuality as a distinct form of sexual agency" (2012: 116). Indeed, *Top 10*'s emphasis on non-normative sexual identities makes queer subtexts running throughout the superhero genre tradition legible. On this point, Ramzi Fawaz argues that the comic book superhero is itself a queer figure, from its celebration of diverse embodiments to its "implicitly queer and nonnormative affiliations that exceeded the bounds of traditional social arrangements such as the nuclear family and the national community" (2016: n. pag.). *Top 10*'s characterizations therefore interrogate the genre's sublimated sexual dynamics.

These themes continue in a spin-off miniseries, *Smax*, illustrated in a cartoonish style by Zander Cannon. In *Smax*, Toybox accompanies her partner to his home dimension. After the events of *Top 10*, the two of them have a genuine mutual respect, even if Smax's frosty temperament still strains their friendship. Their relationship, though, is platonic: Toybox's asexuality means that sexual tension "is simply removed from the central duo of the entire comic, replaced with a complex asexual relationship" (Torner 2012: 116). Yet, once they arrive in his home-world, Smax implores Toybox to pretend to be his wife to avoid family pressure to follow custom and marry his sister.

The seeming backwardness of Smax's home culture adds to *Top 10*'s genre play, for whereas Neopolis' majority population is superheroes Smax comes from a world patterned after fantasy and sword-and-sorcery series like *Elfquest* or *Conan the Barbarian*. Tim Callahan notes, "Jeff Smax, no-nonsense officer of the law in Neopolis, sees himself as a hillbilly who has escaped his embarrassing past" (2012b: n. pag.). *Smax* juggles several genre elements and tones—gesturing not only to superheroes and fantasy, but also to screwball comedies and social drama—and, like *Top 10*, imbricates them with questions of sexual mores, identities, violence, and experiences. In *Smax*, this thematic thread touches on questions of race, too: in the end, Smax and his sister Rexa do pursue their romantic relationship—uncontroversial in their home culture—after realizing they can avoid Neopolis' legal and social prohibitions against incest by not acknowledging that they are siblings. Toybox is the one who proposes this elegant solution, noting that she is the only one "that knows you guys are related" and that they could simply tell others they are members of the same tribe. Rexa objects, "we're both blue giants with white hair. We look alike"; however, Toybox rebuts, "So do most foreigners to Americans" (Moore 2004d: n. pag.). Smax and Rexa, ironically, are able to share a non-normative partnership free from prejudice thanks to the racist blind spots of Neopolis' citizens.

Top 10's playful examination of identity constellates it with other sideways perspectives on superheroes in the ABC line. After Moore quit ABC, Wildstorm published two miniseries: Paul Di Filippo and Jerry Ordway's *Top 10: Beyond the Farthest Precinct* (2005) and *Top 10: Season Two* (2008) by Zander Cannon and Gene Ha. These sequels kept *Top 10*'s balanced narratives, zaniness, and visual density, but lost Moore's sensitive, witty, and humane characterizations.

Promethea

Promethea is Moore's collaboration with artist J. H. Williams. The series' thirty-two issues are divided, roughly, into three informal acts. *Promethea*'s first dozen issues give an extended origin story for the titular protagonist. Next is a twelve-issue story in which Promethea explores the structure of reality based on Kabbalah cosmology. During this second act, per Christine Hoff Kraemer and J. Lawton Winslade, "the series abandoned any pretense of being a traditional superhero book and . . . become an outlet for exploring the key concepts of magic and occultism that Moore himself has studied" (2010: 275). The final act returns to plot-driven storytelling, centering on an impending apocalypse that reels in guests from other ABC books before its climactic finale.

Who is Promethea? A prologue in the first issue introduces Promethea as a little girl in fifth-century Alexandria. She is the daughter of a pagan magician attacked by a Christian mob. To save his daughter from a violent death, the magician sends Promethea to the desert where she meets two of his gods, the conjoined Thoth-Hermes, who ferries Promethea to a magical realm. The Immateria—yet another representation of Moore's concept of Ideaspace—is an unearthly realm that houses stories, ideas, feelings, and sensations. In the Immateria, Promethea will become a living story and therefore will "live eternally, as stories do" (Moore 1999b: n. pag.). The main story set up by this prelude occurs in "New York City, 1999 A.D," but it is a futuristic New York home to superheroes, akin to *Watchmen*'s alternate reality. The story focuses on Sophie Bangs, a mousy college student who is researching a fictional character named Promethea—this same name, Sophie explains to her friend Stacia, "turns up in 18th century poems, early newspaper strips, pulp magazines and comic books" (Moore 1999b: n. pag.). Oddly, these different depictions of Promethea seem largely independent of each other.

By the end of the first issue, Sophie learns that artists can become imaginatively attuned to Promethea, the young girl who entered the Immateria. Following Moore's theory of Ideaspace, the Immateria and material world interact when people act creatively. Acts of invention are explained as roundtrip mental excursions to the Immateria: a person's consciousness taps into a collective repository of ideas, and then ideas extracted from the Immateria are put into material form by the creator. As a denizen of the Immateria, Promethea is now "made of imagination" and hence accessible to artists who open themselves up to ideas and values she represents. Astoundingly, Sophie learns, some artists become so overcome by the idea of Promethea that they bring Promethea into material existence, either transforming into Promethea themselves or projecting her upon the body of a woman close to them. Promethea is an idea come to life, and Sophie becomes the next Promethea.

In the series' first act, Sophie faces longtime enemies of Promethea and learns more about the Immateria and her predecessors. Previous Promethea often used their magical powers for benevolent ends: one version brought comfort to soldiers during the First World War and a midcentury Promethea served alongside Tom Strong in a superhero team. Promethea's partnership with Tom Strong is just one indication of how the comic registers with the superhero tradition. To be sure, many critics read *Promethea* specifically as a superhero narrative, albeit a subversive or revisionist one. Annalisa Di Liddo's reading of *Promethea* is premised on the claim that "despite the prominence the authors [Moore and Williams] attach to abstract and Kabbalistic aspects, *Promethea* is also the tale of a superheroine and a self-reflective deliberation about the power of narration, the role of the artist, and the modes of representation of comics" (2009: 87). Geoff Klock places

Promethea in his study of superhero comics, contending that it "struggles with the status of a female superhero in a masculine continuity, and attempts to carve out a space for a genuinely female superhero narrative" (2003: 98–9). *Promethea* contends with and examines genre questions.

To this end, *Promethea* aligns superhero comics with other cultural forms. The character, after all, traverses middlebrow poetry, newspaper comic strips, and pulp fiction before appearing in comic books. Even as it puts cultural forms into conversation, however, in terms of genre *Promethea*'s critical eye is trained on superhero comics, especially the maleness—and frequently misogyny—of the genre. Within *Promethea*'s narrative, the comic book "science heroine" version of Promethea appears from 1938 to 1996, making the comics format the most enduring medium for any fictional representation of her. Promethea's diegetic tenure as a fictional comics superhero is divided into two runs, the first by artist-writer William "Bill" Wollcott, a gay man and only male whose body is inhabited by Promethea in her "real world" manifestations. The second run is by writer Steven Shelley, who based his Promethea on his wife, Barbara, which in turn projected Promethea's spirit onto her, making Barbara the last Promethea before Sophie.

Stewards of this female superhero, then, are male comics creators. Previous iterations, such as the newspaper strip Promethea and the heroine on memorable painted covers of pulp magazines, were rendered by women artists. The shift to male creative workers points to the comics industry's inhospitality to women creators compared to other realms of popular culture. Promethea's history as a comic book character also registers sexism in the marketplace. Issue #1's paratextual history notes that "apparently it's well known that [comic] books with a female title character have never performed well in a male-oriented marketplace" (Moore 1999b: n. pag.)— an admission that slyly admits *Promethea*'s own commercial liabilities. The origin story told in *Promethea*'s first act thus registers intersections between gender, culture, and creative practices.

Such concerns are centered in the second act. After coming to terms with her powers, identity, and responsibilities, Sophie sojourns through the Kabbalah's Tree of Life in what amounts to Moore's exposition of his magical education. Against criticisms that this material is pedantic and self-indulgent, Moore rebuts, "there are 1000 comic books on the shelves that don't contain a philosophy lecture and one that does. Isn't there room for that one?" (Campbell 2002: n. pag.). The essayistic middle act of *Promethea* drills deep into esoteric lore to detail Moore's conflation of art and magic.

Researching the occult for *From Hell* introduced Moore to magical discourses; a decade later, *Promethea* exhibits his fluency with them. Moore acknowledges that "*Promethea* grew out of research that I was doing already" and a desire "to have a comic where I can release some of the steam of my magical researches" (Robinson 2012: 107). Promethea's immersion in esoteric metaphysics narrates Moore's own commitment to magic and his related theories about creativity, language, and culture. By the series' final issue, in a direct address to the reader, Promethea declares, "The only reality we can ever truly know is that of our perceptions, our own consciousness, while that consciousness, and thus our entire reality, is made of nothing but signs and symbols. Nothing but language" (Moore 2005a: n. pag.). Marc Singer writes that *Promethea* offers an "extreme interpretation of the idea . . . that our experience of the world is always shaped by languages whose signs can only refer to other linguistic signs. *Promethea* literalizes this interpretation, suggesting that the world is materially as well as socially and psychologically created by language" (2011: 102). In *Promethea*, reality is consciousness, consciousness rests on language, and language needs imagination: Moore's "magic" names this cluster of meaning-making principles.

Promethea's representations of magical concepts, moreover, are inextricable from the comics form in which they appear: it makes a case that knowledge of magic, and the heightened forms of consciousness that studies in magic allegedly facilitate, correspond with the affordances of comics. On this note, Kraemer and Winslade maintain, "Using the unique artistic advantages of the comics medium, the comic itself becomes a potential tool for creating the positive shift in consciousness portrayed in its conclusion" (2010: 277). Since the magical schema posited by *Promethea* considers "reality" itself to be conscious perception, and consciousness is shaped by language, then the language of comics has the power to reshape consciousness and, in turn, reality.

To this end, Williams consistently defies conventional comics art techniques. His lush, ornate pages frequently eschew any type of grid-like composition of panels, instead organizing a sequence of images in a fractal pattern or around a central image. While issue #11 uses rigid gridded panels, they are arranged as vertical bands so to read them one must turn the comic ninety degrees. Issue #7 features Sophie's dreamlike visit to the "earthly memories" of former Promethea Bill Woolcott, which are rendered using photographs of live actors. While these techniques are not at all wholly original they are atypical, especially for the type of mainstream superhero comic that *Promethea* superficial resembles. Such defamiliarizing techniques visually thematize the comic's arguments about comics form as a vehicle to new ways of seeing. Nick Sousanis makes a similar argument in *Unflattening*, his pioneering philosophical study composed in comics form. Sousanis argues that the image is as essential as the word for modes of thinking and creation of mental models. "Unflattening," as he defines it, is "a simultaneous engagement of multiple vantage points from which to engender new ways of seeing" (2015: 32). *Promethea* too figures comics as able to provoke new perceptions.

Consequently, in *Promethea* magic and comics are entwined. Sophie and Barbara trace comics' history to Egyptian hieroglyphics, suggesting that pictorial representation is the first form of human language. These purported origins in foundational forms of human communication and understanding lend comics primal energy and power. Singer avers that *Promethea* "positions comics as the repository of our most primal written communications" and "elevates comics as one of the most privileged and perfect forms of language since it combines visual and verbal signs" (2011: 101–2). Comics is an early language system and living language with unrealized potential, and the comics form is aligned with Sophie's spiritual enlightenment in the second act.

After returning to the earthly plane, the third and final act of *Promethea* commences. This act begins with Sophie living in hiding in Tom Strong's Millennium City, temporarily cowed by hostile forces arrayed against her. Eventually, however, she resumes her identity as Promethea and embraces her prophesized destiny as midwife to the end of the world. The "end of the world" in *Promethea*, however, refers not to physical destruction and death, but ideological transformation and rebirth. In the end, Promethea unleashes a revelatory moment of collective clarity and oneness. Afterward, in issue #31, she explains, "the world was all still there. It all looked just the same . . . except it didn't" (Moore 2004c: n. pag.). While this new world is not a total utopia, Promethea's apocalyptic event inspires widespread interest in spirituality, pursued with pantheistic openness: "It's okay to worship everything," Sophie explains (Moore 2004c: n. pag.). As Rikke Platz Cortsen writes, "Moore intends the reader to realise the potential of an apocalypse of this kind, that changing the ideological structures through imaginative force can change the world" (2014: 407). By the end of the series, this transformation is replicated in changes to the materiality of the comic itself: if the pages of *Promethea*'s final issue are detached from their binding, they can be reassembled to produce a poster with portraits of Promethea on either side.

By linking the narrative's radical transformation of the world with *Promethea*'s radical transformation of comics form, not to mention the superhero genre, Moore posits a relationship between experimental forms of expression and creative acts with personal and political change. This dynamic is triangulated with magic, since the second act of *Promethea* encourages an understanding of magic as analogous to art. Such a constellation occurs at a plain plot level, too: Cortsen writes, "In *Promethea*, Sophie's enlightenment and education in magic and myth serves as a way to prepare her for the end of the world" (2014: 407). One final element to this mix is sex.

Sexual experience is positioned as a key part of Sophie's magical education. In the controversial issue #10, Sophie begins her magical learning by agreeing to have sex, while in her Promethea form, with a decrepit, older, and paunchy occultist named Jack Faust. This issue links transcendent magical experiences with ecstasies of sexual experiences, echoing *Lost Girls'* parallels between sexual and artistic imaginations. *Promethea*, then, triangulates sex, magic, and art. And since part of Moore's reason for writing *Promethea* was a feminist motivation to make "a comic with a strong female character" (Robinson 2012: 107), the series is also in line with another ABC character, *Cobweb*, which likewise roots feminist liberation in women's bodily autonomy symbolized by sexual freedom.

Accordingly, preoccupations with sex, sexual and gender identities, and sexual bodies recur in *Promethea*. A slow subplot with Sophie's best friend Stacia, for instance, follows major changes to her sexual identity: during Sophie's time in the Kabbalah's Tree of Life, Stacia becomes a vessel for a former Promethea, pulp artist Grace Brannagh. Sharing body and mind, Stacia and Grace fall in love; Stacia's story in the series is her journey toward identifying as queer. Bill Wollcott, the one biologically male character who could channel and embody Promethea, is an example of the series' consistent narrative emphasis on fluid, non-normative embodiments. Notably, Bill is the first Promethea whose imaginative engagements with the character occur via the comics medium.

Bill's transgender identification with Promethea returns us to the latent queerness in the superhero figure, itself a motif in *Promethea*: the overt superhero elements in the series routinely point to queer and trans subjectivities. For instance, one member of New York's resident superhero team, the Five Swell Guys, was biologically male until a mostly unexplained mishap transformed his embodiment into a woman. Five Swell Guys' fiercest opponent, moreover, is The Painted Doll, an anarchic villain based on one of Moore's unrealized proposals from the 1980s for a "transsexual terrorist" called the Doll (Parkin 2013: 48). These mutable and fluid bodies and identities not only underscore the ways that the superhero genre is rich for interrogations of queer and trans subjectivities, but also are homologous with the cultural and political transformations that *Promethea* identifies as the potential effects of artistic creation's magic.

Histories of Horror

In recent years, Moore's comics are marked by a turn to horror, which stands as the primary genre for the final phase of his comics career. Of course, Moore has worked within horror since the start of his career, but a late wave of horror comics suggests he sees the genre as apt for the conditions of the early twenty-first century. This section's readings of these comics analyze Moore's late return to horror alongside his grim sense of the ill health of contemporary culture.

Lovecraft Cycle: The Courtyard, Neonomicon, *and* Providence

Moore's late-career embrace of horror commences with *The Courtyard*, a two-issue miniseries that engages with the early twentieth-century "weird fiction" of H. P. Lovecraft. *The Courtyard* is followed by two sequels: *Neonomicon*, from 2010 to 2011, and *Providence*, 2015–17. These interconnected miniseries revisit Lovecraft's fiction and legacy. Their violence and bleakness, moreover, convey what Moore sees as the horrific realities of contemporary culture. This Lovecraft trilogy traces to 1994, when Moore contributed "The Courtyard" as a prose story to *The Starry Wisdom*, a collection that paid tribute to Lovecraft's legacy. Nearly a decade later, Avatar Press released *Alan Moore's Yuggoth Cultures and Other Growths*, an anthology series with comics adaptations of Moore miscellany, including two Lovecraft-inspired poems. Writer Antony Johnston and artist Jacen Burrows' comics adaptation of "The Courtyard," for which Moore is listed as consulting editor, was going to be included in the *Yuggoth Cultures* anthology, but was published later as a separate series instead.

The Courtyard focuses on undercover Federal Bureau of Investigation (FBI) agent Aldo Sax's investigation of a wave of gruesome murders tied to a rumored new drug called Aklo. This premise is set in 2004 of an alternate timeline, one whose dystopian tenor is visually captured in the domes covering cities to protect citizens from pollution. The domes, then, are a symbol of entrapment and environmental decay. In this setting, Sax is a cruel and racist protagonist, a man who despises the poor and hard luck residents of Red Hook where his investigation is based. Following leads to a mysterious, masked man named Johnny Carcossa, Sax learns that street rumors of "Aklo" refer not to a new narcotic, but an occult language. When Carcossa speaks this eldritch tongue to Sax, the FBI agent experiences a traumatizing hallucination. For this dreamlike sequence, Burrows renders tentacled monsters and other macabre imagery that allude to Lovecraft's famous tales of cosmic demons and eerie planes. *The Courtyard* ends with a maddened Sax killing a neighbor in the same gruesome fashion as the crimes he is investigating, pointing to a Lovecraftian Satanic cult as the culprits.

After serving as creative consultant on Johnston and Burrows' comics version of *Courtyard*, in 2010 Moore returned to its Lovecraftian world in the four-issue miniseries *Neonomicon*, which he scripted for Burrows. In it, FBI Agents Brears and Lamper link *Courtyard*'s Sax case to an underground sex cult. The cultists capture the agents after a botched infiltration of the group. Lamper is killed and Brears is raped by the cultists before given to a Lovecraftian monster, a huge fishlike creature that rapes her repeatedly. These graphic and prolonged rape scenes, ideologically complicated by Brears' characterization as a recovering sex addict, sparked controversy; see Critical Questions for attention to this debate. As for *Neonomicon*'s narrative development, Brears subdues the creature and even empathetically feels that he too is a victim of the cult. As Adam Kozaczk observes, the violent contact between Brears and the monster inverts the consensual interspecies sex that is found in Moore's *Saga of the Swamp Thing*, yet shares some of the earlier depiction's sense of connection (2015: 497). Brears eventually escapes captivity, but learns that she is pregnant and will soon give birth to Cthulhu, the signature monstrous cosmic entity of Lovecraftian mythos.

Moore concluded his excavation of Lovecraft's Cthulhu stories in *Providence*. This third and last Lovecraft series expands *Neonomicon*'s narrative, functioning as both prequel and sequel: the majority of *Providence* is set in New England in 1919 and even introduces Lovecraft himself as a character. By moving backward chronologically to Lovecraft's time, *Providence* provides backstory for the diabolical, scheming occultists of *The Courtyard* and *Neonomicon*. *Providence*'s finale, however, returns to the modern era for the apocalyptic event of Cthulhu's birth by Brears.

By reworking elements and themes from Lovecraft's fiction, Moore's horror trilogy joins the so-called Cthulhu Mythos. Antony Johnston, who adapted Moore's prose "The Courtyard" into comics, explains: "During his life [Lovecraft] welcomed other writers who wanted to spend time in the universe he'd created, and at times positively encouraged it. . . . The Mythos is a growing entity, larger now than any one writer" (2004: 7). The Cthulhu Mythos chimes with Moore's intertextual practices: Lovecraft's openness to other writers' work with his concepts speaks to the acts of creative borrowing and revision that are fundamental to Moore's comics work. Such resonances are deepened by Lovecraft's investments in the occult discourses of interest to Moore.

If Lovecraft is one of Moore's spiritual artistic ancestors, then Moore's horror trilogy might be seen as a reckoning with his own artistic genealogy. To this point, this cycle of horror comics draws out the ideological subtexts of Lovecraft's fiction. Sax's racism in *The Courtyard*, for one, indicts the xenophobic Lovecraft himself, whose anxieties about New York's multiethnic neighborhoods during his time in the city are grafted onto Sax. *Neonomicon* goes even further to pursue the sexual subtexts of Lovecraft's writings and contend with the misogyny and racism laden within Lovecraftian horror. As Moore puts it, one of his goals with *Neonomicon* was to do a "modernization of Lovecraft" rather than a "strictly by-the-book pastiche" (Thill 2010: n. pag.). For Moore, this approach means confronting "all of the things that tend to be glossed over in Lovecraft: the racism, the suppressed sex" (Thill 2010: n. pag.). Given the expansiveness of the Cthulhu Mythos and the extent of Lovecraft's cultural influence, however, Moore's interrogation of "suppressed" elements buried in Lovecraft's work engages a tradition that goes beyond one particular cult writer. Textual and cultural lineages in fact link Lovecraft's pulpy weird fiction to the comics genre traditions within which Moore has worked, obviously horror yet also science fiction and even superheroes. Moore's Cthulhu comics tacitly admit that any objectionable elements of the Cthulhu Mythos are inherited by wider literary and genre traditions—legacies of which Moore's comics are a part.

A sense of complicity therefore registers in the cycle. For example, Annalisa Di Liddo concedes that *Neonomicon*'s controversial rape scenes are unsettling, but argues that the "extent of the rape scene"—that is to say, its extreme duration—functions as a "critique of [the reader's] own voyeurism" (2012: 203). Kozaczka contends that Moore's strategic use of genre clichés, like Brears' nymphomania and appearance as conventionally attractive white woman, fuels the exploitative excitement common to the horror genre, but its explicitness and her superior's regret over assigning her this case act as "critique of the plotlines that deliver that excitement" (2015: 491). These generous readings take Moore's horror comics as critical metafictional exercises: they indulge Lovecraft's racism and dysfunctional sexuality to subvert those elements. While such defenses of *Neonomicon*'s shocking representation of sexual violence are debatable, they rightly underscore how Moore's trilogy offers a critical revision of Lovecraft's horror stories and their legacies that implicates *Neonomicon*'s participation in the tradition despite its critique.

Joining a popular culture tradition in order to unpack its ideological underpinnings calls to mind the superhero revisionism on which Moore built his reputation. Interestingly, Moore's return to earlier revisionist strategies seems motivated by a return to his state of mind in the 1980s. In 2003, Moore reflects on his dystopian revisionist superhero comics like *Watchmen*, *Miracleman*, and *V for Vendetta*, noting they reflected his outlook at the time: "I was in a bad mood, politically and socially and in most other ways" (Robinson 2011: n. pag.). Likewise, Moore calls *Neonomicon* an expression of his current "very, very bad mood" (Gieben 2010: n. pag.). In both cases, the locution "bad mood" indexes Moore's anger with the conditions surrounding and informing his creative activity.

Like Moore's 1980s superhero comics, the trilogy of *Courtyard*, *Neonomicon*, and *Providence* use revisionism to paint a dreadful portrait of the present. To see the Lovecraft cycle as allegory, consider how Moore negatively casts recent political developments in terms of magic:

> The slogans "Brexit Means Brexit" or "Let's Make America Great Again," while they mean precisely nothing, if repeated enough times with steadily increasing volume will come to seem like profound eternal truths. And of course, the purpose of repeated incantation in magical practice is to raise or evoke some specific kind of energy. (Ó Méalóid 2017: n. pag.)

Moore's sense that recent political demagoguery can be taken as form of dark magic has an allegorical counterpart in his trilogy's rendering of dark magic as cause for collective suffering.

This allegory becomes clear at the end of *Providence*, the trilogy's final installment. *Providence* and thus the trilogy ends with an assortment of characters, from the FBI agents featured throughout the series—including *Courtyard*'s Aldo Sax—to S. T. Joshi, based on the real Lovecraft scholar and biographer, whom Brears refers to as "the old world's foremost Lovecraft scholar." Brears makes this assignation as she stands nude, prepared to birth Cthulhu. Her casual use of "old world" here is telling, pointing to the wholesale reordering of reality occurring in this finale (Moore 2017a: n. pag.). In this scene, we have another example of the apocalyptic moment in Moore's comics. Regarding this motif, Rikke Platz Cortsen writes: "The apocalypses in Moore's works are concerned with transformation . . . whether of one's self or of the imagined world" (2014: 408–9). The birth of Cthulhu is an apocalyptic transformation that is sublime in the romantic sense of being both awesome and terrifying. When Brears' superior officer sees her on the bridge he describes her as "radiant" and the skies above are filled with beautiful celestial patterns, but at the same time Lovecraftian monsters roam the streets and all the characters admit feelings of dread (Moore 2017a: n. pag.).

Once the apocalypse is upon them, Joshi leads the assembled characters in analysis of Lovecraft's fiction as a way to explain the bizarre phenomena before their eyes. Brears and others realize, at this moment, that Lovecraft's writings described a fundamentally chaotic and mystical true reality obscured only by the "fragile construct" of "human reality" (Moore 2017a: n. pag.). Now that the Lovecraftian occultists have lifted the veil, Earth's awful essence is apparent. To see allegory at work in this scene, Moore's public statement on his decision to vote for Labour in the UK's 2019 general election is instructive. In a public letter, Moore warns, "I do not believe that four more years of these rapacious, smirking right-wing parasites will leave us with a culture, a society, or an environment in which we have the luxury of even imagining alternatives" (Flood 2019: n. pag.). Moore's argument is that the UK, like other governments facing similar political turbulence, is at a tipping point: if its current leadership continues, Moore fears, the current ills and dysfunctions created by that leadership will become so entrenched that they will become the new normal conditions for the world. In other worlds, Moore sees an unconscionable political regime giving birth to a new future world in its vile image.

Likewise, Cthulhu's birth heralds the arrival of a terrifying new order. Looking at the eerie illuminations in the sky and strange creatures rapidly appearing across the landscape, Joshi asks, "Is this our new world?" Brears answers with a reference to a remote planet in Lovecraft's canon: "I think it's Yuggoth now. I think maybe it's always been Yuggoth." (Moore 2017a: n. pag.). The horror is not that Earth has been deformed into something Lovecraftian, but that Lovecraftian wickedness has always been there, in need of agents to activate it. This line not only suggests the danger of rabblerousing politicians who Moore believes cultivate peoples' worst impulses, but also Lovecraft since Moore's engagement with the writer is rooted in drawing out racist and misogynist subtexts that were always present, presumably having unconscious effects upon readers, but never made overt.

Ultimately, the human response to Lovecraftian apocalypse is the series' most horrifying moment. In *Providence*'s final pages, Joshi the Lovecraft scholar, Brears the FBI agent, and Brears' superior officer Carl Perlman all wearily contemplate their futures in this grim emergent reality. Since Lovecraft's fiction, in Moore's narrative, is treated as a Rosetta stone for decoding occult activity, the trio turns to Lovecraft's characters as guides to know what fates they can expect. Joshi notes that Lovecraft's characters confront chthonic horror and end up mad or suicidal. When Lovecraft's narrators seem to display acceptance, Joshi clarifies, Lovecraft is "indicating that his [the narrator's] mind is changing, emphasising the horror" (Moore 2017a: n. pag.). Acceptance, in this schema, is actually the more unnerving response, for it means that horror itself is no longer recognizable as such. Here, then, we return to Moore's fear that continued rule by "rapacious" Tories will turn their unscrupulous values into the accepted common sense of the future.

And indeed, this reconciliation with horror is precisely what Brears and Joshi do at the end of *Providence*. Perlman possesses a journal that might hold information that can be used to reverse the apocalypse. Brears and Joshi, however, insist that it best to embrace a changed reality and find new roles for themselves in it. "It's all destiny. It's all providence" (Moore 2017a: n. pag.), Brears tells Perlman as she departs. Dispirited, Perlman gives up hope and shreds the one remaining artifact from the past that might be able to preserve a world that is slipping away. This melancholic finale displays Moore's skepticism that reversing a frightening political tide is possible—and, indeed, the Tories won a clear majority in the 2019 election, confirming Moore's angry trepidations. When Perlman desperately offers the diary as a key to "save the world," Brears ruefully responds, "I don't think this is that kind of story. It's not about what humans want anymore" (Moore 2017a: n. pag.). Dark occult forces are now charging ahead, changing reality and—in the most horrifying development of all—acquiescing humans are accepting this dismal new world as inevitable and irreversible. When read in the context of British politics and Moore's views on them, his Lovecraftian cycle is a darkling view of the road ahead.

Crossed + 100

Crossed + 100 is a six-issue miniseries set in the fictional universe created by writer Garth Ennis and artist Jacen Burrows' *Crossed*, which debuted in 2008 from Avatar Press. The series is a postapocalyptic narrative: following genre conventions, a viral outbreak infects a huge percentage of the world population, turning them into ravaging monsters. Rather than the mindless living dead of zombie tales, the series' undead—named "the Crossed" due to a cross-shaped sore that marks infected persons' faces—remain physically human in appearance and retain human cleverness and skills, yet are transformed into relentless, psychopathic, and cannibalistic killers. The *Crossed* franchise is notorious for stomach-churning violence. Crossed "zombies" rape and maim their victims, and graphic images of sexual violence, mutilations, and other bodily violations appear unceasingly. The series easily matches *Neonomicon* for its depraved and disturbing content.

Moore, along with artist Gabriel Andrade, embraces such unrestrained ugliness in *Crossed + 100*, a miniseries set in 2108, a century after the initial outbreak depicted in the original *Crossed* volume. In it, human civilization is slowly rebuilding. Though humans still live in small, semi-nomadic survivalist communities, the tide has turned for the humans in large part due to natural selection: around 2050, the numbers of Crossed began declining since their cannibalism led them to turn on each other. Unable to sustain their numbers, the Crossed in 2108 are near extinction. In this context, *Crossed + 100* follows a band of humans settled in the area formerly called Tennessee.

Crossed + 100 adds some distinctive touches to its postapocalyptic world. For example, Islam's prominence is a detail inspired by the contemporary Muslim community in rural Tennessee. The most striking world-building gesture, however, is the series' treatment of language. Characters speak a new English dialect characterized by the use of standard nouns as verbs ("sexed" or "accident" as verbs), abbreviated or other economical locutions ("afawk" as verb form of "as far as we know"), and simplified usages ("skull" as verb meaning "to think" and "bird-bunk" for "pen"). Moore's defamiliarizing language implies a correspondence between a society and the forms of communication found within it: the crude but inventive dialect is an apt match for a harsh environment in which resourcefulness and efficiency are essential. *Crossed + 100* therefore reflects Moore's interest in the relations between language and cultural values.

Another significant feature of the *Crossed + 100* world is the change to attitudes and mores about sex. Norms surrounding sex, sexual identity, sexual partnering and monogamy, and sexual bodies are noticeably progressive compared to a present-day referent. Interestingly, the relatively enlightened sexual behaviors center on shared pleasure and mutual consent. In issue #2, the series protagonist, an archivist named Future Taylor, recounts in her diary a coupling that occurs among two of her squadron members, women with the respective names Cautious and Ho-Ho: "Cautious was rashing because Archie Keller sex-declined her. I said how some olds don't feel tight, sexing young. Ho-Ho said she was bunking single if Cautious wanted to sex with her. Cautious said okay" (Moore 2015a: n. pag.). Consent, physical pleasure, and companionship drive human sexual activity, a contrast with the sexual violence of the Crossed, who rape and brutalize their victims in horrific acts of domination.

On a related note, issue #4 features an extended sex scene between Taylor and a fellow archivist named Mustaqba. These four pages, divided evenly in their compositions using a six-panel grid pattern, depict sex in explicitly rendered, wordless drawings by artist Andrade (Moore 2015a: n. pag.). This prolonged representation of sexual pleasure contrasts with the violent rapes that characterize the *Crossed* franchise—and much of Moore's own work. Indeed, responding testily to allegations that his comics dwell in images of sexual violence against women, Moore rebuts "that there is a far greater prevalence of consensual and relatively joyous sexual relationships in my work than there are instances of sexual violence" (Méalóid 2014: n. pag.). *Crossed + 100* illustrates this tension: the threat of sexual aggression and violence contrasts with healthy and satisfying sexual behavior. In this tension, moreover, we see an initial undercurrent of hope that runs throughout *Crossed + 100*. Speaking to the optimistic spirit in its early chapters, the story focuses on the archival work of the fittingly named Future Taylor, suggesting a link between the creation of a better future with the continuity that comes from preservation of the past.

This hope, however, is negated in the end. A mysteriously resurgent Crossed population is explained when Taylor and her team locate the diaries of Beauregard Salt, a vicious serial killer from the twenty-first century who was infected during the initial outbreak. Because Salt was psychopathic, not dissimilar in personality to the Crossed themselves, he retained more of his mental acuity than other Crossed zombies. His foresight allowed him to realize that this new world of the Crossed, which he considered paradisiacal, was unsustainable. He therefore began selective breeding experiments to create a new strain of the Crossed population, one conditioned to have the wherewithal and restraint needed for long-term survival. He even created an elaborate plan for his enclaves of evolved Crossed to stay hidden, encouraging human populations to grow complacent from false security, before launching sneak attacks on the anniversary of the initial outbreak. Salt's twisted plan, then, means that humanity's future triumph is thwarted by the past—or, our present.

Crossed + 100 ends with Taylor's despairing diary entries, dismissing humanity's recent "build-back" as a fleeting false start. Hope for the future was a "wishful fiction" because now there will be "no more later" (Moore 2015a: n. pag.). This lost future is made even more painful since it is entirely the result of human venality: Salt's byzantine plot preserves hostile conditions that could not survive on their own. Keeping with the dark tone of the *Crossed* franchise, the series suggests the intransigence of human viciousness and violence. But, significantly, such savagery is not positioned as an essential, universal human quality; rather, it is a revanchist remnant from the degraded culture of the early twenty-first century.

Cinema Purgatorio

Cinema Purgatorio is a horror comic done with Moore's *League of Extraordinary Gentlemen* co-creator Kevin O'Neill, and it is the lead feature in a black-and-white anthology of the same name. If *Crossed + 100* narrates future progress sabotaged by the present, *Cinema Purgatorio* excavates the past and renders historical memory as nightmare from which the present cannot awaken. The horror of *Cinema Purgatorio* centers on a stasis that comes from being trapped in the past; or, put differently, surviving a present that cannot exorcise the ghosts of its past. Moore and O'Neill present this horror in short episodes unified by the conceit of a haunted movie theatre.

Each episode of *Cinema Purgatorio* begins in a seedy movie theatre. Entering this cinema is a narrator, unseen other than her limbs, for O'Neill's artwork frames panels as her field of vision. The reader thus shares her point of view, positioning the narrator's experience as representative of a general condition or shared experience. Moore's first caption for the first installment reads, "Are there really such things as recurring dreams?" (Moore 2016b: n. pag.). This question distills the strip's surreal atmosphere and thematic emphasis on repetition. Every time the narrator enters this cinema, she vaguely recalls sensations of having done so before, but does not trust her perceptions. Adding to the dreamlike ambiance, this cinema still operates with old-fashioned accoutrements like ticket-taking ushers and curtains for the screen. The cinema, then, is charmingly outdated but also decrepit, pointing to the strip's attempts to undercut nostalgia for older popular cultural artifacts, figures, and experiences.

Classic Hollywood film serves as a metonym for this nightmarish cultural nostalgia. Each strip's prelude ends by turning to the screen, with the comic transitioning into the feature itself. For the middle portion of the strip, before a return to the cinema frame narrative, the comic's panels "become" the film our narrator is viewing. These films visually refer to older Hollywood eras and styles and feature caricatures of historical figures from the film industry. The films rewrite memories of classic Hollywood in an oppressive, violent, and exploitative key. Episodes retell true scandals such as the arrest of film comedian Fatty Arbuckle for manslaughter and the "Black Dahlia" murder of aspiring actress Elizabeth Short. Moore and O'Neill retell such controversies with surrealist imagery and disjointed narratives that replicate dreamlike logics and sensations.

A running theme is the exploitative nature of work in Hollywood. "A King at Twilight" from *Cinema Purgatorio* #4, for instance, relays the story of Willis "Obie" O'Brien, a pioneer in stop-motion animation and other visual effects. The strip's film tells the story of O'Brien's career through his most famous stop-animation creation, King Kong. The giant ape from 1933's classic *King Kong* explains how he, speaking as O'Brien, was an innovator—"I like to think I showed the film world something it had never seen before"—until personal tragedies and a series of lackluster projects left him a has-been (Moore 2016: n. pag.). In the strip's finale, Kong-O'Brien falls from a jungle ledge: paralyzed, a swarm of giant spiders consumes him. As he is eaten alive, Kong-O'Brien laments, "I was an artist, in an industry. It's a beast. It knows nothing of love . . . and it always kills the beauty" (Moore 2016c: n. pag.). This dialogue, recalling the famous closing lines of *King Kong*, points to the strip's theme of creative exploitation: the criminal violence of Hollywood scandals chimes with the everyday violence of Hollywood's exploitation of creative labor. This theme resonates with Moore's harsh critiques of the comic book industry, based on his frustrating experiences with large publishers.

To this point, *Cinema Purgatorio* focuses on the film industry, but it resonates with other media, especially comic books. "The Last Adventure" from issue #16 retells the sordid story of actor George Reeves, who played Superman on the 1950s' television series *Adventures of Superman*. Shortly after show's end, Reeves died by gunshot wound in a death ruled a suicide but one that remains shrouded in uncertainty. "The Last Adventure" parallels

Reeves with Superman. A caption describing "the one lethal substance to which he was vulnerable"—alluding to Kryptonite, the one element that harms Superman—joins an image of Reeves' binge drinking (Moore 2018a: n. pag.). Such paralleling extends into commentary on the contexts of the superhero's creation. In a panel depicting Reeves' funeral, the actor's corpse wears his Superman costume as one of his mourning costars says, "Probably suicide, over our lousy comic-company contracts" (Moore 2018a: n. pag.). "The Last Adventure" implies that *Cinema Purgatorio*'s lurid portrait of Hollywood applies to the comics industry as well, and that exploitative industry practices are source of abuses capable of killing creative talent.

Cinema Purgatorio deglamorizes cultural memories of yesteryear Hollywood. The images, figures, and products that are a foundation for much of contemporary popular culture are replayed in grotesque ways. These retellings draw out the hidden violence and exploitation lingering beneath the surface of a modern commercial culture epitomized by Hollywood. *Cinema Purgatorio*'s rejection of nostalgia for old Hollywood is captured in a faux magazine cover for *Screen Regrets* that recurs in the strip: the cover features Marilyn Monroe, altered to look more aged than she ever did in her tragically short life, with an accompanying quotation, "Sometimes I wish I was just dead." This sentiment—"just" or merely dead—speaks to the strip's demythologizing of icons like Monroe, whose posthumous mystique distorts and obscures a darker reality.

The films revisit the cultural past, and the narrator is trapped in a perpetual present that replays that past. In the closing bookend to issue #1's episode, the narrator muses, "This is all so old-fashioned when these days, what you want is something modern." Yet, the narrator remains, for she has "paid to get in" (Moore 2016b: n. pag.). The frame narrative and the films together render a portrait of the present stuck within a hellish past. *Cinema Purgatorio*'s title telegraphs its vision of the present as limbo. Ultimately, obliteration is the only escape. The final strip ends with the narrator in the cinema's stockroom, reviewing piles of film canisters. In the last panel, a caption reading "There's no exit" accompanies a film canister, which appears to be smoking, labeled "Nitrate" (Moore 2019). Nitrate film, the outdated technology used for early film, is extremely flammable. This finale—Moore's penultimate comic book before his retirement with the end of *The League of Extraordinary Gentlemen: Tempest*—implies that, for the narrator, the only escape from the nightmare of the present is to burn it down.

CHAPTER 4
CRITICAL QUESTIONS

Critical Questions is the first of two chapters that build on Key Texts' overviews of Alan Moore's major comics. This chapter outlines issues prominent within scholarship on Moore's comics and their legacies, identifies critical concerns that run throughout Moore's career, and attends to questions that animate existing and emergent critical work on Moore's comics.

Themes and Techniques

Several themes predominate in Moore's comics. Major themes include sexuality, especially sexual activity's emancipating potentials; power and its capacities for liberation as well as corruption; the nature of culture and conditions under which culture thrives or deadens; politics, especially regarding what might constitute just rule; the workings of perception and consciousness; relations between individual experiences and collective formations; and representations of and meditations on the nature of history and historical narratives. These themes cut across his comics.

Sean Carney spotlights Moore's interest in history, calling it the "single thematic concern that ties Moore's work together into a coherent oeuvre" (2006: para. 2). Questions of history concern history's content, apparent in Moore's historical comics, and ontological explorations of history itself. Carney elaborates,

> Moore offers a vision of human history in which metaphysics and materiality are identical. This contradictory identity is . . . made by human beings in historical moments, but is also the seemingly transhistorical force that makes and drives humanity forward, and so it takes on the appearance of an impersonal tide even while this tide remains the result of human agency. (para. 3)

This view of history intersects with concerns about temporality. Moore muses that "what we *perceive* as time" (Khoury 2008: 187) may be his great theme.

This investment in questions of how time is perceived slides into his comics' characteristic formal techniques, namely experiments with how time is represented on the comics page. Examples addressed in the preceding Key Texts chapters include the equivalence of Dr. Manhattan's quantum perception with the comics page in *Watchmen* (1987d); the kitchen table scene in *Big Numbers* #2 (1990c); and the tiered, cross-decades panels in "How Things Work Out" from *Tomorrow Stories* #2 (1999g). These instances and more show Moore and his artists playing with comics' ability to represent the passage and experience of time, which in turn spur reflections on time itself.

Moore's comics favor other formal characteristics, storytelling techniques, and stylistic features. The technique perhaps most associated with Moore's comics writing is ironic counterpoint. Lance Parkin calls ironic counterpoint "the artistic effect to be gained by combining a picture and text" (2013: 91), typically in ways that produce rich contrasts or parallels between visual imagery and language. Per Annalisa Di Liddo, this practice enables Moore to "take advantage of the possibility to manipulate the time of narrative by peculiarly orienting the reader's attention on the page, or he might play with the juxtaposition of seemingly unconnected words and pictures, whose association will only become clear in the following pages" (2009: 35). Ironic juxtapositions layer meanings, resonances that collectively create patterns of significations. The technique exemplifies Moore's attunement to possibilities inhering in comics' formal interplay between text and image.

Moore's comics are tightly structured. They are built around a refracting image or idea—such as *Big Numbers*' design inspired by chaos mathematical principles—and follow discernible patterns, like *Lost Girls*' strict eight-page chapters. Moore's comics are famous for their intricate page layouts, typically prescribed in his script or composed in collaboration with his artist. Panel compositions are loaded with visual detail, and they use mirroring or contrast to make meaningful transitions from panel to panel.

The overt "literariness" of Moore's writing is another widely noted trait. Mazur and Danner locate in Moore's often florid writing a mixture of "lyrical narration and pointed social commentary" (2017: 72). Douglas Wolk identifies Moore's penchant for "describing quotidian or ghastly things in jeweled language" that always verges on "purple prose" (2003: n. pag.). Of course, such elements seen in traditionally "literary" terms have prompted critics to read Moore's comics within the boundaries of a definition of "the literary" not constructed with comics in mind, a move no doubt often made in order to draw on the cultural prestige of "literature." The very title of Sara Ness' monograph, *Watchmen as Literature* (2010) speaks to this critical tendency. Criticism that puts Moore's work in conversation with literary conventions and discourses is valuable and has yielded a great deal of important insights, but such work also risks overinvesting in the concept of "literature" itself, reinforcing cultural hierarchies and obscuring comics' distinct formal properties.

On a related note, Moore regularly integrates other forms into the textual body of his comics, moves that experiment with genre, form, and medium. A key technique here involves paratexts that dialogue with the primary comics text. For example, most volumes of *League of Extraordinary Gentlemen* include installments of a prose back-up story in the serialized issues, each of which is narratively separate from the comics narrative but includes events and character developments that are canonical for the franchise's overall continuity. *The Black Dossier*, a "sourcebook" for the *League* franchise, takes this use of paratexts further. In *Black Dossier*, a comics frame narrative centers on the existence of the titular portfolio, one that details the exploits of the League's incarnations dating back to Elizabethan England. When characters in the framing narrative read the dossier, the form of the graphic novel changes to reflect the dossier's contents, including a "lost" Shakespeare folio, government reports, maps, postcards, memoir, and more. Philip Wegner argues that these paratexts' interruptions of the "main" narrative underline the inherent hybridity of the comics form. Moreover, since its paratexts are "essential to grasping the work as a whole" (2010: para. 12), *Dossier* demands readers draw on a self-conscious awareness of their "placement and connection in much larger spatial and collective networks forged through the media(tions) of [digital and electronic] technologies" (2010: para. 8). Moore's paratexts thus enact new forms of cognitive mapping.

Moore's engagements with genre extend to the other sense of the term: plots, narrative codes, conventions, and tropes. For example, Lance Parkin contends that while *Watchmen* is a superhero narrative, it is "also a science fiction story. It's a detective story, a conspiracy thriller, a political satire, a historical family saga. It has elements of romance stories and war stories. It contains a comic-within-a-comic, a pirate adventure. It is packed with all manner of jokes" (2013: 184–5). The generic eclecticism and range of *Watchmen*, according to Parkin, represents Moore's creative praxis generally. Indeed, the formal transgressions noted in this section, from paratexts to genre hybridity, speak to an intertextual sensibility—ethos and aesthetics—informing his comics.

Intertextuality

Intertextuality may be the defining feature of Moore's comics: Annalisa Di Liddo argues that intertextuality is "pervasive" and "permeates" (2009: 35–6) his corpus. The term "intertextuality" can be attributed to Julia Kristeva; her 1966 essay "Word, Dialogue, and the Novel" argues that "any text is constructed as a mosaic of quotations; any text is the absorption and transformation of another. The notion of *intertextuality* replaces that of intersubjectivity, and poetic language is read as at least *double*" (1986: 37). Per Kristeva, texts are more like nodes in cultural networks than acts of individual expression. Later usages, however, shift intertextuality from condition to practice, one typified by playful (self-)referentiality: intertextuality amounts to "pastiches, imitation and the mixing of already established styles and practices" (Allen 2000: 5). Intertextuality as acts of self-aware borrowing and revision is usually the meaning used vis-à-vis Moore. Di Liddo finds Moore's intertextuality "in the form of quotation, allusion, parody, or as happens most often, the revisiting of well-known works or patterns" (2009: 35). This sense of intertextuality covers a raft of strategic engagements with other texts informing Moore's comics work.

Reconciling these senses of intertextuality into a coherent praxis is Moore's own theory of the case, one that emerges inductively from his comics themselves and is centered on a concept he deems Ideaspace. Moore explains that

> the terrain that I term "Idea Space" [is] a kind of medium or field or space or dimension in which thoughts occur. I believe this space to be at least in part mutual, rather than discrete, which is to say that I believe that this "space" impinges to some degree upon all consciousness and that it is co-accessible. ("Correspondence" 2015: n. pag.)

Lance Parkin refers to Ideaspace as "an individual mental landscape" that "is connected to that of others, so it may be something like Jung's collective unconscious" (2013: 284–5). Similarly, Eric Berlatsky calls it "a neo-Platonic realm of imaginative 'forms' more real than reality itself from which artists and writers derive their inspiration" (*Time* 1652). Ideaspace underpins Moore's intertextual theory and practice. We see Moore work through his notion of Ideaspace within his comics in two chief ways.

First, Moore often literalizes accounts of Ideaspace as an accessible "realm" or cohabitated "landscape." Marc Singer finds Moore's "idea of an otherworldly repository for fiction" (2019: 103) recurring in his comics. In *League*, the Blazing World is fictions' sanctuary from a debased physical world. *Promethea*'s Immateria and *Supreme*'s Supremacy allow those books' title characters to interact with previous iterations of their superhero personae. "In Pictopia" features comics and comic strip characters living in an eerie urban sprawl. Relatedly, *From Hell* posits "the 'idea' of Jack the Ripper as, ironically, far more compelling, important, and 'real,' than the real Ripper, whoever he may have been" (Berlatsky 2014: 1652), allegorizing Ideaspace's core tenet: fictions and ideas "live on" in an ether that transcends materiality even as they travel to and intervene in a material world. These metaphysical havens for fictions and ideas found throughout Moore's comics, which resonate with Moore's Ideaspace concept, allow ideas not only to traverse into the physical world and back but also to interact freely with each other. Such depictions of Ideaspace chime with Kristeva's theorization of intertextuality as the substance of cultural activity.

Second, Moore habitually takes existing texts, narratives, characters, or some other cultural artifact as starting point for his art. As Douglas Wolk puts it, "Virtually every comic Moore has written is inspired by some kind of pop-culture source of the past that he can elaborate and improve on" (2008: 230). *Miracleman*, *Captain Britain*, and his work at DC revise characters created by others; *Supreme*, *1963*, *Watchmen*, and his ABC titles rely on pastiches of prominent characters or character types; and *League of Extraordinary Gentlemen* and *Lost Girls* mix and match characters from the public domain with analogues of copyrighted ones. Berlatsky utilizes Moore's terminology to describe this practice, noting that Moore "often draws others' characters from shared 'Ideaspace' and redeploys them for his own purposes" (2014: 1652). For example, Bertatsky cites *Lost Girls*, which he claims enacts Moore's notions of the collective imagination by "drawing its principal characters . . . from shared Ideaspace" (2014: 1652). *Lost Girls*, then, relies on Ideaspace for its premise, one that, as Berlatsky notes, is "the same intertextual logic" (2014: 1654) that Moore extends in *League of Extraordinary Gentlemen* and, implicitly, animates much of

Moore's franchise work. This "intertextual logic" entails free movement of characters across texts, granting license for writers and artists to appropriate existing characters, texts, and other artworks as they see fit. Here, then, we see intertextuality as borrowing, allusion, and parody.

Taking Moore's borrowed characters alongside his narrative "Ideaspaces" suggest a sense of intertextuality that aims to blend, if uneasily, Kristeva's relocation of autonomy from author to text with author-centric practices like pastiche. This model of intertextuality draws on Kristeva's diminution of authorial intersubjectivity by suggesting that artists ultimately channel Ideaspace's fictions and concepts, thus granting those fictions a sort of agency and integrity. At the same time, Moore foregrounds the cleverness and critical purposes of his authorial appropriations, moves that speak to the other notion of "intertextuality" as a virtuosic technique deployed by a knowing artist.

These dimensions to Moore's intertextual practice cannot be disentangled from the comics medium and the publishing practices that structure it. Serialized comics are inherently intertextual, dialoguing with previous stories and incarnations as well as other characters in a publisher's line. Yet, many comics-specific intertextual practices derive from publishers' ownership of characters created by their employees who labored under work-for-hire contracts. Extraliterary factors, like corporate authorship and copyright law, also necessarily structure Moore's intertextual practices.

Copyright mediates and mitigates Moore's intertextual practice, and Moore's comics directly attend to questions of copyright. Here we return to Moore's representations of Ideaspace, for these unearthly spaces of freedom for fictions are typically wielded, allegorically, to defend a creatively and culturally sustaining model of intertextuality against the constrictions of maximalist copyright regimes and corporate comics practices such as corporate authorship. I have argued, for instance, that the *League*'s transdimensional Blazing World amounts to "an ideal public domain: in this metaphysical realm, fictions are freed of any temporal or spatial bounds and enabled to crisscross and comingle without limitation" (Ayres 2016: 153). Overseeing the Blazing World and leading its inhabitants is Prospero from Shakespeare's *The Tempest*, a temperamental magician with bushy beard who seems to be an "authorial stand-in" for Moore (Singer 2019: 104); thus, even a utopian zone of autonomous fictions contains an author-figure guiding their movements. Again, we see in Moore's intertextuality tension between art's autonomy and an author's primacy.

Magic

Moore's identification as a magician changed how he sees himself as an artist. This transformation occurred in large part while writing *From Hell*. Moore explains that research into esoteric traditions for *From Hell* "pointed me towards the occult pursuits that I'm now increasingly immersed in, which are obviously having a significant impact on the kind of artwork that I produce" (*Feature* 1997: 9). Here Moore refers not only to content but also to form, for much of his investigations into magic and its artistic ramifications are found in his projects outside comics. For example, see Moore's spoken word performance, *The Birth Caul*, staged and recorded in 1995 and adapted to comics by Eddie Campbell in 1999. *The Birth Caul* is "a moving meditation on the loss of Moore's mother . . . that examines the connections between our language, our identity, and our perceptions of the world" (Singer, 2004: 236). Other performances—*The Moon and Serpent Grand Egyptian Theatre of Marvels* (1995), *The Highbury Working* (1997), *Snakes and Ladders* (1999), and *Angel Passage* (2001)—explore similar magical themes and use hypnotic incantations and the collective experience of performance generally to enact a ceremonial magic ritual of sorts.

Yet Moore's magical investigations register across his comics, too: *Promethea*, the *League* series, and his Lovecraft cycle all weave occultism into their narratives. *Saga of the Swamp Thing*, a title that Moore wrote prior to his turn to magic, debuted the English wizard John Constantine, a figure who is hard not to see as an authorial projection. So, even before Moore declares himself an actual magician, magic and magicians feature as a specific narrative device and thematic preoccupation; still, it becomes more pronounced and detailed as his knowledge of magic deepens.

For Moore, magic is art—full stop. In *The Mindscape of Alan Moore*, a 2005 film profile, Moore directly equates magic with art writ large—he points out that "in its earliest form, [magic] is often referred to as 'the art'"— but he draws special attention to magical practices' resonances with writing. Operating at an etymological level, Moore notes, "A grimoire, for example, the book of spells, is simply a fancy way of saying 'grammar.' Indeed, to cast a spell is simply to spell, to manipulate words, to change people's consciousness." In an interview with Eddie Campbell, Moore observes that "magic is indeed mostly a linguistic phenomenon and was therefore what had been lying at the end of the path beyond mere craft all along" (Campbell 2002: 4). Ultimately, Moore sees art as extension of ancient shamanistic traditions. Timothy Materer draws a similar conclusion in his study, *Modernist Alchemy*, noting that "the ancient connection between poetry and religious ritual suggests a natural link between poetry and occultism" (1996: xiv). Much of Moore's comics work after his 1993 self-identification as a magician is prompted by, and focused on examining, this understanding of magic as art and vice versa.

From Hell, the comic that facilitated his conversion to magic, arguably gives the rawest expression of Moore's understanding of magic and its relation to art. The magician figure in *From Hell* is Jack the Ripper, Royal physician William Gull. Like Moore's own comparisons between magicians with poets and magical acts with metaphors, Gull compares magic with writing. During his tour of London's occult monuments, Gull, speaking to his coachmen, uses a literary vocabulary, calling London "a literature of stone, of place-names and associations" and promising that they will "penetrate its metaphors, lay bare its structure and thus come at last upon its meaning" (2006: Chapter 4, page 9). Gull invites us to see acts of ceremonial magic embedded in London's streets as creative writing, and see his decoding of those symbols as akin to acts of deft literary criticism.

Promethea, written later in Moore's own magical training, takes *From Hell*'s associations of art and magic further. Early in Promethea's magical education, the enchanted snakes that make up her staff's caduceus take her into a "theater of the mind" to learn about magic. This initiation appears in issue #12, in which artist Williams employs only full-page images as the snakes, named Mike and Mack, guide Promethea through the cards of the Tarot. Mike and Mack's metaphorical reading of the Tarot gives a history of the universe, one in which humanity's relationship to magic functions as the narrative axis. According to this account, the mystical pursuits of magicians drove humanity beyond "the tribal hunter-gatherer stage" into more advanced societies, for "all culture must arise from cult." Promethea muses, "everything in our culture, including language and art, arose from the drugged-out insights of the first magicians" (2001: n. pag.). *Promethea* therefore boldly posits magic as the fundamental source of all human cultural activity.

The core substance or crux of Moore's equation of magic with art is the capacity for transformation—of consciousness and society. Leigh Wilson, focusing on modernist writers who drew upon occultist discourses, contends that "claims at the heart of modernist mimesis" hinge upon the notion that "the copying of the world inherent in aesthetic representation constitutes an act of transformation that changes not just the art but the world itself" (2012: 21). In a similar vein, Moore insists that magic and art are "transformative forces that can change a human being, that can change a society" (*Mindscape* 2008). In *From Hell*, Gull calls magic "the will made manifest; our inmost dreams externalized, to work their influence upon the world" (2006a: Chapter Four, page 26). Moore seems to derive Gull's conception of magic from British occultist Aleister Crowley, who, in Moore's words, "defined magic as bringing about change in accordance with the will" (De Abaitua 2012: 84). Moore's view of magic, however, "is a bit less invasive and intrusive" and instead "more exploratory" (2012: 84). Still, Moore admits that enacting change in the world is "certainly part of [magic's definition]" (2012: 84). These dual aspects of magic—on one hand, stepping outside one's conscious self, and on the other hand channeling conscious desires into material reality—resonate with the potency that symbols and stories have for human experience and consciousness, individual as well as collective.

Art and magic are in this way political, for their practices involve wielding signs to shape collective perceptions of reality, processes that likewise underpin and drive all political action. Changing perceptions, views, and consciousness—remit of magic and art—is also the core predicate for political change. Such political ends are apparent in *From Hell*. Gull rails against the social upheavals of the late-Victorian era, lamenting that "man's pattern of control grows faint amidst the tumult of these times" (2006a: Chapter Four, page 31). His ritual murders aim to shore up the power of a threatened ruling order: "Gull's urge to dominate is bound up with a macho philosophy of male dominance, which is in turn intimately connected to nineteenth century visions of history and progress" (Brigley-Thomson 2012: 77). The Ripper as reactionary returns us to the comic's presentism—as Moore puts it, *From Hell* uses "the 1880s to represent the Twentieth century" and "the Whitechapel murders to represent the 1880s" (*Feature* 1997: 13)—suggesting that Gull's regressive political vision still haunts Britain. Moore views contemporary Britain as socially and culturally debauched, victim of a political dark magic of sorts; in response, such oppressive sorcery must be met by counter-symbols and stories.

From Hell's political theme reinforces magic as a metaphor for art's capacity to change how consciousness perceives and engages with reality. Although Moore, especially in *From Hell*, does posit magic as metaphor for art, over time the metaphor dissolves into equivalence. Sean Carney writes, "Moore's use of words like 'magic' . . . is a rhetorical strategy meant to refuse the easy binary oppositions of 'true' and 'false,' 'reality' and 'fiction' which are employed to subjugate fiction to a position of insignificance" (2006:

para. 22). Art and magic, in this schema, are not practices that provide alternative ways of perceiving and experiencing reality, but rather they give the means by which reality itself is constructed and thus lived. Boundaries between fact and fiction are blurred, and Moore's magical discourse is a language that circumvents such restrictive binaries.

Psychogeography

Closely related to Moore's magical practice are his engagements with psychogeography. In "Coal Memory," an essay for the 2016 collection *Spirits of Place*, Moore attends to the significance of places and spaces for cultural production. Moore contends, "Landscape is memory . . . and only artists of one stripe or other will feel the necessity to dig, to excavate, to willingly immerse themselves" (2106a: 270) within its freighted terrain. Moore's own creative praxis invests in environments and their meanings, pronouncedly so in his experiments with psychogeography.

A. E. Souzis defines psychogeography as "an open-ended, deliberately vague phenomena designed to encourage people to explore their environment—usually the streets of a city—as a way to open themselves up to play and chance" (2522015: 194). Annalisa Di Liddo similarly contends that, in psychogeographical writing, "The geographical experience—be it urban or not—becomes a palimpsest where a fictional map, both subjective and universal, is traced for the reader to confront and to recognize his/her own cultural references and identity" (2009: 127). Parkin writes, "Moore uses psychogeography to draw attention to the history of an area, to map the deep roots of history and culture" (2013: 274). For Moore, it is "the understanding that in our experience of any place, it is the associations, the dreams, the imaginings, the history—it is all the information that is relevant to that place which is what we experience when we talk about a place" (Vollmer 2016: n. pag.). The stories that emerge from and are told about a place actualize it *qua* place; once imbued within a place, these haunting stories inform experiences of it. Psychogeography unearths such dynamics.

An emphasis on environments and locales as rich and evocative settings has long been part of Moore's method, dating back at least to his work on *2000 A.D.* serials: the blighted streets of Birmingham and symbolic closed loop structure of the Hoop respectively contribute to *Skizz*'s and *Halo Jones*' class critiques. Later, the specificity of the Louisiana bayou informs the Southern Gothic atmosphere of horror in Moore's *Saga of the Swamp*

Thing. By the late-1980s, however, influenced by a psychogeographic wave in English fiction and poetry, Moore turns his attention to interrogations of place itself. Indeed, Annalisa Di Liddo identifies Moore's unfinished 1990 comic *Big Numbers* as "site of the first manifestation of the quasi-archeological investigation of English spaces that has frequently appeared in Moore's work, especially from the nineties onwards" (2009: 126). Such investigations persist throughout Moore's artistic career, but among Moore's comics *From Hell* arguably has the most striking overt demonstration of psychogeography's practices and power.

Moore's sense of psychogeography is on display in *From Hell*'s celebrated fourth chapter, in which William Gull—Royal physician who is Jack the Ripper—tours London. Embarking on this excursion, Gull insists that London "is symbol, history and myth" (2006a: Chapter 4, page 6), with meanings "encoded in this city's stones"; sites and monuments form an "earthbound constellation" that "yield a wealth of knowledge past imagining if properly divined" (2006a: Chapter Four, page 19). Gull's tour focuses on sites linked to Freemasonry, and in turn Masonry's lasting influence on London. Elizabeth Ho calls Chapter Four "a tour of the psychogeography of London" (2006: 110), for its occult mapping is a psychogeographical performance par excellence.

Psychogeography oscillates between sensitivity to the existing energies of a place with the ability to redescribe and transform that place, a movement that aligns it with Moore's sense of magic. Gull's tour of London in Chapter Four is a virtuoso act of psychogeography, but cabbalistic magic is framework for Gull and the narrative to explain this activity. Gull explains how magicians enchant physical environments to tap into as well as shape human memories, myths, and histories. Like Gull's account of magic, psychogeography posits the potency of symbols and stories for human experience and consciousness—individual as well as collective experiences and consciousness—and how refashioning those symbols and stories can have transformative effects.

As examples from *Big Numbers* and *From Hell* attest, Moore's interest in psychogeography registers in his comics—but it is more prominent in his work beyond comics. Alongside "Coal Memory," another piece of nonfiction, *Unearthing* (2010) profiles Moore's friend and mentor Steve Moore (no relation). This book, an expanded version of Moore's essay from Iain Sinclair's collection *London: City of Disappearances* (2006), features vivid photographs from Mitch Jenkins. *Unearthing* entwines the story of Steve Moore's life with the history of South London. Much of Moore's psychogeographical art, moreover, hits close to home. His novels, *Voice of the Fire* (1996) and *Jerusalem* (2016), explore the history and mythology of Moore's place of birth, Northampton. His short-lived underground magazine, *Dodgem Logic* (2010–11) attended to Northampton's energies by spotlighting its arts and culture scenes. *The Show*, an upcoming film written by Moore is poised to be his next artistic representation and excavation of Northampton.

From his interrogations of Northampton, Moore extrapolates broader conclusions. Indeed, Moore notes his hometown is the "median of England geographically, culturally, economically, and politically" (Millidge 2011: 13); he maintains that these forms of centrality enhance his artistic development, for they position him to understand English culture at its core. While such grand claims for Northampton's affordances are dubious and likely not fully sincere, they nonetheless reveal the degree to which Moore locates power in place's exertions and effects on the creative imagination.

Englishness

Alan Moore's relationships to England and Englishness are complicated. He is rooted in provincial Northampton with little taste for travel, yet his cultural and political perspectives are cosmopolitan. His comics often follow "specifically American comic narrative patterns" (Di Liddo 2009: 102), but their receptions are informed by Moore's role in the "British Invasion" of US comics. As Bart Beaty and Benjamin Woo aver, British Invasion writers "were aided by their 'Britishness': For American audiences, the UK is, above all, the land of culture and good taste, and there is, for instance, a long-standing tendency to see British popular culture as more sophisticated than its US counterparts" (2016: 63–4). Writing for an American market in which the audience held assumptions about British culture's inherent superiority gave Moore some leeway for mounting his critiques of American culture and politics, critiques made from the perspective of an outsider. At the same time, Moore's comics often confront England and Englishness directly, interrogating English history, culture, and identity.

We see Moore's focus on England across his career. The superhero narratives of *Captain Britain* and *Miracleman* rely heavily on their characters' Englishness; relatedly, in 2005–6, Moore plotted a miniseries (fully scripted by Leah Moore) called *Albion*, which revived defunct British superheroes. *Big Numbers*, *A Small Killing*, and—despite its Victorian setting—*From Hell* give trenchant visions of late-twentieth-century Britain, in some ways fitting within the storied tradition of panoramic "Condition of England" novels. Among Moore's objections to the 2006 film adaptation of *V for Vendetta* is that Hollywood repurposed the comic's critique of 1980s Britain and Prime Minister Margaret Thatcher into a commentary on then-US president George W. Bush and his administration's "War on Terror." Moore, then, routinely centers English questions.

How might we critically read Moore's investments in Englishness? Annalisa Di Liddo argues that Moore's comics "retain a very tight bond with distinctly English cultural, social, and aesthetic contexts" (2009: 102), and, ultimately, these engagements confront crises of English values and identity. Her analyses, however, miss how Moore's critiques go hand-in-glove with his fondness and nostalgia for Englishness. Two long-running series serve as test cases here: *League of Extraordinary Gentlemen* and *The Bojeffries Saga*. Both series were produced with a single artistic collaborator—Kevin O'Neill on *League* and Steve Parkhouse on *Bojeffries*—each of whom has an art style that Moore has praised for reflecting traditions of caricature in English visual culture. Along with their visual roots in English cartooning, both *League* and *Bojeffries* display Moore's perspectives on English identity.

Consider first *League of Extraordinary Gentlemen*. In it, especially its first two volumes, Moore focuses his attention on British, primarily English, literary and cultural histories. *League*'s emphasis on Britannia is not merely incidental: questions and concerns about national identity pervade the series. At one level, the comic is *about* British culture and identity. On this note, Moore has expressed pleasure that the response to *League* from US readers has been positive, though it "is all set in Britain, and where there's hardly an American influence to be seen" (Khoury 2008: 181). This sentiment registers not only a justifiable chastisement for American audiences' parochialism and chauvinism, but also a reassertion of British cultural superiority. Despite Moore's satisfaction that non-British audiences respond approvingly to *League*'s showcase of British literary culture, Di Liddo reads *League* specifically for "its critical vision of English imperial culture" that discloses how this "legacy of imperial culture still lurks in dark corners of contemporary English society" (2009: 103). How might Di Liddo's reading of *League* as censure of Britain's imperial inheritances square with the series' apparent celebration of that same culture?

On this question, we see both critique and recovery in Moore's characterizations. While Moore insists that his appropriations of British culture and cultural figures are fair extensions of the depictions and logics from his source materials, his versions plainly revise and recontextualize them. *League*'s primary protagonist is Mina Murray from Bram Stoker's *Dracula*, who Alison Halsall argues "is recast as a resistant and transgressive Victorian woman" (256). Mina and her romantic relationship with explorer Allan Quatermain, Halsall continues, "pillory Victorian discourses of femininity and Empire while using these two particular characters to show the legacy of imperialism that lasts throughout the long twentieth century" (2015: 256). In contrast to the heroic shading of Mina Murray, *Black Dossier*'s secret agent "Jimmy" Bond is a vile tool of an oppressive political culture. *League*'s Bond takes an internationally famous British hero and makes the character's obvious but regularly overlooked misogyny and racism his defining characteristics.

The dueling strategies of recuperation and indictment that we see in *League*'s revisions to Murray and Bond, respectively, repeat throughout the series' representations. In some cases, then, Moore draws out heroic qualities buried within British literary and popular culture, whereas in other cases he identifies its dysfunctions. The ideological effects of this patterning, however, are less consistently critical and resistant to Britain's imperial legacy than critics like Di Liddo and others allow. *League* indeed critiques the pernicious ideologies running throughout canonical British literary and popular cultures—ideologies that are transmitted via enduring figures and texts and hence retain their purchase today. However, such critical moves counterpoise with revisionist appropriations of characters, recuperations that contribute to the series' implicit commemorations of British literary and popular culture's verve and power.

In a telling example of this dynamic, the main villain behind the plot against London in Volume I turns out to be not the Fu Manchu-inspired "Devil Doctor," as the team is initially led to believe, but Sherlock Holmes' perennial nemesis, Professor Moriarty—who also happens to be the shadowy "M," head of MI6 and thus the League's commander. Moriarty, we learn, has maintained his criminal enterprise while at the same time risen in the ranks of British Intelligence. He muses, "Am I, for example, a Director of military intelligence posing as a criminal . . . or a criminal posing as a Director of military intelligence . . . or both?" (2002b: n. pag.) Moriarty's dual identity comes close to equating Victorian Britain's imperial government as a criminal enterprise; furthermore, the fact that the League must in the end combat their own boss, Moriarty, suggests the Empire's invention of its own enemies and a need for Britain to fight back against such diabolical internal threats. On one hand, Moriarty's duality blurs distinctions between British governmentality and criminality, and suggests that British imperialism is the actual source of threats, real or perceived, to Britain itself. But, on the other hand, Moriarty is ultimately defeated by the League, agents of MI6: the same dominant imperialist culture represented by Moriarty contains forces needed to undo it. Imperialist culture is emancipatory: only British culture can save British culture from itself.

As the series goes on, however, its allegorical narrative gets increasingly skeptical that contemporary British culture retains its redemptive capabilities. In 2011, Moore explained that as the narrative moves through time into twenty-first century it will show "contrasts . . . between the different eras," namely the "bleaker cultural landscape" of the present against the "richness of the Victorian or the Edwardian era" (Banerjee 2011: n. pag.). *League* thus has shades of "Merrie England" nostalgia.

Contrasts between a culturally vital Victorian past with a culturally stagnant present have ideological effects seemingly at odds with the series' anti-imperialist gestures. The final image of the *Century* trilogy is Quatermain's burial site in Africa, in which a hazy lion is perceptible in the sky. According to Marc Singer, this finale "serves as a belated elegy for a dead genre"; he adds,

> the apparition of the heraldic symbol of Britain over the skies of Africa also reads as a sincere and even affectionate tribute to the imperial heroes of old. This puzzling image demonstrates the comic's uncomfortable relation to imperialism: *The League of Extraordinary Gentlemen* condemns Britain's imperial adventures while breathing new life into its antiquated views of foreigners, and lays its heroes to rest without questioning their ideological foundations. (2019: 119–20)

A similar sentiment of wistful nostalgia in the midst of decline and loss can be detected over the long course of Moore's occasional installments of *The Bojeffries Saga*, done with Steve Parkhouse.

The Bojeffries Saga is perhaps Moore's most distinctly English strip, steeped in English idiomatic life, experience, and frames of reference. Episodes often depict customs and features of the landscape whose origins are hazy yet have persisted. If the absurdist sensibilities of *Bojeffries'* tales of an English family of monsters yield affectionate snapshots of life in the English Midlands, it balances its fondness and charm with withering honesty—several strips, including the standout "Raoul's Night Out" from 1984, display the racism endemic within British society. In its entirety, however, *The Bojeffries Saga* tells a story of England's gradual cultural decline and diminution.

Consider 1986's "Batfishing in Suburbia." In this short strip, Jobremus takes his son Reth onto a rooftop in order to "batfish," which as its name suggests involves casting a fishing line into the air, with moth as bait, to catch a bat. The activity is a bonding experience for Jobremus, for he waxes nostalgic about batfishing as a young man and quotes his own father's saying that the first time father and son partake in batfishing together is "a turning point in a boy's life" (2014a: 6). The joke of the strip arrives in its final panels, as Jobremus pontificates on "the way this family's fished for bats since time immemorial" (2014a: 8), to which Reth asks, "Yiss, but . . . well, what's the point exactly?" (2014a: 8). After a panel depicting an awkward silent pause, the final panel zooms out to depict the building in silhouette, with two shadowy figures on top, plus a word balloon with Jobremus' non-answer to his son's query: "Drink your Bovril, son" (2014a: 8) (Figure 4.1). "Batfishing" exemplifies how, in *Bojeffries*, Englishness consists of rituals and iconographies that are deeply held, even if these folkways' origins are obscure and their practice is ostensibly pointless. Such arcane customs inhere meaning through maintenance and inheritance.

By the time *The Bojeffries Saga* concludes, however, these traditions and more are lost. In 2013, Moore and Parkhouse provided a capstone to their paranormal soap opera with a final strip, set in 2009, entitled "After They Were Famous." This finale shares the charm and humor of previous installments, but its tone is more bitter and cynical. Narrated by a television reporter, the strip depicts the Bojeffries clan's dissolution: each member has charted a new path, and while some found seeming success—from celebrity writer to Blairite MP—every one of them is now living in some state of ignominy. Not only has the family drifted apart, but their former community and its social world, too, are dissipated. "After They Were Famous" (2014a) opens with a panel showing the Bojeffries' home in total disrepair, and later in the episode a background gag shows a doghouse on sale for £200,000, grimly indicating the disappearance of council estate housing and the affordable housing opportunities they gave. *Bojeffries'* finale depicts an erosion of the features, habits, and personalities of working-class life that earlier strips found inscrutable yet appealing. The end of "After They Were Famous," the end of the strip itself, involves the Bojeffries family's accidental reunion, for each of them has independently been cast on the crass reality television series *Big Brother*. Their home has relocated from the imperfect and bizarre but intimate and sustaining council estate to an exploitative, voyeuristic, and artificial household. The family's precarious

Figure 4.1 "Bat-fishing," an eccentric tradition, from *The Bojeffries Saga*. Art by Steve Parkhouse. *The Bojeffries Saga*. © Alan Moore and Steve Parkhouse. Courtesy of Top Shelf Productions. Used with permission.

upward mobility is therefore shown to have been underwritten by horrific cultural and social deterioration.

In retrospect, *The Bojeffries Saga* serves as a sort of chronicle of the transformation of English culture over recent decades. As Moore puts it, within *Bojeffries* there is "a kind of history of British culture, the incidental British culture that is kind of embedded in that narrative. . . . It's these ephemeral things about our culture and the way it's changed over the years that end up being the most poignant things about the Bojeffries" (Boyle 2014: n. pag.). Yet, this change is hardly progress: like *League*, *The Bojeffries Saga* narrates cultural deterioration. *League of Extraordinary Gentlemen* and *Bojeffries* thus disclose Moore's integral if often overlooked cultural conservatism. Moore's politics are Left, yet his political critiques contain a nostalgic construction of Englishness.

Representations

In late 2013, an uproar over one of Alan Moore's public appearances erupted online. The controversy began after a comics scholar, Will Brooker, posted his misgivings about an event entitled "An Evening with Alan Moore." This event, held November 26, 2013, featured a conversation between Moore and his biographer, Lance Parkin, as well as screenings of two Moore-penned short films (*Jimmy's End* and *Act of Faith*) and audience questions. In his Tweets, Brooker lamented forum panelists' defenses of the racist caricature Golliwog's inclusion (and recuperation) in *The League of Extraordinary Gentlemen*, as well as ableist jokes made by Moore and the alleged misogyny of the short films. Brooker added that he intended to ask Moore about possible regrets over the depiction of gendered violence in *Batman: The Killing Joke*, but he instead left the event in disgust and disappointment.

Online responses to Brooker's Tweets proliferated, and the commentaries quickly moved beyond direct responses to Brooker's criticisms of the "Evening with Alan Moore" event into more comprehensive and retrospective examinations of representations in Moore's comics work: representations of race, gender and sexuality, and violence—especially sexual violence against women. Indeed, Brooker's Tweets were less the start of a sudden firestorm than the final spark on simmering kindling. For years before the 2013 ruckus, commentators such as Pam Noles and Laura Sneddon gave thoughtful critiques of Moore's treatments of race and sexual violence in his comics. Brooker's posts unified and magnified these critiques into a wider reassessment of Moore's work.

After an invitation by blogger Pádraig Ó Méalóid to respond to his critics, Moore defended his creative decisions forcefully. The interview ends with Moore declaring his exit from public life (Ó Méalóid 2014). As it turned out, Moore did not withdraw from interview opportunities or public appearances, and the controversy's intensity subsided after its peak in late 2013 and early 2014. Still, reader qualms and critical reassessments of representations in Moore's comics linger. Marc Singer takes comics scholars to task for overlooking or pardoning "racist, heteronormative, or misogynistic representations" (2019: 125) when they occur in Moore's work. Such critics, Singer alleges, tend to contort such problematic representations into examples of critiques of racism, homophobia, or misogyny—moves that uncritically reinforce Moore's own self-exculpations. This section attends to these elements in Moore's comics and their impacts on his work's legacy in turn.

Race

Much of the critique of Moore's history with racial representations in his comics centers on the inclusion of the notoriously racist Golliwog character in *League of Extraordinary Gentlemen*. The use of this character in a visual narrative like comics—he appeared in the prose paratext for Volume II, but debuted in the comics narrative with *Black Dossier*—itself reproduces the character's racist iconography and, in turn, racist ideological messaging. Moore and O'Neill insist, however, that the early depictions of Golliwog in illustrated stories for children by creator Florence Kate Upton are separable from the figure's vile legacy as a racist stereotype. According to Moore and O'Neill, Upton's Golliwog is unfairly tarnished by the racist associations that have accrued around the character. Since *League's* appropriations of existing literary and cultural figures intend to be faithful to their creator's original and therefore most "true" depictions, even if they go against the impressions of the character most deeply lodged in the popular imagination, Moore and O'Neill see their version of Golliwog as a recuperation that counters racist caricatures.

Moore and O'Neill seem to think their representation of Golliwog in *League* "recovers" the character's past and thus detaches it from racist ideologies that the Golliwog visually embodies. However generous we are to Moore and O'Neill's intentions, the effects of their creative decisions with Golliwog are complicated at best. In a set of online posts from 2007, blogger Pam Noles—a Black feminist comics fan and critic—challenges

Moore and O'Neill's equivocations about racism in Upton's text and situates Golliwog in a context of racist cultural practices like blackface and minstrelsy that make the racist meanings of the original Golliwog legible. From her overview, Noles concludes that for *League* "to deliberately take a racist construct like the Golli, refuse to engage with where it came from and what it meant, and then attempt to pass it off as some sort of heroic wonder free of cultural baggage is a putrid act of profound corruption. Alan Moore and Kevin O'Neill should be shamed for it" (2007: Part 5). Singer adds to Noles' critique, noting that not only does *League*'s visual representation of the Golliwog reproduce the racial stereotyping of the illustrations in Upton's children's books, but also Moore's tongue-in-cheek characterization of Golliwog "as a prodigiously endowed, oversexed lover" (2019: 122) speaks to a racist trope of hypersexualized black men. While the intensity of criticism against Moore for *League*'s use of Golliwog has largely waned, the vexed dynamics of *League*'s complicity with anti-black racism, centered on but not exclusive to the Golliwog, speak to tensions felt across Moore's comics work.

Critical interest in the tensions of Moore's representations of race has in fact been reignited recently by the critical success of the HBO television series, *Watchmen*, which updates the comic book's focus on Cold War conflicts into a narrative about a dire contemporary US political context: white supremacy and the rise and normalization of white nationalism. This approach drove fans and critics to an obscure 2017 interview with Moore. In this conversation, Moore rehearses his arguments against the current popularity of superheroes, adding in an aside that "save for a smattering of non-white characters (and non-white creators) these books and these iconic characters are still very much white supremacist dreams of the master race. In fact, I think a good argument can be made for D. W. Griffith's *Birth of a Nation* as the point of origin for all those capes and masks" ("Eternalism" 2019: n. pag.). The *Watchmen* show leverages its superhero source for an allegorical commentary on race, pointedly in its disclosure that Hooded Justice, whose face and identity go unrevealed in the comic, is a Black, queer man. Moore's comments in the resurfaced 2017 interview, however, prompted critics to return to *Watchmen* and Moore's other superhero comics for indications of a racial critique. Was the show's rewriting less novel than seemed?

Turning to *Watchmen* the comic, racism is found among both generations of superheroes. In Hollis Mason's memoir of his time as the first superhero codenamed Nite-Owl—the contents of which constitute the paratexts for the first three issues of *Watchmen*—he discloses, "Before Pearl Harbor, I heard

Hooded Justice openly expressing approval for the activities of Hitler's Third Reich, and Captain Metropolis has gone on record as making statements about black and Hispanic Americans that have been viewed as both racially prejudiced and inflammatory, charges that it is difficult to argue or deny" (1987d: n. pag.). When Captain Metropolis attempts to recruit a second generation of masked vigilantes into a new superhero team, none bat an eye at his identification of "black unrest" as a social ill in need of correction. And Dr. Manhattan and Comedian, respectively, representatives of second- and first-generation cohorts of superheroes, unquestioningly participate in President Nixon's neo-imperialist war in Vietnam; both Dr. Manhattan and Comedian are depicted committing acts of racialized violence against Asian soldiers and civilians.

Perhaps the most patently racist of *Watchmen*'s vigilantes is Rorschach, disturbingly also a fan-favorite breakout character from the comic book. In one of his diary entries from *Watchmen*'s first issue, for example, Rorschach complains about his landlady: "She has five children by five different fathers. I am sure she cheats on welfare" (1987d: n. pag.). While this comment avoids mention of his landlady's race, the language echoes then-US president Ronald Reagan's rhetorical construct of "the welfare queen" exploiting social services, a figure clearly racially coded as black. Furthermore, Rorschach's favored newspaper is the right-wing *New Frontiersman*, which runs a piece (appearing as issue #8's paratext) that addresses leftists' view of "costumed heroes as direct descendants of the Ku Klux Klan" (1987d: n. pag.). Far from disputing the lineage, the editorial argues that, "despite what some might view as their later excesses, the Klan originally came into being because decent people had perfectly reasonable fears for the safety of their persons and belongings when forced into proximity with people from a culture less morally advanced" (1987d). In this passage equating superhero vigilante justice with Klan terrorism, we see a preview of Moore's 2017 comment about *Birth of a Nation* as antecedent for superhero cinema. In a review of the *Watchmen* show that compares it to the comic, Aaron Bady contends that Moore and Gibbons' *Watchmen* posits superheroes as a "wish-fulfillment fantasy of a white supremacist state, libidinal violence utterly typical of white men of their era" (2019: n. pag.). At a broader level, Qiana Whitted argues that *Watchmen*'s revisionist critique of the superhero genre "has its counterpart in the subversive practices of African American storytelling traditions" (2015: 237). While *Watchmen* the TV show breaks ground by centering Black characters and experiences in its revisionist superhero narrative, it seems invested in the legitimacy of superheroes;

Moore and Gibbons's *Watchmen*, by contrast, unsparingly undoes the myths of the superhero in part by conjoining those genre myths with the white supremacist racial myths pervasive in the United States.

Such commentaries are not exclusive to *Watchmen*, but are actually common in Moore's superhero narratives. *Miracleman*'s vile creator of the Miracle family of superhumans, Dr. Gargunza, has ties to Nazi Germany, thus linking his bioengineering of a new superpowered race with Nazi eugenics and belief in Aryan racial supremacy. Likewise, the classic *Saga of the Swamp Thing* #24 refers to its guest stars from the Justice League as "the Overpeople," a term laden with fascist connotations. Suggesting that the Justice League's protection of humanity is also a form of fascistic domination of the world cannot be divorced from the racial identities of these heroes, all of whom—with the exception of the green extraterrestrial hero, Martian Manhunter—are rendered as white characters.

Elsewhere in Moore's comics, we see tensions between Moore's apparent progressive, even at times more purposefully anti-racist, views and politics with the contradictory meanings and effects of his representations of race themselves. *V for Vendetta*, for instance, makes clear that white supremacy is integral to the ruling ideology underpinning its vision of a dystopian England. The sole political party in control of the narrative's authoritarian government is called "Norsefire," reflecting neo-Nazi's affinities for Germanic mythological iconographies, and its members use Nazism's outstretched arm salute. A popular entertainment within *Vendetta*'s narrative world is *Storm Saxon*, a television series whose titular Aryan hero fights "black cannibal filth" (1990d: 108). The comic's protagonist, V, not only fights against these racist forces but also is implied to be a member of a marginalized group targeted by Norsefire. His ostensible origin story is set in a labor camp imprisoning and torturing ethnic, racial, sexual, and religious minorities.

No matter V's "actual" identity or heritage, however, we only ever see him visualized as a white (by virtue of his Guy Fawkes mask) and able-bodied man. V's acts of rebellion occur in a nation effectively devoid of ethnic and racial minorities—"There's mischiefs and malarkies / but no queers or Yids or darkies" (1990d: 92), V sings—making *V for Vendetta* a narrative that sympathizes with the injustices inflicted on marginalized, minoritized communities, but one absent any representations of agential members of those communities. In a somewhat similar vein, although *Supreme*'s transdimensional kingdom populated by variants of the hero Supreme certainly contains Supremes of diverse ethnicities, genders, body types, abilities, and other identity markers, by using a white, muscular design for the protagonist Supreme, and by rendering the "original Supreme" in a visually similar way, *Supreme* thus suggests that while superheroes may appear in countless embodiments the superhero template is male, able-bodied, cisgender-heterosexual, and white.

The whiteness of the superhero, however, is complicated in Moore and Chris Sprouse's *Tom Strong*. If that series' draws on older colonial adventure stories like *Tarzan* for inspiration, it resists its genre predecessors by depicting the black islanders among whom Tom Strong is raised with comparative dignity and depth. One of the final stories for *Tom Strong* written by Moore, moreover, is an alternate history narrative in which Tom Strong's mother is impregnated not by a white, American scientist but by a Black, West Indian sailor. The revised story of Tomas Stone posits a superhero world in which whiteness is not presumed to be a default. *Tom Strong's* opening for the possibility of more inclusive histories and mindful representations of race might apply to Moore's comics generally. While his engagements with race at times counterproductively draw on and reproduce the very racist iconographies and ideologies he might be intending to subvert—the effects of which cannot be ignored, downplayed, or rationalized, despite any presumed intention—running across his comics work are also attempts to rupture and revise racist cultural narratives.

Sexuality

Representations of sex and sexuality in Moore's comics are similarly vexed. Without question, Moore's comics offer varied, nuanced, and complex representations of gay characters and queer experiences: Captain Steve Traynor in *Top 10*, Robert Black in *Providence*, Stacia in *Promethea*, and Valerie in *V for Vendetta*, to name a few. Moreover, Moore himself has long identified as a queer ally and, in 1988, organized a fundraising comic, *AARGH!*, to protest homophobic legislation. Moore's contribution to that anthology, "The Mirror of Love," is a poetic paean to gay love and eroticism. Yet, at the same time, Moore's tendency to thematize sexuality, especially gay, queer, and non-normative sexualities, frequently have counterproductive unintended effects.

Consider *Watchmen*'s account of sex and sexuality. While its overt representations of queer love and experience are minimal, the comic nevertheless features gay and lesbian supporting characters, including several members of the first generation of superheroes: Captain Metropolis,

Hooded Justice, and Silhouette. Treatments of these characters, overall, reflect Moore's attempts to take sex seriously, affirm varieties of sexual experience and identity, and think about genre conventions and tropes as metaphors for sexuality. *Watchmen* draws out superhero comics' queer subtexts as part of its interrogation of the superhero figure and genre, and it leverages them for its social and political commentaries. If the comic makes such moves for apparently progressive ends, it also traffics in troubling representations of sexual violence and non-normative sexual identities.

Watchmen seems to strive to depict its gay characters with dignity and acknowledge the injustices of homophobia. The paratexts in issue #9 include an interview that Sally Jupiter gave to a fictional magazine, *Probe*, in 1976. Reflecting on her years as a crime-fighter in the 1940s, Sally notes that several of her comrades were gay: "Some professions, I don't know, they attract a certain type" (1987d: n. pag.). One of Sally's compatriots whose homosexuality was made public is Ursula Zandt, codenamed Silhouette, who was murdered alongside her lover in a vicious and bloody hate crime. In the *Probe* interview, Sally admits that she and Silhouette did not get along, personally, but looking back the treatment that Silhouette, after being outed, received from the press and her fellow superheroes "wasn't fair" and "wasn't honest" (1987d: n. pag.). Sally's sympathies and attitudes toward gay superheroes seem to be shared by the text and Moore. In an interview, Moore echoes his dialogue for Sally, musing that "certain professions might attract a higher percentage of gays than other professions. It seemed sensible to me that costumed crime fighting might be one of those professions" (Sharrett 2012: 51). Moore in one sense downplays his characters' sexualities, insisting *Watchmen*'s world simply contains "roughly the same percentage of gay people as in our own world" (Sharrett 2012: 51), but his observation that superhero activity might "attract" queer people plays out problematically.

Looking at the relationship between superhero identities and queerness in *Watchmen*, we see that many of the queered forms of superhero sexuality represented in the comic are dysfunctional and destructive. Moore himself points to this dynamic, acknowledging that while he made sure to include several gay characters in *Watchmen* in part to recognize their existence— important for a genre in which explicitly gay characters had been largely invisible—he also notes,

> yes, there is a sexual element to costumed adventuring, and this becomes a subtext to the book. The sexual element takes various forms. It can be argued that Rorschach's energies must surely be

displaced sexual energies. In writing him, it was plainly obvious that he never had any relations with anyone at all, and furthermore viewed the entire subject with violent distaste, presumably because of his experience with his mother. (Sharrett 2012: 51)

Rorschach, in Moore's account, is not healthily asexual or nonsexual; rather, he is a violent virgin whose anti-social behaviors, psychotic tendencies, and harsh worldview flow from his sublimated sexuality. This link is reinforced by the Rorschach test's cultural associations with Freudian psychoanalysis that is invested in repressed sexual desires. Rorschach undergoes psychotherapy in *Watchmen*, and the paratexts from issue #6 include a childhood drawing done by Rorschach of his mother, a prostitute, having sex. In this garish rendering, sex is nightmarish: two monstrous figures meshed together at the waist in a symmetrical composition that resembles an inkblot.

Another character whose superhero identity intersects with an unhealthy sexuality is the second Nite-Owl, Dan Dreiberg. An altogether decent and honorable person, in his superhero retirement Dan finds himself sexually impotent and frustrated. He and the second Silk Spectre, Laurie Juspeczyk, begin a romantic relationship, but it is only after the two of them readopt their superhero personae in order to conduct a rescue operation that Dan is able to perform sexually. In an earlier, failed attempt at intercourse on Dan's couch, their fumbling efforts are contrasted with a television announcer providing commentary for a gymnast's remarkable athletic feats. That gymnast, pointedly, is the former superhero Ozymandias. The announcer's descriptions of Ozymandias' physical prowess contrasts the virility of the superhero with the impotence of Dan's mild-mannered normality. When Dan and Laurie's consummated sexual encounter does happen, it occurs in Dan's owl-shaped airship, and the moment of climax is signified by Laurie's accidental firing of the ship's flame-throwers. The image of the bird-themed ship spewing a stream of fire into the night sky amusingly, if heavy-handedly, grounds Dan's sexuality in his superhero identity.

In a more fleeting example, sexual dysfunction, confusion, or maladjustment becomes a source of humor. At the end of the first issue, Dan and Laurie reminisce about their superhero days. Laurie remembers an antagonist, one with the moniker Captain Carnage, "who pretended to be a super-villain so he could get beaten up" (1987d: n. pag.). "Captain Carnage" was apparently a sadomasochist who wanted superheroes to subdue him, thus gratifying him sexually. Dan recalls that he foiled this enemy by simply walking away, ignoring the plea to "Punish me!" Laurie wonders what happened to Captain Carnage, to which Dan answers, "Rorschach dropped him down an elevator shaft" (1987d: n. pag.). Responding to the gallows humor, Dan and Laurie laugh even as they admit the inappropriateness of that response. While this moment is played for comedy, like the murdered lesbian Silhouette, Captain Carnage is killed over his non-normative sexuality. While Captain Carnage is an offhand joke, it is of a piece with characterizations like Nite-Owl's impotence and Rorschach's sublimated sex drive. *Watchmen* aligns non-normative sexuality with the superhero, blurring distinctions between sexual identity, dysfunction, and deviance. Since *Watchmen* also aligns superheroes with queerness, homosexuality is constellated with unhealthy and violent sexualities.

Perhaps the most fraught triangulation of superheroes, violence, and sex centers on the relationship between Edward Blake, or the Comedian, and the first Silk Spectre, Sally Jupiter. In a flashback to the 1940s, the Comedian assaults Silk Spectre, attempting to rape her. This attack occurs after The Minutemen team takes a photograph, an image that recurs in the series and recalls the posed "group shot" visual convention for superhero team comic books. In this way, placing Comedian's brutal assault in the moments after that photo shoot returns us to *Watchmen*'s theme of the hidden violence behind the iconography of the superhero figure and genre. Along these lines, in the aftermath of the assault Comedian leaves the Minutemen and becomes an agent of the US military, eventually recognized as a war hero. Karl Martin describes Comedian as a defender of the nation-state form and as such finds continuity across Comedian's attack on Silk Spectre and his military conquests—he is "an agent of violence and a potent symbol of American power" (2012: 68)—thereby aligning imperialist US foreign policy and military interventionism with sexual violence. This linkage is driven home in a flashback to the Vietnam War, appearing in issue #2: in a fit of anger, the Comedian brutally murders a local woman whom he has impregnated.

Comedian's sexual violence joins the broader motif of superheroes' non-normative and problematic sexualities. In the rape scene, Hooded Justice intervenes; as Hooded Justice beats Comedian to a bloody mess, Comedian sneers, "This is what you like, huh? This is what gets you hot" (1987d: n. pag.). Comedian's remark eroticizes superhero violence and takes on an additional resonance given the series' later disclosures, via paratexts, that Hooded Justice is gay. Ultimately, *Watchmen*'s grafts of non-normative sexual identity to a non-normative social identity aligns homosexuality with deviant, violent, and dysfunctional expressions of sexuality. As in later attempts to represent nuanced sexualities in *League of Extraordinary Gentlemen* and *Promethea*, as well as the emancipatory potential of transgressive sex in *Lost Girls*, Moore can be blind to the unintended consequences of his representations. In *Watchmen*, we see Moore's interest in the sexual subtexts of fictions and fictional forms, but also the tendency of his comics work to reproduce ideas and assumptions about normative sexualities despite his attempts at subversion.

Sexual Violence

Watchmen's dysfunctional relationship between Comedian and Silk Spectre does not end with the assault scene discussed in the previous subsection. Late in the narrative, Laurie learns that her mother eventually did engage in consensual intercourse with Comedian, and he is in fact her biological father. Sally admits to Laurie that she cannot justify her feelings for Blake, which persist: near the end of the series, Sally kisses a picture of Blake and weeps. Moore denies suggesting that Sally desired the "dreadful" rape attempt (Khoury 2008: 118), explaining that the Blake-Jupiter dynamic captures a nuanced characterization he wanted to grant superheroes. If Moore is correct that "people's behavior often is counter-intuitive, particularly when it comes to sex and love" (Khoury 2008: 118), it is also true that in discourses around rape and sexual harassment women are often alleged to have secretly enjoyed an assault or to have misled or encouraged their attacker. Here, Moore's theme of ambiguity joins damaging assumptions about women and sexual violence.

Throughout Moore's comics, we see other complicated engagements with sexual violence. *From Hell*, for instance, features graphic renderings of Jack the Ripper's murders and vivisections, but artist Eddie Campbell deliberately avoids the visual motifs of horror that might allow for vicarious pleasure in the violence. Moore devotes considerable character development to these women so that they are seen as rounded, complex humans with identities that are not reducible to their statuses as sex workers and victims. *Watchmen* gives due attention to the lingering traumas and coping strategies of sexual assault, even if its results are questionable. In a critique of Moore's problematic representations, Laura Sneddon acknowledges that "Moore is a big supporter of women in the arts, equal rights, feminism, and so on, and has condemned the underlying misogyny and lack of diversity in the industry" (2011: n. pag.). Little doubt exists that Moore is attuned and responsive to feminist concerns about representation and equity.

Depictions of rape and sexual violence, nevertheless, are rampant across Moore's comics. *League of Extraordinary Gentlemen* is rife with depictions of violence against women, most of it targeted against series protagonist Mina Murray; as Marc Singer writes, "Almost every woman seen in volume 1 is either a prostitute, a fetish object, or a victim of sexual assault, and Mina plays all these parts in turn" (2019: 115). Such figurations for women have pervaded Moore's comics from the earliest stages of his career. In *Miracleman*, Miraclewoman's desire for power is fueled in part by her anger at Dr. Gargunza, the villainous scientist who created the "Marvel family" of superhumans, for he raped her repeatedly while she was comatose. Likewise, Evey from *V for Vendetta* is transformed into a revolutionary only after V subjects her to torture and humiliation.

More recently, Moore has amplified the stakes by way of his late-career turn to horror. For instance, *Crossed + 100* is Moore's contribution to the *Crossed* franchise, which is notorious for its extraordinarily graphic and revolting depictions of zombies raping and mutilating (simultaneously) their victims. *Neonomicon*, notoriously, features a federal agent repeatedly raped by a Lovecraftian reptilian monster in an extended ten-page scene. Laura Sneddon writes, "The rape scene in *Neonomicon* is disgusting, debased and horrifying. To call it a 'scene' is misleading; the horror goes on for pages and pages. . . . This comic is sick and wrong and horrible, and you are supposed to feel ill reading it" (2011: n. pag.). As Sneddon's scathing condemnation admits ("the horror goes on," "you are supposed to feel ill"), *Neonomicon* is working within a framework of horror and as such intends to cause revulsion and dismay. Yet, as in *Crossed + 100*, *Neonomicon* instrumentalizes rape to fulfil genre expectations of horror rather than disclose the horrors of rape.

Perhaps the test case for critical interrogations of gendered violence in Moore's comics is *Batman: The Killing Joke*, in part because with this example Moore has expressed regret over his creative choices. In a 2008 interview with George Khoury, Moore admits that the violent content of *Joke*, upon reflection, is gratuitous: "Don't do something horrible and nasty [in a story] just because you couldn't think of anything interesting. That's easy and cheap. And I think that's probably, at the end of the day, what happened with *The Killing Joke*" (123). Ultimately, Moore admits, *Killing Joke* contains "some very nasty things" disconnected from any "important human information being imparted" (123). While Moore has given varied reasons for distancing himself from *Joke*, the exchange with Khoury is noteworthy for in it Moore's retrospective reservations about the comic center on the apparent purposeless of its "nasty things." Moore's view seems to be that graphic representations of violence are justifiable if they convey some meaningful idea.

Yet, not tending to qualify as "important human information" imparted by Moore's many representations of violence, especially gendered and sexual violence, are the causes, experiences, and traumatic aftereffects—including survival mechanisms—of the violence. For Moore, in other words, representations of rape, sexual humiliation, and violence against women generally are justifiable if leveraged toward some narrative purpose, thematic effect, or political commentary *apart from* but not necessarily *about* rape, sexual humiliation, violence against women, and the cultural conditions and contexts that (re)produce and define those gendered threats.

Critics and fan communities, however, have contextualized Moore's representations within a problematic genre history for superhero comics. These critics note how superhero comics, to the point of cliché, depict female characters as objects fit for bodily harm. Writer Gail Simone called out the prevalence of this narrative strategy in 1999, posting on her website an inventory of female supporting characters who have been subject to brutal violence as merely a device for advancing the narratives of male protagonists. Simone prefaces her catalog by writing, "This is a list . . . [of] superheroines who have been either depowered, raped, or cut up and stuck in the refrigerator" (1990: n. pag.). *Killing Joke* fits within this disturbing trend: the narrative purpose behind Joker's attack on Barbara Gordon is to propel the conflicts between the three men in the story.

Moore's prestige as a writer compounds the problem, for the symbolic capital his name carries arguably imparts a gravitas to its explicit violence. In this way, graphic violence, especially violence against women, within superhero narratives has acquired an association with seriousness and profundity. And this dubious relationship between violent content and literary or aesthetic quality, unfortunately, might be *The Killing Joke*'s most enduring contribution to superhero comics, a legacy that spreads from the comics readership and into broader public knowledge of the genre. Indeed, *The Killing Joke* was recently adapted into an animated feature that, in its desire for fidelity to its source material, replicates rather than mitigates the comic's problematic violence.

Joke's status as flashpoint for ongoing arguments over representation in superhero comics is exemplified by a 2015 mini-controversy that erupted among fan communities over an alternate cover. Artist Rafael Albuquerque was commissioned by DC to create a variant cover image for *Batgirl* #41. The cover paid homage to *The Killing Joke* by showing a menacing Joker with his arms around a visibly terrified Barbara Gordon—a version of the character who, due to a 2011 continuity reboot in the style of *Crisis on Infinite Earths*, is once again a teenager and active as Batgirl, no longer paralyzed as she was in the aftermath of *Killing Joke*. This art spurred a backlash from fans, who saw it as glorifying violence against women, and Albuquerque quickly asked DC to recall his own artwork. Uproar over this cover indicates how *Killing Joke*'s legacy now seems tarnished.

These questions of representation and race, sexuality, and violence, are thorny and, in most cases, are not easily resolvable. Even Moore's most unrelenting critics on these matters tend to admit discrepancies between, on the one hand, Moore's apparent intentions and publicly stated (and acted-upon) political commitments with, on other hand, the actual effects and implications of his comics' representations. Along similar lines, surveying the body of comics produced by Moore over the course of his career will yield divergent representations with contradictory ideologies attached to them. Furthermore, the vexing problems of representation raised by Moore's comics extend well beyond Moore's comics themselves; rather, Moore's comparatively intelligent and reflexive genre comics index representational dilemmas endemic in comics' very form and history.

CHAPTER 5
SOCIAL AND CULTURAL IMPACT

This chapter attends to the reverberations of Moore's comics. How are the effects of his work felt and where are those effects seen? To what developments have his comics contributed? What discursive and material changes have his comics wrought? These significances are found in the comics field and different areas of cultural production and other spheres. A final section, which reflects on the canonical status of Moore's comics, acts as conclusion for this book.

Authorship and Ownership

Over the course of Moore's career, what it means to be a comics author—how "authorship" is defined and the cultural capital granted that label—has changed. By no means is Moore responsible for this transformation, but he has been key to the process. Shifting notions of comics authorship have been driven by comics professionals reimagining the values of their work and contesting their labor statuses, efforts buttressed by fan communities' advocacy for varied forms of recognition and compensations owed creators. This section situates Moore within the intersection of the creator rights movement and changing ideas of comics authorship.

Moore's own comments on comics authorship can be confused. Consider Moore's extended essay on his method, *Writing for Comics,* originally published in 1985. In *Writing for Comics,* Moore emphasizes the need to understand visual narrative, insisting that "it is vital that a writer thinks visually and takes advantage of how much information it is possible to casually convey within an image without overburdening either the picture with extraneous detail or the captions with lengthy descriptions" (2010e: 41). He recommends comics writers draft thumbnail page layouts to aid pacing and provide "a solid jumping-off point for whatever visual input he or she may care to add to the art and design" though "the artist will almost certainly have visual sensibilities 50 times more sound and reliable"

(2010e: 41). The essay thus challenges hard separations of verbal and visual elements and takes collaboration on comics as a porous exchange.

Nevertheless, *Writing for Comics* ultimately conceives comic book writing and illustrating as discrete, sequential acts. Moore assumes that "the writer is at the beginning of the whole creative process" (2010e: 6), an ordering that positions writing as the fount for comics authorship. Moore's suggestion that "writing" is an origination point means that "comic writing is perhaps even a greater cause for concern than comic book drawing" because, he maintains, "[i]f the thinking behind the writing is inadequate, the script is inadequate. Consequently, even in the hands of the best artist in the world, the finished comic will lack something that no amount of flashy coloring or printing can hope to compensate for" (2010e: 3). Moore revisits this line of thought when he identifies "the very heart of any creative process: the idea. The idea is what the story is about; not the plot of the story, or the unfolding of events within that story, but what the story is essentially *about*" (2010e: 6). The impression made here is that authorship rests on an idea, and ideas originate with a writer.

Visual art sustains and enhances the idea, Moore suggests, but does not generate the idea nor can art overcome a weak idea. By yoking writing with invention and alleging that visuals cannot offset the script's deficits, Moore privileges writing. The implied linearity of his account, moreover, glosses over generative activity between collaborators as well as recursive creative developments. *Writing for Comics* discloses a tension: on one hand, the essay stresses the hybrid nature of comics and collaborative authorship, while on the other hand it suggests that the writing of a comic precedes subsequent stages and is hence the chief act of invention for comic book creation.

To be fair to Moore's essay, questions of authorship and attribution for comics are complicated and not easily unpicked. Indeed, Corey Creekmur's observation from 2004 that "the theoretical issues around [comics] authorship, and what remains an industrial model of collaboration, remain unexplored" (2004: 287) still holds true, for the most part, today. An influential if informal theorization of comics authorship, however, took shape around the early 1970s, when a groundswell of comics fans began championing the idiosyncratic styles and specific contributions of creators. Mobilized fandoms dovetailed with activist professionals during this period, since both constituencies—which interacted at conventions and in forums like letters pages and fanzines, and overlapped when fans became professionals—shared investments in a model of authorship that centers individual vision and sensibility. This framework is akin to film studies' auteur model, which focuses on patterns across the work of a single creative voice. Whereas in film studies, in which the auteur is almost always the director, in comics studies the auteur may be a writer-artist, a writer, an artist, or, in rare cases, an editor; complicating matters further are specific writer-artist partnerships—say, Stan Lee and Jack Kirby—taken as one creative voice.

Even when it considers work done in collaboration, implicit within comics' auteur model is a privileging and elevation of notions of individuality. Creekmur refers to this critical assumption with respect to Moore, when he questions the widespread fan and critical contention

> that [Moore's] high artistry can in itself lift a lowbrow, blatantly commercial artform. Again, were this asserted of any popular form other than mainstream comics, it would seem retrograde. It is certainly nothing new in the comics field: the cult of the individual creative artist has always been central to the appreciation of independent comics creators, from Robert Crumb to the Hernandez Brothers and Chris Ware. (2004: 287)

This "cult of the individual" rebuts comics' histories of production and reception, in which many creators worked anonymously and under factory-like conditions of mass production. Championing single creators humanizes the workers and honors artistry occurring within a mass culture industry.

This case for artistry is made against lingering prejudicial commonplaces about comics. As Bart Beaty puts it in *Comics versus Art*, "the simple fact of corporate control of the material"—a fact for most US publishers—"is frequently assumed to lead to uninspired hackwork" (2012: 81). Beaty shows the challenge made by fan communities to such assumptions via the case study of Carl Barks, a writer-artist who worked uncredited for Disney but whose "distinct visual style" was hailed by fans in the late-1960s for its originality against the "constraints of the anonymous Disney machine" (2012: 80). Fan recognition of Barks "illustrates one of the first, and central, accomplishments of organized comics fandom—the identification of individual creators within the entertainment industry, the compilation of bibliographies of their works, and the recognition of their creative labour" (2012: 80). The case of Barks exemplifies a view of comics "as a form of creative self-expression rather than as mass-produced pulp widgets" (2012: 82). This emergent sense of artistic integrity, notably, dialogues directly with the field's commercial imperatives, since calls for attribution and validation of creative work slide into demands for proper compensation and ownership rights of that material.

Organized fandoms and creator rights advocates sought critical legitimacy for comics by pointing to and elevating the status of distinguished practitioners, and they attempted to leverage those gains in the critical recognition of comics talent toward the redressing of economic injustices committed against all comics producers. Despite its many shortcomings as an accurate representation of the complexities of comics authorship, the dominant auteur model of comics authorship becomes, for the comics field, one that performs a key legitimizing function as well as a labor-activist function.

Moore's comics regularly represent, allegorize, or thematize such dynamics. Andrew Hoberek, for instance, sees some of the central character conflicts in *Watchmen* amounting to "an allegory of the conflict between the work-for-hire creative talent of the comics industry and the corporations which by and large controlled and profited from their creations" (2014: n. pag). *Watchmen*, he continues, "does not treat this allegory consistently but rather remains torn between Moore's idea of comics as literature, which . . . allows him to relocate agency to creators, and a more medium-specific celebration of the aesthetics and modes of production of comics themselves" (2014: n. pag.). *Watchmen*'s allegorical engagement with these questions demonstrates how Moore relates comics' creation to the labor contexts of that creation.

We might even take Moore's career itself as index of changes to how comics authorship is conceived and how it functions within the comics industry. By the mid-1980s, when Moore began writing for the US comics market, Marvel and DC Comics were experimenting with creator-owned projects like Frank Miller's *Ronin* (1983–4) at DC and creator-owned titles at Marvel's Epic Comics imprint, launched in 1982. Such examples do not suggest DC's or Marvel's enlightenment on the justness of creator ownership or artistic freedom; rather, they reflect a star system burgeoning in US comics, a phenomenon intertwined with the rise in the 1970s of the direct-market distribution system. In Creekmur's words, "The direct market, while dependent on the appeal of brand names, has encouraged the rise of a star system of comics creators, which first developed around the figures of Frank Miller and Alan Moore" (2004: 285). A tenet of the independent comics scene that transferred to mainstream fare was the value placed on the creative visions of individual creators, resulting in "creative growth and, to a degree, diversification" (Hatfield 2005: 25). At the same time, as audiences increasingly made comics purchases based on the creators involved, Marvel and DC realized that accommodations for creator rights were necessary incentives for top talent. Here, again, creative and market developments coproduce each other.

Effects of the nascent star system register early in Moore's US comics career. By the sixth issue of Moore's *Saga of the Swamp Thing*, its covers began featuring authorial attributions. Issue #25, dated June 1984, first adds the credits, "By Alan Moore, Stephen Bissette, and John Totleben" to its cover. The addition of cover credits was not exclusive to *Swamp Thing*, but was a rare new practice at DC. When credits began appearing on the covers of issues of *Swamp Thing* they were used inconsistently, only becoming a permanent fixture on covers about a year after their debut.

Cover credits on *Swamp Thing* indicate DC's confidence in the clout and market viability of Moore's name. Capitalizing on the drawing power of Moore's name demonstrates how the industry adapted demands for greater creator freedom and recognition into branding and marketing practices. Such a dialectic between creative achievement and market incentives, of course, is not unique to Moore or comics. Bart Beaty and Benjamin Woo in fact remind us "that all cultural goods are produced by the push and pull of 'art' and 'commerce'" (2016: 74). Moore's career, which traverses independent as well as mainstream comics, indexes this dynamic; indeed, Douglas Wolk argues that Moore's work is a "bellwether for comics' path between commerce and art" (2003: n. pag.). Wolk's assessment obtains at multiple levels—most obviously, Moore's fusion of traditional notions of literariness with popular, commercial genres—and includes his role in the creator rights movement. By championing publishing models that validate and properly compensate creative talent, and by using his comics themselves to confront questions of artistic integrity and labor, Moore has been central to comics creators' quest for recognition, remuneration, and even dignity.

These efforts, however, have not led to a robust theory of comics authorship that adequately contends with comics' specific aesthetics, histories, and contexts for production, dissemination, and reception. Instead, Moore's comments on comics authorship and his contributions to the creator rights movement draw on and reinforce auteur models that emphasize individual artistic visions—a conception that, despite its limitations, still prevails within comics studies and, frankly, animates much of this book. Though Moore is implicated in the "British Invasion" of US comics that factors into the comics' literary turn and privileging of the writer, as Key Texts' readings of *1963* and some of Moore's other comics at Image indicate, Moore often champions the authorial visions of comics artists. Auteur logics and the cult of the individual, however, persist either way.

Moore's approach to comics authorship, part of a far wider creator rights movement, was meant to change perceptions of comics from assembly line products to works with artistic merit. While this goal is by and large achieved—comics' cultural legitimation being basically complete and any remaining status anxiety being primarily a residual phenomenon—the view of authorship associated with Moore has not fully reckoned with the collaborative nature of comics authorship. Large corporate publishers, moreover, co-opted comics' cult of the individual into a reigning star system that capitalizes on creators' names while mostly preserving inequitable industry practices.

The Revised Superhero

In early March 2009, during the week that director Zack Snyder's film adaptation of *Watchmen* hit cinemas, *The Baltimore Sun* newspaper ran a piece by Michael Sragow entitled, "*Watchmen* vs. *The Incredibles*: It's Really No Contest." The article takes as its impetus online discussion, propelled by Snyder's film, on the similarities between the plots of *Watchmen* and the 2004 Disney-Pixar animated superhero movie *The Incredibles*. Sragow reads *The Incredibles* as an homage to the *Watchmen* comic, stressing that director Brad Bird's "ebullient" feature film "probably wouldn't have been possible were it not for the example of Alan Moore's original *Watchmen* comic book" (2009: n. pag.). Both texts, per Sragow, consider the social and political implications of superheroes, were they to exist, and probe the psychologies of characters whose senses of self are grounded in their exceptional powers and secret superhero identities.

The surprising *Incredibles-Watchmen* parallels disclose the pervasiveness of Moore's work in the superhero genre. Bird's lighthearted film is tonally distant from *Watchmen*, but the notable symmetries in characterizations, plot, and themes all suggest that Moore's skewed perspective on superheroes has been so influential that his revisionism has found its way, improbably, into family-friendly blockbuster films. In short, the ironic distance and deconstructionism that made Moore's take on superheroes seem so revolutionary might now in fact be the genre's new status quo.

But how, exactly, are we to define Moore's transformative take on the genre? Typically, "revisionist" is the term and rubric used to describe the approach that Moore popularized. Sragow even says explicitly that *Incredibles* "offers a revisionist view of superheroes" (2009: n. pag.). Darren Harris-Fain etymologically aligns revisionism with "re-vision," a practice of "looking again at something familiar and seeing it with new eyes" (2017: 97). Geoff Klock explains this mode of genre storytelling in a more taxonomic way using his variant term, "revisionary." Klock defines revisionist superhero storytelling by textual self-awareness, which is to say that revisionist narratives reflect on, reorganize, and allegorize their own franchise and genre histories. A revisionist narrative, in Klock's formulation, "makes sense of its [genre] history, rather than mechanically adding another story" (2003: 28) to the tradition. Revisionist storytelling's self-consciousness about its narrative and genre histories, then, makes claims for what the genre means, what it can be, and why it matters. In short, a revisionist superhero narrative makes "a judgment" (2003: 26) related to genre or a character.

Consider *Watchmen*, Moore's most acclaimed and influential revisionist narrative. For Klock, the meta-commentary of *Watchmen* "sends a wave of disruption back through superhero history" (2003: 63) that questions the genre's moral bases. Harris-Fain similarly concludes that "*Watchmen* undermines the veneration typically granted to superheroes by readers and forces them to question the entire concept of the superhero" (2017: 107). A revisionist superhero narrative, then, offers a perspective on itself, even if the judgment on the genre is critical or condemnatory.

Of course, successful revisionist superhero comics are not solely genre commentaries. To this point, in a 1988 interview, Moore clarifies that "*Watchmen* is a moral and political story with superheroes" (Sharrett 2012: 56). Here, Moore stresses that along with its inward-looking genre reflections, *Watchmen* also repurposes genre tropes and motifs for deliberate, outward-looking engagements with broader issues, leveraging genre conventions toward deliberate thematic ends.

One final aspect of the revisionist approach pioneered by Moore is tone. A darker or "grittier" tone is associated with the revisionist model, and much has been made of the cynicism and violence of Moore's 1980s superhero texts. Yet, the significance of tone to Moore's revisionist model can be overstated. After all, revisionist tendencies can be found in tonally diverse narratives like *Kingdom Come*, *Astro City*, and *Planetary*, among others. Indeed, Moore cites the influence of comics parody magazine *Mad*, naming Harvey Kurtzman's superhero spoof *Superduperman* as an inspiration for his work on *Miracleman*—also cited by artist Dave Gibbons as an influence on *Watchmen*. Self-referential revisionism thus derives from humorous parodies and is tonally adaptable.

Moore's revisionist comics in fact encompass a range of tones and perspectives. *Watchmen* and *Miracleman* do evince a deep suspicion toward the ideologies lurking behind the superhero figure and genre tropes, and both (along with, notoriously, *Killing Joke*) contain graphic, realistic depictions of violence and sex. Yet, those texts are a small share of Moore's total revisionist output. By contrast, Moore's revisionist work at Image, like *Supreme* and *1963*, and his America's Best Comics line of titles, joyously recuperate the kitsch and innocence of classic superhero comics.

Even Moore's initial superhero revisionism during the 1980s is more tonally varied than often remembered. Most of his stories for DC—the Superman tale, "For the Man Who Has Everything," and his stories for the Green Lantern franchise—show Moore's revisionist tendencies but stay within the typical content boundaries for superhero comics. And though his Superman opus, *Whatever Happened to the Man of Tomorrow?*, does indeed feature amplified violence, it does so in a way that meta-textually confronts the question of violence for the superhero genre and reconciles its depictions of violence with wistful affection for the genre's lighthearted past. Revisionism's crux is critical engagement with genre history, not a particular tone or content.

Unfortunately, in Moore's estimation, his fellow creators have not pursued the full potential offered by revisionism. Moore has said he hoped *Watchmen* would inspire others to realize superheroes' potential as a "vehicle for the imagination" that affords radical experimentation; instead, in Moore's unhappy view, came "retreads of *Watchmen*" (Khoury 2008: 120). In his review of the recent *Watchmen* television series, Aaron Bady notes that the original comic's "once-novel idea" of anti-superheroes "has been absurdly generative and influential to the point of cliché" (2019: n. pag.). One explanation for the weak imitations of Moore's revisionist approach to superheroes is a misunderstanding of Moore's model. Corey Creekmur boils down Moore's endeavors in the superhero genre by identifying Moore's prevailing interests in "the superhero as a social problem (what would their political function be, if they really existed?) and narrative concern (how should we continue to tell their stories?)" (2004: 287). Many of Moore's inheritors have been preoccupied by the first plank of Moore's revisionist project; too few, however, have taken up the challenge of the second plank. Yet, ultimately, questions about how—and why, if at all—to tell superhero stories might be the essence of Moore's genre contributions.

Mature Readers?

Allegedly, the ultimate legacy of Moore's superhero revisionism has been derivative comics defined by a cynical tone as well as gratuitous sex and violence. As Jack Teiwes writes, by the mid-1990s

> Moore had grown dismayed . . . by the influence that his own work had exerted on the industry. He perceived, rightly or wrongly, that the unrelentingly "grim and gritty" direction that comics had taken since the late 1980s was largely a result of other creators (poorly) imitating the superficial results of his deconstructionist style—i.e. overt depictions of violence, sexuality and character neuroses, rather than Moore's more complex conceptual motives behind composing these representations. (2011: para. 45)

Watchmen artist Dave Gibbons too laments that "other people in the business [took *Watchmen*] to mean 'ah this is how you must make comics'" and so, as a result, "there was a decade of grim, gritty and nihilistic comics, which wasn't what we intended at all" (Holub 2018: n. pag.). This view contends that wrongheaded (mis)interpretations of Moore's breakout work, especially *Watchmen*, brought about a wave of shallow, nihilistic comics with amoral antiheroes, gratuitous sex, and glamorized violence, which were erroneously seen as signs of seriousness and subversion.

Moore's innovation was not the inclusion of controversial subject matter and explicit depictions, which his comics do feature, but rather his revisionist storytelling techniques. Many of his fellow comics creators, however, displayed a misplaced belief that explicitness of content was itself artistic sophistication. Most commentators do not fault Moore for his imitators' excesses and weaknesses. Even Grant Morrison, rival comics writer who has professionally and publicly feuded with Moore, describes the grim and gritty era that followed Moore's milestone texts as a story of decline: "The subtle psychological insights of the Moore advance were replaced with feverish inner monologues detailing the inner agony of being a superhero crime fighter in one more crumbling sewer of a city" (2012: 251). Beaty and Woo note the many misguided creators "who larded their work with a newfound grimness and grittiness, often resulting in comics that seemed more sophomoric than sophisticate" (2016: 57). Speaking to the period's broad trends, Beaty and Woo add that "prestige often accrues around works that are perceived as subversive, and the combination of 'adult' content in a 'kids' medium" (2016: 57) exerted a powerful force on the field. This confusion over what earned the label "mature readers" meant that Moore's imitators in fact arguably made their work more juvenile than the older superhero comics that were the subject of Moore's revision!

Such (mis)readings of Moore's comics go hand-in-hand with comics' cultural legitimation. This process was propelled by a wave of comics, comix, and graphic novels that amounted to "the modernist moment of the comics medium—that of its great auteurs and the emergence of a new self-reflexivity within the form" (Wegner 2010: para. 4). *Watchmen*, in particular, is consistently placed among the mid-1980s texts that are "credited with kickstarting the newfound perception that comics were 'not just for kids anymore' and would henceforth be taken seriously" (Berlatsky 2012b: vii). This shift inspired what Beaty and Woo call the seemingly endless wave of "execrable 'Bam! Pow! Comics Aren't for Kids Anymore' headlines" (2016: 57). Notably, the lame and now-clichéd crux of such headlines—"comics aren't for kids"—contains a telling double meaning for "mature," one that registers as both "complex" and "explicit." This rhetorical move signals a slippage between "maturity" as formal and thematic construction with "maturity" as explicitness of content.

These dual senses of "mature" thus form a major facet of Moore's comics legacy, and one that ultimately centers on *Watchmen* and its reception. Mathew Levy and Heather Mathews argue that "*Watchmen* produced a new, wider appreciation of comics as a popular and serious art form for adults" (2013: para. 1). Following this comment about *Watchmen*'s legitimacy, Levy and Mathews contend that plot elements and characterizations as executed by Moore and Gibbons "problematize the heroism of comic book characters" (2013: para. 4) and reveal "the dark side of comics" (2013: para. 3). *Watchmen* shows "that comics are not just 'funnies'" but rather—catch the implied opposition—art objects that "demand serious critical attention" (2013: para. 3). Here we see slippages between meanings of "mature" as it refers to complexity— formal difficulty, narrative depth, and thematic sophistication—and imagery, subject matter, and tone, or what Levy and Mathews deem comics' "dark side." Such oscillations between our two inflections of "mature" signal how graphic violence and sex, while not the source of *Watchmen*'s sophistication, were not incidental to comics' rising cultural status.

First, consider "mature" in terms of complexity Writing for the Culture section of *BBC*'s website in 2016, Nicholas Barber declares *Watchmen*'s arrival in 1986 to be "the moment comic books grew up" (2016: n. pag.). Barber expresses a commonplace when he claims *Watchmen* elevates comics "to the level of literature," one that "proved that superhero comics could be as sophisticated as any novel or film" (2016: n. pag.). Barber's piece is consistent with popular writing about Moore that positions his comics as a "maturation" of a medium assumed to produce only juvenile, in the sense of unsophisticated, fare. This view can be found in academic scholarship on Moore as well. Tim Summers, for instance, cites *Watchmen* for its role, during the 1980s, in transforming "the cultural reception of comic books": he writes, "The popular understanding of the comic as a disposable picture book that contained nonsensical cliché-ridden stories for children changed as the medium began to attain new credibility as a form of popular art" (2015: 121). "Maturation" here refers to the advancement of the form by its practitioners and, in turn, a new appeal to older readers; the maturation of form parallels the maturation of audience.

Coexisting with this sense of mature is its usage in "For Mature Readers" content warning labels, which is to say "mature" in terms of the explicitness of a comic book's content. Certainly, Moore was not the first comics creator to include graphic content in a graphic narrative: the aesthetics and ideologies of underground comix were propelled by deliberately provocative depictions of sex, drug use, profanity, and violence. And lurid material in comic books aimed ostensibly at younger readers—notoriously, EC Comics' horror titles like *Tales from the Crypt*—was at the center of a national debate on juvenile delinquency. This controversy led to the creation of the Comics Code Authority (CCA) as a self-censoring body. The CCA's strict and often by any measure excessive restrictions on content entrenched impressions of comics as juvenile by definition.

More than thirty years later another national outcry over comics content occurred, and in this case Moore's work was at its heart. As Jean-Paul Gabilliet details in his cultural history, *Of Comics and Men*, a sequence of panels accurately depicting childbirth in *Miracleman* #9 was one cited by influential retailers and distributors who argued for the need for a comics rating system akin to the one used by the film industry. As a result, large publishers including DC announced content guidelines as well as their participation in a new ratings classification system. The general reaction from comics creators was hostility: "a petition signed by twenty-four of the most popular creators appeared in

The Comics Buyer's Guide, while Alan Moore and Frank Miller decided to cease working for DC" (2010: 91). The industry's use of ratings and content warning labels has since waxed and waned, but questions of "appropriateness" persist.

Ultimately, these discourses of "maturity" are rooted in comic books' historical association with children and childhood. Though greatly diminished, the conflation of "comics" with "kids" lingers still today. This impression forms the basis for pervasive condescension about comics' intrinsically sub-literary status—not to mention the astonished excitement when a text like *Watchmen* challenges that view—as well as puritanical attitudes about the appropriateness of certain content for a comic book. These intersecting senses of "mature" reflect the narrowness of established critical values, for they at once ignore the complexity of comics' multimodal significations as well as patronizingly deny the readerly sophistication of children and intellectual, aesthetic, and emotional depths of children's literatures.

Respect for the legitimacy of children's literatures registers, in a roundabout way, in the new stance Moore has taken on audiences for superhero comics. Speaking with the website *Vulture* in 2016, Moore bemoans the realignment of superhero narratives for older, or "mature," audiences. He reminisces, "[W]hen I was a child, from about 7 to 12 reading *Superman*, comics were an incredible stimulus for my imagination. They were brilliant. They were cheap. They were readily available. I don't think that superheroes or superhero comics of today are aimed at children anymore." Instead, Moore continues, superhero narratives—in comics as well as (or, perhaps, especially) in film and television are aimed at far older audiences, which, to him, looks "slightly unhealthy" (Marchese 2016: n. pag.). Whether Moore's dim view of superheroes in the twenty-first century is fair or accurate, it honors the validity and potencies of children's reading material not beholden to literary criteria crafted for "adult" literatures. His attitude about superhero narratives and their audiences, however, has looked differently in the past. More generous, or at least more conflicted, views about popular comics genres and older readerships are apparent in his comments from earlier interviews and implicit in his contributions to popular comics genres like superheroes.

Take, for instance, Moore's first major revisionist superhero narrative, *Miracleman*. Moore, in the *Vulture* interview cited earlier, refers to *Miracleman* as being "critical of the idea of superheroes" that was not intended "to be a reinvigoration of the genre" (Marchese 2016: n. pag.), but this demurral flattens out the actual comic's engagement with superheroes and audience. Early in *Miracleman*, Miracleman reveals his identity to Liz, the wife of his human host Mike Moran. Upon recounting his childhood adventures as Miracleman—which is to say, describing the narratives of the *Marvelman* comics read by Moore in his own youth—Liz laughs at their silliness. Miracleman lashes out in response to this condescending incredulity, smashing the floor and screaming, "Damn you, Liz. You're laughing at my life!" (Moore 2014d: 28). This outburst might be taken as standing in for the frustration that adult comic book readers—at least, before the mainstreaming of the superhero genre in the twenty-first century—feel when the narratives that are most meaningful to them ("my life!") are held up for ridicule and scorn. Of course, Miracleman's reaction is excessive and it leaves Liz visibly frightened, foreshadowing the decidedly ominous turn his character takes later in the series.

And yet, in the context of the narrative, Miracleman is in the right: the events he recounts, however absurd, *are* his life, and the scene's sympathies seem to reside with Miracleman's defensiveness: it hurts to have your childhood's formative experiences mocked. *Miracleman*, a comic that narrativizes what happens when a superhero literally grows up, captures a vexed attitude toward the genre and its audience. The series reaffirms a view of superhero comics as naïve, juvenile power fantasies, but the comic also implicitly contends that latent within even the crudest examples of the genre, like Mick Anglo's derivative *Marvelman*, exist complex and relevant meditations on human experience that speak to an adult readership's presumably more nuanced perspective and refined tastes. The complexity that Moore's revisionist comics like *Miracleman* and *The Killing Joke* make visible was in fact already present in earlier comics, only unrecognized.

Lastly, while discussions on Moore's work for "mature readers" often focus on *Watchmen* and superheroes, it is true that the superhero genre is not the only site for Moore's interrogations of comics and the overlapping notions of "mature." His early 1990s ventures into less fashionable comics genres, such as historical drama and political fiction, might in and of itself be taken as a rebuke to the dominance of comics genres like superheroes, fantasies, and science fiction, all of which have associations with youthful readers. But, perhaps the most obvious synthesis and exploration of "mature" in terms of content and "mature" in terms of complexity and depth would be *Lost Girls*, his controversial collaboration with artist Melinda Gebbie. To talk about *Lost Girls*, in fact, the more appropriate term may be "adult," since the three-volume graphic novel has been described by Moore as an attempt to produce "intelligent pornography" (Baker 2005: 35).

Lost Girls is undeniably graphic in its depictions of sex and sexual taboo, but it also relishes high modernist literariness: it is a celebration of avant-garde artistic experimentation telegraphed by its setting in Austria in 1913, the year identified by Jean-Michel Rabaté as "the cradle of modernism" (2007). The comic thus weaves together revolutionary, high-minded artistry with grubby, mass-produced titillation, a move complicated further still by the narrative co-options of popular tales from the golden age of Anglo-American children's literature: *Peter Pan*, *Alice's Adventures in Wonderland*, and *The Wizard of Oz*. This combination, for Kenneth Kidd, means that "*Lost Girls* moves at once toward the pornographic and toward the literary, echoing more highbrow forms of pornography (erotica) and engaging the productive tensions in yet another unsettling (if not impossible) genre, children's literature" (2007: para. 10). Perhaps more than any superhero comic by Moore, *Lost Girls* confronts and complicates, directly and overtly—daresay, explicitly—discourses of literariness and audience that have pervaded and informed cultural understandings of American comic books. *Lost Girls*, and Moore's corpus generally, compels reassessment of terms like "mature" as a critical rubric, namely a disentanglement of misguidedly ageist associations of adulthood with formal complexity.

Politics and/of Comics

Moore's essay, "Buster Brown at the Barricades," argues that a defining feature of the comics form is its utility for—and history of—expressing political dissent and populist discontent:

> In the derivation of the word *cartoon* itself we see the art-form's insurrectionary origins: during the tumults and upheavals of a volatile seventeenth century Italy, it became both expedient and popular to scrawl satirical depictions of political opponents on the sides of cardboard packages, otherwise known as cartons. . . . As a method of communicating revolutionary ideas in a few crude lampooning strokes, often to an intended audience whose reading skills were limited, the power and effectiveness of the new medium was made immediately apparent. (Moore 2014b: n. pag.)

Comics and cartooning's antiauthoritarian, populist, and oppositional tradition is held at bay, however, by a comics *industry* that develops around the comic book, primarily in the United States, during the 1930s. "Buster Brown" argues that the comic book industry's capitalist imperatives demanded it aspire for bourgeois respectability; comics' slow march to cultural legitimacy, Moore concludes, sacrifices the form's historical disregard for conventional tastes, rootedness with marginalized populations (for production and consumption), and efficacy for social protest. This section considers how Moore's comics fit within an *engagé* comics tradition that "Buster Brown" outlines.

Notably, much of Moore's own comics writing walks a line between traditional literary values and commercial appeal, eschewing the type of subversively lowbrow aesthetics that he celebrates in his "Buster Brown" essay. As Hatfield says of Moore and Melinda Gebbie's attempt at "intellectual pornography," *Lost Girls* refuses to "be thoroughly about sex" but instead offers "a vision of sex as imaginative, liberatory, and . . . improving" that "ends up just barely skirting a kind of middlebrow earnestness, in spite of the radical obscenity that Moore and Gebbie so clearly intend" (2007: n. pag.). In short, Moore's deliberately transgressive comics still shy away from fully investing in the subaltern aesthetics that he identifies, in "Buster Brown," as the historical source of comics' political energies and potentials. Nevertheless, even Moore's most mainstream comics display a clear social conscience that reflects his anarchist, left-libertarian politics. In this way, Moore's comics carry on the tradition of comics as site for social protest.

But the politics of Moore's comics are not, in fact, clear-cut. Ideological readings of Moore's comics underscore their contradictions. Hoberek, for instance, notes that *Watchmen*'s anti-Cold War critique is underpinned by Moore's anarchist suspicion of institutions per se, a radical posture that "surreptitiously reproduces a key tenet of [Conservative prime minister Margaret] Thatcher's own rhetoric, in the process demonstrating the link between the postwar countercultures, literary and social, in which Moore cut his teeth and the emergent neoliberalism of the mid-1980s" (2014: n. pag.). While Hoberek is sure to avoid conflating Moore's Leftist politics with Thatcherite neoliberalism, the resonance between the two postures "suggests a certain ironic complicity on *Watchmen*'s part with the very order it seems to be critiquing" (2014: n. pag.). If Moore's comics display Left and bohemian sensibilities, Hoberek suggests, they do not offer a consistent or untroubled politics. At times, however, the contradictions are intentional. Speaking of *V for Vendetta* in a 1984 interview, Moore admits that the project was conceived as "a pretty trite piece of propaganda. But it didn't work like that" (Lawley and Whitaker 2012: 32); Moore found that *Vendetta*'s sites of contradiction and ambiguity were the more compelling areas to explore. As he puts it later in that same interview, "I'm not so much interested in coming to a conclusion as in examining the problem thoroughly" (2012: 34). When crafting his comics, Moore sees political fidelity and coherency as less important than, and at times even contrary to, intellectual honesty and artistic complexity.

Even so, Moore's comics oeuvre also has a strong didactic streak running through it. This thread is most prominent in the several comics Moore has contributed to activist fundraising projects. Examples of this sort of engaged comics work include "This is Information," an entreaty for historical awareness and recognition of common humanity that concluded the post-9/11 tribute collection, *Heroes*, as well as the more polemical denunciation of British economic austerity programs in "If Einstein's Right . . ." for *24 Panels*, a collection of comics that raised money for victims of the Grenfell Tower, a London council estate devastated by fire in 2017. Both strips were co-created and illustrated by Melinda Gebbie. Earlier in his career, Moore organized and published *AARGH!*, a comics anthology produced in opposition to 1988 legislation that Moore saw as homophobic and heterosexist. Such projects draw attention to a cause and contribute materially to it.

Moore's comics have sustained social causes and activist movements in ways beyond donations. On this point, we return to Moore's long prose essay, "Buster Brown at the Barricades." In it, Moore valorizes comics as "a genuine art-form of the people, . . . [capable] of becoming, in the right hands, a supremely powerful instrument for social change" (2014b: n. pag.). This portrait of comics as an especially potent tool of political action is deeply contextual, for the piece was serialized in *Occupy Comics*, a series produced in support of the "Occupy" political movement opposed to economic inequality and committed to open democracy. Moore's choice of *Occupy Comics* as the venue for "Buster Brown" not only signals his support for the movement but also points toward Occupy's own visible sign of affiliation with Moore's comics: the adoption of *V for Vendetta*'s Guy Fawkes mask and rhetoric by Occupy protestors, an appropriation preceded by the Occupy-adjacent hacktivist ("hacker activist") collective known as Anonymous.

The mask is styled after Lloyd's design for the *V for Vendetta* comic, but popularized by (and sold as merchandise for) the 2006 film. In an article on this phenomenon in *The Independent*, Tom Ough roughly dates Anonymous' adoption of the Fawkes mask to 2008. "Since then," Ough writes, the use of Fawkes' visage as political protest symbol "has skyrocketed, and the mask has been commonplace at protests, especially those affiliated to Anonymous, and online, where it accompanies Anonymous projects and is the centrepiece of memorabilia stores devoted to the hacking group" (2015: n. pag.). When Occupy demonstrations broke out internationally in 2011, the Fawkes mask—described by Jonathan Jones as "an eerie phantom face of a diabolical musketeer, a cheerfully sinister underground d'Artagnan" (2011: n. pag.)—seemed ubiquitous.

Any actual correspondence between the politics of *V for Vendetta* (the comic book or the film adaptation) with Anonymous and Occupy is tenuous. The ideologically splintered politics of Anonymous and Occupy seem to align more closely with the film version of *Vendetta*, which turns V into a left-libertarian champion of civil liberties in the film's displaced critique of the modern surveillance-security state. Lance Parkin notes these discrepancies, maintaining that one can detect "some evidence that representatives of Anonymous are familiar with the philosophy behind *V for Vendetta*" since the "nature of the group is anarchic"; however, Parkin continues, such is not "always the case with the street protests" (2013: 371) in which participants wear Fawkes masks, for in its depiction of resistance to tyranny, Moore and Lloyd's comic "stresses the role of individuals, rather than any mass protest" (2013: 373). Ironically, the masks worn in these protests are trademarked products of Time Warner, the corporate entity that owns *V for Vendetta* the comic and movie, thus implicating the anti-corporate Occupy protestors' use of the mask within the capitalist structures they oppose. But, if nothing else, these groups' use of V's mask translates the image, in both comics and film, as a symbol of countercultural and anti-establishment ethos. In short, the adoption of Lloyd's Fawkes mask keeps with the spirit, if not the letter, of *V for Vendetta*.

Moore, for his part, has expressed approval of the Fawkes mask's entrance into a twenty-first-century political consciousness. Parkin cites Moore admitting that seeing the masks worn by Anonymous gave him "a warm little glow" (qtd. Parkin 2013: 370); likewise, when Britain's *Channel 4 News* asked Moore for his response to the presence of Fawkes masks at Occupy protests, he responded,

It's a bit surprising when some of your characters who you thought you'd made up suddenly seem to escape into ordinary reality . . . I'm amazed, I'm very impressed and I'm rather touched. The people here are amazing. I think that this is the probably the best-organised and most forward-thinking protest that I've ever had experience of. (qtd. Parkin 2013: 371)

As these comments suggest, while he refrains from giving blanket endorsements to Anonymous, Occupy, or their offshoots, Moore has largely welcomed their appropriation of *Vendetta*'s Fawkes imagery.

This support can be traced to what, for Moore, is a fundamental way that comics can make political and social interventions. At the end of his "Buster Brown" essay, Moore postulates that a

long-term strategy would surely be to occupy the medium itself. . . . Thus armed, with nothing more than a blank page and some variety of drawing implement, dissenting voices can refine and broadcast their ideas more widely and compellingly, while at the same time possibly making their protest into an enduring work of art that can enrich the medium and the broader culture in which it exists. (2014b: n. pag.)

Experiments with the comics form, Moore contends, not only elevate the comics medium but also reorients readers' political imaginations and thus the bases for activism. In a 2005 documentary spotlighting his views and career, Moore describes art and writing as "transformative forces that can change a human being, that can change a society" (*Mindscape* 2008). Comics, then, have potential to shape consciousness and alter the very ground on which political action occurs.

Cultural Remixing

Alan Moore hates film adaptations of his comics. Much of Moore's distaste for cinematic versions of his comics narratives stems from his disappointing experiences with Hollywood, including what he saw as bad faith negotiations, distrustful people, and a pervasive commercial ethos that disregarded creative intentions. His direct negative experiences likely inform his dim appraisals of adaptations of his work. Regardless, in interviews Moore has not held back: he has widely badmouthed the efforts of filmmakers adapting his work. For instance, his assessment of the screenplay for *V for Vendetta* is that it is "rubbish" (Itzkoff 2006: n. pag.).

He has also weaved parodies of adaptations of his work into his comics: later installments in the *League* series feature "wry digs at the critically reviled 2003 film adaptation" (Singer 2019: 101). He even wields his magical practices against the films, claiming to have "cursed" the *Watchmen* film, a movie over which he also swore to be "spitting venom" (Boucher 2008: n. pag.). The effectiveness of Moore's efforts is unclear, but it is true that none of the adaptations of his comics has received serious critical acclaim, and even the two most commercially successful films—*V for Vendetta* and *Watchmen*—were, by Hollywood blockbuster standards, modest hits.

Of course, Moore's resistance to adaptations is somewhat ironic given the extent to which he himself employs adaptation in his work. To this point, Moore's hostility toward adaptation is an entry point into a review of broader trends in contemporary cultural production, specifically, a contemporary form of (quasi-)adaptation that mixes and matches elements from its source texts.

Moore's antipathy toward film adaptations of his work has only grown. From the beginning, he has had little to no direct involvement in any of the productions. However, after the disappointments and failures of the *League* film (its title lamely stylized as *LXG* in promotional materials) and, before it, 2001's loose adaptation of *From Hell*, Moore went a step further and declared that he would never option the rights to any comic for which he had legal control. Arguably the real breaking point in Moore's interactions with Hollywood came in 2003, when he was implicated in a lawsuit by screenwriters Larry Cohen and Martin Poll that alleged his *League of Extraordinary Gentlemen* plagiarized their work ("Studio Sued" 2003: n. pag.). This aggravating experience gave Moore reason to insulate himself from Hollywood film culture altogether.

From that point on, for adaptations of texts that he wrote but does not control, such as *Watchmen*, *V for Vendetta*, as well as the recent *Watchmen* television series for HBO, he refuses to have his name appear in the credits or to receive compensation, instead reallocating his royalties to his comics collaborators. Moore explains this drastic decision: "And that struck me as the best solution so that I could put as much distance between myself and Hollywood as possible, and make it clear that I had nothing to do with these movies, that I was not profiting from them, and that I didn't want my name on them" (Khoury 2008: 200). Moore's attitudes toward cross-media adaptation, then, seem to be clear-cut.

Yet, basic familiarity with Moore's body of work makes visible the apparent contradictions and potential hypocrisies of Moore's hostilities toward adaptation. Indeed, Moore himself is a master adapter, given his talent for taking existing texts and reimagining them into something fresh, potent, and in productive dialogue with their sources. Douglas Wolk observes, "The totally original major creations in [Moore's] bibliography can be counted on the fingers of one hand" (2008: 230), adding—using an apt wizard analogy—that Moore's great strength as a writer is "transmuting base metal into gold" (2008: 229). When one considers Moore's habit of reworking or adapting texts, then, is he employing a double standard by rejecting adaptations of his work?

Several critics have confronted this incongruity. For some, the explanation is simple: Mark Hughes, writing for *Forbes*, perceives Moore's attitude toward adaptation as no more than rank hypocrisy. In a biting commentary, Hughes segues into a direct address to Moore: "Your work is great—including all of those many pieces of work lifting and borrowing and based on other people's work, even when they might strongly denounce what you did with their characters—but your attitude about this whole situation is hypocritical and wrong" (2012: n. pag.). Are the disjunctions between Moore's word and practice so cut and dry, and explained away so pithily, as Hughes suggests?

While Hughes and likeminded critics of Moore might see it as splitting hairs, other critics attempt to treat discrepancies between word and actions with more nuance. Hoberek, citing the *League* series' appropriation of established characters for a comic book adventure, first recognizes the surface tensions between Moore's work in adaptation and his rejection of adaptations of his work: "On one hand Moore opposes others' adaptions of his creations, especially *Watchmen*, which he sees as a sacrosanct work of art comparable to *Moby-Dick*; on the other hand he seeks to make other works of art grist for his own mill" (2014: n. pag.). But, for Hoberek, the third volume of *League* narrates a conflict between prior volumes' Victorian-era characters versus contemporary, corporate-owned franchise characters, like James Bond and Harry Potter. While the older characters are in the public domain—thus available for Moore and O'Neill to use directly—their more recent counterparts must be represented with lookalikes to avoid copyright infringements.

League, in Hoberek's reading, provides a distinction with a difference vis-à-vis Moore and adaptation. According to Hoberek, the conflict between these sets of characters analogizes "the conflict between corporations' desire to profit from characters and stories (what we might understand as the economics of the comics industry) and artists' desire to revise them creatively (which is central to the aesthetics of the comics medium)" (2014: n. pag.). Marc Singer, building on Hoberek's analysis, maintains that as *League* goes on it "pit[s] the franchised avatars of corporate ownership (art as commercial property) against representations of the artist's participation in and revision of prior traditions (art as common property)" (2019: 106). These readings suggest that Moore is by no means opposed to the notion of adaptation per se, but rather he is angered by what he sees as the unscrupulous, mercenary, even culturally destructive motivations behind corporate ownership and franchising—base motivations that he believes also animate most film adaptations of his comics work. Hughes, though totally unsympathetic to Moore's position, acknowledges that Moore hates the film versions of his work "on sheer principle, in part because he thinks the film medium is mostly so worthless and commercialized" (2012: n. pag.). Although Hughes is dismissive of this logic, he is essentially correct: any potential merits of the film adaptations themselves are undercut, even made irrelevant, by what Moore sees as the unjust means by which the rights to an adaptation are secured and the impure, that is to say strictly commercial, aims of the filmmakers. Moore's principled objection to film adaptations is a proxy stance against exploitation of artists.

We can get further insight into Moore's views on adaptation by attending to his own adaptation strategies, which themselves resonate with developments in other realms of literary and popular culture. For instance, Hoberek ends his study of *Watchmen* with a review of "the graphic novel's influence on contemporary American fiction. This influence was mostly indirect and has to do with Moore and Gibbons's role in bringing greater realism and formal sophistication not just to comic books but to the superhero genre in particular" (2014: n. pag.). According to Hoberek, novels by Michael Chabon, Junot Díaz, Aimee Bender, among others, take up *Watchmen*'s audacious "idea that the mass fantasy of superheroism that arose in the late 1930s and remained for a long time stigmatized as juvenile and preliterate now provides a storehouse of themes and tropes on which serious fiction can draw" (2014: n. pag.). Moore "adapted" comics, especially the superhero comic book, to the intelligence and sensibilities of traditional literature, and now—according to Hoberek—writers working within so-called literary fiction are returning the favor.

Such borrowings seem to extend to other adaptation strategies. A similarity exists between Moore's narrative mixing and recombination and a trend in popular fiction and film: rewriting of canonical tales and historical narratives in the registers of popular "low" genres, such as Seth

Grahame-Smith's *Pride and Prejudice and Zombies* (2009) and *Abraham Lincoln: Vampire Hunter*, both adapted to film. Perhaps the texts that most closely compare to Moore's work, however, come from television. The television series *Penny Dreadful* (2014–16) effectively lifts the premise of *League*: it is about a band of adventurers whose ranks draw from Victorian popular literature. Similarly, in 2011, two networks debuted shows that featured characters from fairy tales, folklore, and public domain popular literature converging together: on NBC was crime-fantasy series *Grimm* (2011–17), and ABC aired *Once Upon a Time* (2011–18), which had more soap opera-style melodramatics. The latter series, notably, faced allegations of plagiarism from fans of the comic book *Fables*, which brings together figures from world folklore, but *Fables* creator Bill Willingham dismissed the similarities. Similarly, Ernest Cline's 2011 novel *Ready Player One*, as well as its 2018 film adaptation directed by Steven Spielberg, organizes its plot around incessant referencing of late-twentieth-century pop culture artifacts. Given the pervasiveness of Moore's method of adaptation across popular culture, how might Moore help us make sense of this practice?

Moore's comics can be an interpretive guide for understanding new and emergent forms of storytelling. In his book, *Projections*, Jared Gardner maintains that "the history of comics and its readers offers a treasure chest of experience, cautionary tales, and possibilities for engaging with new narrative media" and that this "history helps us imagine the future of storytelling going forward" (2012: xiii). Gardner ends his book with a defense of Zack Snyder's accomplishment with his *Watchmen* film, noting that the movie's extended cut DVD and supplemental releases (such as the animated film *The Black Freighter* and the short film *Under the Hood*) adapt to film the paratextual storytelling techniques of the graphic novel. Locating Moore's strategy of paratexts—integrating noncomics forms into his comics—in media like film is a curious example of "comicity," Colin Beineke's term for "the presence of 'comics-like' operations at work within objects belonging to discrete ('non-comics') art forms and traditions" (2017: 227): Moore's genre and formal mixing have moved to other genres, media, and creative industries.

The rise of comic book film underscores the significance of this appropriation. Consider the massive success of Marvel Studios' "Marvel Cinematic Universe" (MCU), and other Hollywood studios' attempts at interconnected film franchises inspired by the MCU's success. In the MCU cycle of films, putatively separate film franchises reference each other and occasionally converge in the studio's tent-pole franchise-of-franchises, *The*

Avengers. Matthias Stork describes the MCU as "an experimental exercise in mainstream storytelling, pushing the boundaries of character licensing and industrial content flow" (2014: 79); this experiment, moreover, "adapts the logic of comics production and is designed to update and energize the genre and its commodity value" (2014: 79). Although the MCU films rarely retool comics' formal storytelling properties of the kind that interest Gardner, they adapt the narrative and promotional interconnectedness of superhero comics.

Moore's career in comics features a series of meditations on such storytelling practices. His many metafictional commentaries on superhero comics continuity, such as *Killing Joke* and *Supreme*, reflect on the roles of revision and adaptation to comic book storytelling and meaning-making. These ideas are expanded in projects like *Lost Girls*, *Promethea*, and the *League* volumes, extending the logic of superhero continuity and intertwined storytelling to all forms and realms of cultural production. Moore's self-reflexive comics' engagements of continuity, genre histories, and cultural relevance can be resources for analyzing contemporary cross-media culture.

Moore After Comics, Comics After Moore

The finale of *League of Extraordinary Gentlemen: Tempest*, a six-issue miniseries, marked not only the end of the *League* saga but also Moore's comics career. In advance of that series' debut, Moore announced that the fourth volume of *League* would be his final comics work altogether. Reviews of *Tempest* therefore tended to include retrospective looks at Moore's comics career and legacy, ranging from hagiographic to contrarian. One *Guardian* piece, for example, puts Moore among "the most significant fiction writers in English" and refers to *Tempest* as "his final contribution to an art form he utterly transformed, sometimes to his chagrin" (Thielman 2019: n. pag.). Is Moore truly done with comics for good? Time will tell: after all, Moore has made strident declarations about his professional intentions before, only to walk them back. His 1988 assertion that he is finished with superheroes, for instance, was negated just a few years later (Sharrett 2012: 58). Perhaps a more pressing question, however, is whether comics is in fact now done with Moore?

Reputation and influence are not easily measured and tracked, but there are anecdotal signs that Moore's star within comics has dimmed.

Moore's recent comics—only a few, sporadically released titles for the past decade or so—rarely crack industry bestseller lists. Perhaps relatedly, as the years have gone on Moore's tirades against the *industry* have become harder to distinguish from scorn for comic book readers and creators. In early 2011, writer Jason Aaron wrote a column for *Comic Book Resources* entitled, "The Year I Stopped Caring About Alan Moore." In it, Aaron first stipulates that "[a]s a comic book writer, I am mostly definitely a child of Alan Moore, whether it shows in my work or not. He had one of the most profound influences on me of any writer in comics." Yet Aaron now proclaims: "Go fuck yourself, Alan Moore. And also, goodbye" (2011: n. pag.).

This turn from admiration to anger was instigated by harsh comments Moore made regarding DC's plan to produce a series of prequels to *Watchmen*, an initiative entitled *Before Watchmen*. Moore decried *Before Watchmen* as a sign of creative impoverishment symptomatic to the field, and, scoffing at the writers and artists involved, suggested that creators "with an idea of their own" would not agree to "rehash" one of his older works. In an especially spiteful aside in his tirade against *Before Watchmen*, Moore expresses his doubt that "the contemporary industry has a 'top-flight' of talent. I don't think it's even got a middle-flight or a bottom-flight of talent" (Tantimedh 2010: n. pag.). Although Aaron was not a part of *Before Watchmen*, he nonetheless takes Moore's dismissal of fellow comics professionals as a personal insult. He ends his column by writing off Moore, as fan and as ostensible colleague, pledging to never read Moore' comics or pay attention to his press.

To be sure, Aaron's column created something of a stir within comics fandom. Although Moore had long enjoyed a fairly privileged position to say whatever he liked, no matter how caustic, and remain "the good guy" to giant corporate publishers' "bad guys," Aaron's pushback seemed to signal a change. Certainly, Aaron gave no defense of corporate comics practices—he agrees that Moore has "every right to be bitter as the industry has a long track record of fucking over creators" (2011: n. pag.)—but rather expressed exasperation with Moore's denunciations of an industry's low-quality product even though, as Moore often stresses, Moore does not read current comics. While many fans and contemporary creators still deferred to Moore, granting some validity to his dim view of the state of comics, Aaron's willingness to publicly renounce and criticize Moore from the perspective of a fan and professional marked a shift in Moore's reception and stature.

We might see the acclaimed *Watchmen* television show's depiction of Moore's character Ozymandias as an indication of this revised perception of Moore within the comics field. In the comic book, Ozymandias is the child of German immigrants to America; however, the casting of English actor Jeremy Irons marks the character, through his distinct accent, with Moore's own Englishness. *Watchmen* the television series is set thirty years after the events of the comic, and according to its continuity Ozymandias' plot to fool the planet into world peace is a failure. Irons' Ozymandias is still brilliant and cunning, but bitter and haunted by his past. He lives in isolation, surrounded by cloned servants who consistently fail to meet expectations. The show's elderly Ozymandias, then, is a cranky English genius whose inventiveness once made a better world possible, but who is now alone save for a fleet of ineffectual duplicates. Reading this portrayal as sly take on Moore admits the scale of his achievements as well as his successors' failure to make good on those triumphs, but it is also an irreverent portrait of an out-of-touch, beleaguered grump.

This view has a counterpart in comics scholarship. At this point, comics studies is no longer justifying itself; instead, it is *reevaluating* itself, refining its methods and criteria, and rethinking its foundational canon. Take, for example, Bart Beaty and Benjamin Woo's study *The Greatest Comic Book of All Time*, which aims to "imagine the end of this comics world and the beginnings of another" (2016: 16). When Moore as canonical writer and critical standard bearer is assessed in their project, Beaty and Woo note Moore's diminished stature, suggesting that his "ability successfully to navigate a third way between autonomy and heteronomy has waned with time" and that his invective of the type Aaron resents "leave him open to charges of being an irrelevant crank" (2016: 62–3). Beaty and Woo thus endorse decentering Moore from the comics field. Moore's retirement from comics presents an exigence to reassess his contributions to the comics field, for with retirement his corpus has a new coherence and stability. The end to Moore's career allows fresh perspectives and narratives on his comics and their place in the field to take shape.

Alan Moore: A Critical Guide seeks to contribute to this project. Across its chapters, this book has sought to balance: critical consensuses on Moore's comics with novel analyses; dominant organizational frameworks for Moore's body of comics work with alternate arrangements and models; and deference for Moore's current position within the comics field—at least, the English-language comics field—with awareness of that position's impermanence. Indeed, this book fulfils its function if it provides a basis for comics scholars, journalists, and fans to continue the critical work of reading and assessing Moore's comics, even if that works leads to disinvestments in the authority and prestige of Moore's contributions. This book's "map of Moore" aims to propel the ongoing project of comprehending and navigating the work and impact of this intriguing, complicated, and game-changing comics figure.

GLOSSARY

This addendum is a reference for some specialized vocabulary that appears in this book. Some keywords are specific to a study of Alan Moore; others are found in comics studies generally.

§

Anthology is a format for comic books involving multiple stories or other pieces, usually done by different creators. For anthologies that are ongoing series with regular publication schedules, the features comprising it are often serializations, but some anthologies also have done-in-one stories.

British Invasion refers to the impact made by a loosely affiliated cohort of comics creators, from the United Kingdom, that began working for US comics publishers during the mid-1980s and early 1990s. These creators, among other innovations, brought a more ironic perspective to the superhero genre. This aspect of the British Invasion associates it with revisionism and "genre deconstruction." Though the British Invasion cohort included artists, its impact was felt chiefly via its writers; in fact, the British Invasion is now seen as part of US comics' "literary turn."

Comic book is a medium for the comics form, one characterized by its bound, pamphlet-like physical construction. In the US comic books are associated with popular genres, especially superheroes—a genre that originated in the medium—and serialized storytelling. The medium has historical association with young readers, linking it to children's literature traditions, as well as reputations for being "low" art, juvenile, sub-literate, trashy, and even dangerous to young, impressionable readers. However, the cultural prestige of comic books is relatively high at present.

Comic strip, like comic book, is a medium for the comics form, in this case constituted by a discrete set of panels (a single-panel comic is typically differentiated as a "cartoon"). Historically, comic strips are associated with newspaper publishing, but the term is also used for short features that appear in comic book anthologies. A comic book, then, can be comprised of comic strips.

Comics is an expressive cultural form that uses images sequentially arranged and typically but not necessarily includes verbal text. Comics art appears in juxtaposed "frames" or "panels" composed on a page. Strips of negative space called "gutters" usually separate panels. For its text components, comics uses captions (usually for narration), "balloons" for dialogue (with pointer arrows to indicate the speaker), "thought bubbles" to convey characters' unsaid interiority, sound effects (stylized onomatopoeia labels rendered directly atop a visualized action), among other devices. The comics form is used in many comics media, including comic books, comic strips, graphic novels, comics albums, webcomics, manga, and more. Since "sequence" is a significant part of the form's definition, comics are frequently distinguished from single-panel cartoons.

Comics studies is a field of inquiry that takes comics—the form and its media—as its object. If most usages of "comics studies" suggest formalized academic study of comics, in many cases the term also encompasses intellectual work related to comics that comes from fan communities and comics journalism. In the academic context, comics studies reflects comics' hybrid character: the field touches several academic disciplines—literary studies, art history, communications, media studies, and more—and, as a result, involves myriad methodologies and critical perspectives.

Continuity has been adopted within comics' fan and professional discourses as a term to describe internal narrative consistencies and histories for serialized comics. In the early days of comics publishing, unconcerned editors and assumptions about frequent turnover meant stories regularly contradicted each other or failed to acknowledge character or narrative developments. Over time, however, longtime readers began questioning how comics' serialized narratives hung together, both for individual characters and publishers' shared narrative universes. Attempting to maintain a consistent internal continuity for publishing lines eventually became an industry norm, though inevitable contradictions, convolutions, and debates over what stories should or should not be considered as "canonical" parts of this continuity has led several publishers to enact "revamps" or "reboots" that narratively revise characterizations and narrative developments. Questions and practices related to continuity, then, relate closely with comic book revisionism.

Creator Rights functions as a catch-all term for arguments, advocacy, and conflicts related to labor conditions for comic book professionals (generally in the US and UK contexts). Facets to creator rights debates include the limits of free expression protected from censorship, attributions and commensurate compensation for work produced, and industry practices such as corporate authorship and work-for-hire. While an activist "creator rights movement" emerged in the 1980s—symbolized by the 1988 publication of "A Bill of Rights for Comics Creators"—artistic and labor battles over creator rights, for all intents and purposes, are as old as the comics industry itself.

Graphic novel first gained purchase as a neologism starting in the 1970s but usages accelerated in the 1980s and 1990s. This period saw a rise in cultural prestige for comics, but the term "comics" retained juvenile and lowbrow connotations. "Graphic novel" sidestepped such associations and seemed to speak to comics' aspirational cultural status. In retrospect, however, the term seems marked by pretension—not to mention inaccuracy, since many comics forms do not necessarily resemble novels. While "graphic novel" is still at times used interchangeably with "comics," typically the term now designates closed and lengthy comics narratives usually published in their entirety rather than serialized installments.

Ideaspace is a term coined by Alan Moore to name his idiosyncratic views on the relations between fiction and reality or ideas and materiality. For Moore, Ideaspace is an ethereal plane inhabited by concepts, ideas, fictions, and so on. The abstractions of Ideaspace are accessible to the human mind and thus the material realm. Ideaspace figures into Moore's understanding of how language and art mediate consciousness and imagination—collective as well as individual—with physical reality and lived experiences; its emphasis on how ideas converse across time and space makes Ideaspace integral to Moore's intertextual practices. The principles of Ideaspace predate Moore's conversion to magic, but after the fact they have been folded into his philosophy of magic.

Independent or "indie" comics are chiefly defined by the conditions of their production: generally, they are owned and in some cases disseminated by their creator. An indie comic might be a bestseller—like Robert Kirkman's *The Walking Dead*—just as it may sit within popular genres and reflect conventional or trendy aesthetics, as were the Image Comics of the early 1990s. This sense of "independent" distinguishes it from related terms like "alternative comics" or "underground comix," both of which are associated with certain aesthetics (e.g. black-and-white) and genres (e.g. autobiography). The antonym of "independent comics," then, is not "mainstream" or "popular" but rather "corporate comics," a term that suggests corporate authorship and work-for-hire practices. Such divisions in the Anglophone comics field intermingle and cross-fertilize, but the basic distinctions remain.

Intertextuality refers to relationships between cultural texts and the ways in which those relationships produce meaning. In some formulations, intertextuality is the condition in which texts are produced and read. For those working with this model, the meaning of any individual text is not transmitted directly from writer to reader, but is produced out of the reader's mediation of the text through different codes that are created by discourses and organizations of existing texts. "Meaning" does not reside in a text as constructed by an author; rather, meaning emerges out of networks of interacting texts. For later critics and theorists, however, "intertextuality" refers to an effect produced by and within texts, not a system of relationships between texts. In this sense of intertextuality, referential strategies such as parody, pastiche, satire, allusion, quotation, among others, are used by authors to create and activate intertextual networks that shape interpretation.

Magic, in the context of Alan Moore's life and career, refers to a swath of occult, mystical, and spiritual traditions. While he identifies as a practicing ceremonial magician, in theory and practice Moore draws from many esoteric traditions. He also links occultism with contemporary discourses on mind-expansion and altered states. Magic fulfills many purposes for Moore, one of which is the provision of a framework for his ideas about language, art, reality, and consciousness. For Moore, "magic" and "art" are synonymous: both name how symbolic ideas and images can be transplanted into others' minds, transforming consciousness and in turn transforming reality itself.

Mainstream, in many contexts, refers to that which is most popular or commonplace; however, in the Anglophone comics field, the term signifies somewhat differently. If "mainstream comics" meant only the comics with the largest audiences, then Japanese manga in translation and young adult comics by creators like Raina Telgemeier would be considered mainstream. Bart Beaty writes in *Twelve-Cent Archie*, "Arguments about the 'mainstream' of American comic-book publishing are all too often willfully blind, excluding children's comics and humor comics in order to make an artificial argument about the cultural importance of superheroes and their centrality to the economics of the industry in a post–Comics Code publishing period" (2015: n. pag.). Typically, in comics discourse "mainstream" refers to historically significant genres, namely superheroes but also kin genres like adventure and fantasy—despite the misimpressions that the term can produce.

Paratext is a term influentially theorized by the French literary critic Gérard Genette. His 1997 book, *Paratexts: Thresholds of Interpretation* contends with the ways that seemingly supplemental material accompanying a "main" text—epigraphs, tables and charts, prefaces and introductions—mediate the interpretative experience for a reader. Paratexts for comics might include letters pages, editorial pages, advertisements, as well as supplemental content like pin-ups and back-up features.

Psychogeography describes the dynamic between physical environments and consciousness—how spaces, in terms of their designs, aesthetics, and histories, affect perceptions and emotions. The term was coined by Marxist theorist Guy Dubord, whose radical art movement Situationism explored new understandings of the relationship between architecture, everyday life, and the mind. Contemporary psychogeography is largely associated with a cohort of postmodernist English writers and artists including Iain Sinclair, Will Self, Peter Ackroyd, and Pat Barker, all writers who have centered questions of how spatiality structures cultural experiences and meanings. Although this modern, English flourishing of psychogeography—of which Alan Moore is part—is primarily a literary phenomenon, the practice of psychogeography is interdisciplinary, crossing boundaries between history, sociology, political theory, autobiography, art history, and several other fields.

Revisionism, in the context of comics or fiction more broadly, involves the return to an established narrative—whether a specific narrative or a narrative form like genre—and retelling it with changes that are substantial, pointed, and significant enough not only to distinguish the new text from its antecedent, but also "revise" or change the way in which that source is understood. Typically, revisionist narratives employ metafictional techniques in order to foreground the cultural significances or ideological subtexts of the source, often in a critical way.

Serialization is a publication-dissemination strategy commonplace in the comics field. Comics, historically, appear regularly or semi-regularly on monthly, weekly, or in the case of newspaper comics strips, daily, schedules. In some cases, serialized comics have a continuing narrative that stretches across installments, whereas other instances are more episodic. Long-running serials tend to develop a complex continuity that blends the logics of continuing and episodic storytelling. Seriality is entangled with comics' negotiations of cultural capital. Comics presented as complete, beginning-middle-end narratives—even in cases of originally serialized comics collected and repackaged in volumes—acquired more prestige relative to temporary contributions, passed like a baton, on a serialized narrative. Furthermore, beginning around the 1980s, serialized franchise titles saw conflicts between creators and editors over their priorities: more and more comics creators maintained that executing their work according to their artistic standards and visions outweighed the commercial imperative to maintain a consistent publication schedule.

Series refers to a serialized comics narrative. On its own, "series" usually refers to a comic book or strip published on a regular or semi-regular schedule for an indefinite amount of time, without any fixed ending. Variants of the term include "miniseries," which typically means a series set in advance to run six issues or fewer, or "maxiseries," for a finite series of more than six issues.

Thatcherism is a British manifestation of the political-economic ideology called "neoliberalism." Developed by libertarian and right-wing economists and political philosophers starting in the wake of the Second World War, neoliberalism combines unrestrained free market economic principles—such as low taxes, deregulation, and privatization—with strong state power and authority, usually wielded to preserve and expand the power of markets. Margaret Thatcher, the Conservative prime minister of Great Britain from 1979 to 1990, added to neoliberal policy an emphasis on "traditional morality" (associated with the past in her expression "Victorian values"), condescension toward intellectuals and other cultural "elites," a "law and order" rhetoric that contributed to more aggressive forms of policing, and a confrontational political style. An insurgent force upending Britain's midcentury command economy and welfare state, Thatcherism underwrites much of today's political and economic common sense, testifying to her project's success. Thatcherism's influence penetrates the cultural sphere, affecting how the arts are funded and the types of values and representations found in cultural productions.

WORKS CITED

Aaron, Jason (2011), "The Year I Stopped Caring About Alan Moore." *Comic Book Resources*, January 5. https://www.cbr.com/240180-2/.

"Alan Moore" (1997), *Feature*, vol. 3, no. 2, pp. 4–18.

"Alan Moore" (accessed 2019), *Top Shelf Productions*. http://www.topshelfcomix.com/catalog/alan-moore.

"Alan Moore—Critical Perspective" (accessed 2019), *British Council: Literature*. https://literature.britishcouncil.org/writer/alan-moore.

"Alan Moore—*Swamp Thing* Interview 1—1985." *YouTube*, uploaded by A. David Silverman. https://www.youtube.com/watch?v=FJlZUpgXQJI.

Allen, Graham (2000), *Intertextuality*. New York: Routledge.

Artists Against Rampant Government Homophobia (1988), Mad Love.

Ayres, Jackson (2016), "The Integrity of the Work: Alan Moore, Modernism, and the Corporate Author." *Journal of Modern Literature*, vol. 39, no. 2, pp. 144–66.

Bady, Aaron (2019), "Dr. Manhattan is a Cop: 'Watchmen' and Franz Fanon." *Los Angeles Review of Books*, December 31. https://lareviewofbooks.org/article/dr-manhattan-cop-watchmen-frantz-fanon/.

Baker, Bill, ed. (2005), *Alan Moore Spells It Out: On Comics, Creativity, Magic and Much, Much More*. Milford, CT: Regent Publishing Services Limited for Airwave Publishing, LLC.

Banerjee, Subhajit (2011), "Alan Moore: An Extraordinary Gentleman—Q & A." *Guardian*, July 25. https://www.theguardian.com/books/2011/jul/25/alan-moore-league-extraordinary-gentlemen.

Barber, Nicholas (2006), "Our Greatest Graphic Novelist." *Independent*, March 19. https://www.independent.co.uk/news/people/profiles/alan-moore-our-greatest-graphic-novelist-6106279.html.

Barber, Nicholas (2016), "*Watchmen*: The Moment Comic Books Grew Up," BBC, August 9. http://www.bbc.com/culture/story/20160809-watchmen-the-moment-comic-books-grew-up.

Barnes, David (2009), "Time in the Gutter: Temporal Structures in *Watchmen*." *KronoScope*, vol. 9.1, no. 2, pp. 51–60.

Beaty, Bart (2012), *Comics versus Art*. Toronto: University of Toronto Press.

Beaty, Bart (2015), *Twelve-Cent Archie*. Kindle ed. New Brunswick, NJ: Rutgers University Press.

Beaty, Bart and Benjamin Woo (2016), *The Greatest Comic Book of All Time: Symbolic Capital and the Field of American Comic Books*. New York: Palgrave.

Beineke, Colin (2011), "'Her Guardiner': Alan Moore's Swamp Thing as the Green Man." *ImageText*, vol. 5, no. 4. http://imagetext.english.ufl.edu/archives/v5_4/beineke/.

Beineke, Colin (2017), "On Comicity." *Inks: The Journal of the Comics Studies Society*, vol. 1, no. 2, pp. 226–53.

Berlatsky, Eric, ed. (2012a), *Alan Moore: Conversations.* Jackson, MS: University of Mississippi Press.

Berlatsky, Eric (2012b), "Introduction." Berlatsky, pp. vii–xix.

Berlatsky, Eric (2014), "Alan Moore." *Comics Through Time: A History of Icons, Idols, and Ideas.* Ed. M. Keith Booker, Vol. 4. Westport, CT: Greenwood, 1651–5.

Berlatsky, Noah (2016), "How Alan Moore Transformed the Way I Saw Comics (and House Plants)." *Guardian*, September 16, https://www.theguardian.com/books/2016/sep/16/alan-moore-comics-graphic-novels-art-anatomy-lesson.

Bishop, David and Karl Stock (2017), *Thrill-Power Overlord*: 2000 AD—*The First Forty Years*. Rev. ed. London: Rebellion.

Boucher, Geoff (2008), "'Watchmen'? Alan Moore Won't Be Watching." *Chicago Tribune*, September 24. https://www.chicagotribune.com/news/ct-xpm-2008-09-24-0809220295-story.html.

Boyle, Jules (2014), "Unknown Pleasures—Alan Moore Discusses *The Bojeffries Saga*." *Big Comics Page*, October 30. https://bigcomicpage.com/2014/10/30/unknown-pleasures-alan-moore-discusses-the-bojeffries/.

Bredehoft, Thomas A. (2011), "Style, Voice, and Authorship in Harvey Pekar's (Auto)(Bio)Graphical Comics." *College Literature*, vol. 38, no. 3, pp. 97–110.

Brigley-Thompson, Zoe (2012), "Theorizing Sexual Domination in *From Hell* and *Lost Girls*: Jack the Ripper versus Wonderlands of Desire." Comer and Sommers, pp. 76–87.

Callahan, Tim (2012a), "The Great Alan Moore Reread: *In Pictopia*." *Tor*, May 14. https://www.tor.com/2012/05/14/the-great-alan-moore-reread-in-pictopia/.

Callahan, Tim (2012b), "The Great Alan Moore Reread: Smax." *Tor*, October 29. https://www.tor.com/2012/10/29/the-great-alan-moore-reread-smax/.

Callahan, Tim (2012c), "The Great Alan Moore Reread: *The Spirit*." *Tor*, August 21. https://www.tor.com/2012/08/20/the-great-alan-moore-reread-the-spirit/.

Callahan, Tim (2012d), "The Great Alan Moore Reread: *Swamp Thing* Part 2." *Tor*, January 30. https://www.tor.com/2012/01/30/the-great-alan-moore-reread-swamp-thing-part-2/.

Callahan, Tim (2012e), "The Great Alan Moore Reread: *Top 10* Part 1" *Tor*, October 15. https://www.tor.com/2012/10/15/the-great-alan-moore-reread-top-10-part-one/.

Callahan, Tim (2012f), "The Great Alan Moore Reread: *Violator*." *Tor*, June 11. https://www.tor.com/2012/06/11/the-great-alan-moore-reread-violator/.

Campbell, Eddie (1986), "Forward" [sic]. *Alan Moore's Maxwell the Magic Hat.* Vol. I, Acme.

Campbell, Eddie, int. (2002), "Alan Moore Interviewed by Eddie Campbell." *Egomania*, no. 2: 1–32.

Carney, Sean (2006), "The Tides of History: Alan Moore's Historiographic Vision." *ImageText*, vol. 2, no. 2. http://imagetext.english.ufl.edu/archives/v2_2/carney/.

Carpenter, Greg (2016), *The British Invasion: Alan Moore, Neil Gaiman, Grant Morrison, and the Invention of the Modern Comic Book Writer*. Edwardsville, IL: Sequart.

Chapman, James (2011), *British Comics: A Cultural History*. London: Reaktion.

Comer, Todd A. (2012), "Body Politics: Unearthing an Embodied Ethics in *V for Vendetta*." Comer and Sommers, pp. 100–10.

Comer, Todd A. and Joseph Michael Sommers, eds. (2012), *Sexual Ideology in the Works of Alan Moore: Critical Essays on the Graphic Novels*. Durham, NC: McFarland.

"Correspondence from Hell: A Conversation between Dave Sim & Alan Moore— Part 1" (2015), *A Moment of Cerebus*, September 12. http://momentofcerebus.bl ogspot.com/2015/09/correspondence-from-hell-part-1.html.

Cortsen, Rikke Platz (2014), "Full Page Insight: The Apocalyptic Moment in Comics Written by Alan Moore." *Journal of Graphic Novels and Comics*, vol. 5, no. 4, pp. 397–410.

Creekmur, Corey K. (2004), "Review: Superheroes and Science Fiction: Who Watches Comic Books?" *Science Fiction Studies*, vol. 31, no. 2, pp. 283–90.

Cremins, Brian (2014), "Quotations from the Future: Harvey Kurtzman's 'Superduperman,' Nostalgia, and Alan Moore's *Miracleman*." *Studies in American Humor*, new series 3, no. 30, pp. 169–89.

Crowell, Ellen (2009), "Scarlet Carsons, Men in Masks: The Wildean Contexts of *V for Vendetta*." *Neo-Victorian Studies*, vol. 1, no. 2, pp. 17–45.

Daniels, Les (2003), *DC Comics: A Celebration of the World's Greatest Comic Book Heroes*. New York: Watson-Guptill.

Danner, Alexander and Dan Mazur (2014), *Comics: A Global History, 1968 to the Present*. London: Thames and Hudson.

Danner, Alexander and Dan Mazur (2017), "The International Graphic Novel." Tabachnick pp. 58–79.

Davis, Blair and Bart Beaty, Scott Bukatmin, Henry Jenkins, and Benjamin Woo (2017), "Roundtable: Comics and Methodology." *Inks*, vol. 1, no. 1, pp. 56–74.

De Abaitua, Matthew (2012), "Alan Moore Interview." Berlatsky, pp. 61–94.

Di Liddo, Annalisa (2009), *Alan Moore: Comics as Performance, Fiction as Scalpel*. Jackson, MS: University Press of Mississippi.

Di Liddo, Annalisa (2012), "Afterword: Disgust with the Revolution." Comer and Sommers, pp. 202–6.

Fawaz, Ramzi (2016), *The New Mutants: Superheroes and the Radical Imagination of American Comics*. Kindle ed. New York: New York University Press.

Flood, Alison (2019), "Alan Moore Drops Anarchism to Champion Labour Against Tory 'Parasites,'" November 21. https://www.theguardian.com/books/2 019/nov/21/alan-moore-drops-anarchism-to-champion-labour-against-tory-parasites.

Gabilliet, Jean Paul (2010), *Of Comics and Men: A Cultural History of American Comic Books*. Trans. Bart Beaty and Nick Nguyen. Jackson, MS: University Press of Mississippi.

Gallagher, Catherine (2018), *Telling It Like It Wasn't: The Counterfactual Imagination in History and Fiction*. Chicago: University of Chicago Press.

Gardner, Jared (2012), *Projections: Comics and the History of Twenty-First-Century Storytelling*. Stanford University Press.

George, Joe (2017), "*Watchmen*: A Tale of Care and Understanding." *Tor*, December 6. https://www.tor.com/2017/12/06/watchmen-a-tale-of-care-and-u nderstanding/.

George, Richard (2012), "Swamp Thing: The Alan Moore Years." *Ign*, December 20, 2005, updated 18 May 2012, https://www.ign.com/articles/2005/12/21/swamp -thing-the-alan-moore-years.

Georgiou, Bambos (1987), "The Other Alan Moore." *Maxwell the Magic Cat*, Vol. II, Acme. v–viii.

Gieben, Bram (2010), "Choose Your Reality: Alan Moore Unearthed." *The Skinny*, September 1. https://www.theskinny.co.uk/music/interviews/choose-your-rea lity-alan-moore-unearthed.

Gray, Maggie (2017), *Alan Moore: Out from the Underground: Cartooning, Performance, and Dissent*. London: Palgrave.

Groenstein, Thierry (2007), *The System of Comics*. Trans. Bart Beaty and Nick Nguyen. Jackson, MS: University Press of Mississippi.

Groth, Gary (2012), "The Alan Moore Interview." *The Comics Journal*, June 12. http://www.tcj.com/the-alan-moore-interview-118/.

Hague, Ian (2014), *Comics and the Senses: A Multisensory Approach to Comics and Graphic Novels*. New York: Routledge.

Hall, Stuart (1988), "The Great Moving Right Show." *The Hard Road to Renewal: Thatcherism and the Crisis of the Left*. New York: Verso, pp. 39–56.

Hall, Stuart and Martin Jacques (1983), "Introduction." *The Politics of Thatcherism*. Stuart Hall and Martin Jacques, eds. London: Lawrence and Wishart, pp. 9–16.

Halsall, Alison (2015), "'A Parade of Curiosities': Alan Moore's *The League of Extraordinary Gentlemen* and *Lost Girls* as Neo-Victorian Pastiches." *The Journal of Popular Culture*, vol. 48, no. 2, pp. 252–68.

Harris-Fain, Darren (2017), "Revisionist Superheroes, Fantasy, and Science Fiction." Tabachnick, pp. 97–112.

Hatfield, Charles (2005), *Alternative Comics: An Emerging Literature*. Jackson, MS: University Press of Mississippi.

Hatfield, Charles (2007), "A Review and Response." *ImageText*, vol. 3, no. 3, http://imagetext.english.ufl.edu/archives/v3_3/lost_girls/hatfield.shtml.

Ho, Elizabeth (2006), "Postimperial Landscapes: 'Psychogeography' and Englishness in Alan Moore's Graphic Novel *From Hell: A Melodrama in Sixteen Parts*." *Cultural Critique*, no. 63 (spring), pp. 99–121.

Hoberek, Andrew (2014), *Considering Watchmen: Poetics, Property, Politics*. Kindle ed., Rutgers University Press.

Holub, Christian (2018), "Dave Gibbons on the Harvey Hall of Fame and the Continuing Legacy of *Watchmen*." *Entertainment Weekly*, September 7. https ://ew.com/books/2018/09/07/dave-gibbons-harvey-hall-of-fame-watchmen-l egacy/.

Hughes, Mark (2012), "Alan Moore Is Wrong about 'Before Watchmen.'" *Forbes*, February 1. https://www.forbes.com/sites/markhughes/2012/02/01/alan-moore -is-wrong-about-before-watchmen/#6b158e1d65de.

Inge, M. Thomas (2009), "Collaboration and Concepts of Authorship." *PMLA*, vol. 116, no. 3, pp. 623–30.

Itzkoff, Dave (2006), "The Vendetta Behind 'V for Vendetta.'" *New York Times*, March 12. https://www.nytimes.com/2006/03/12/movies/the-vendetta-behind -v-for-vendetta.html.

Jackson, Ben and Robert Saunders (2012), "Introduction: Varieties of Thatcherism." *Making Thatcher's Britain*, eds., Ben Jackson and Robert Saunders. Cambridge: Cambridge University Press.

Johnston, Antony (2004), "The Comic of Cthulhu: Being a Letter of Reminiscence and Recollection Concerning *The Courtyard*." *Alan Moore's* The Courtyard: Companion. Avatar, 4–8.

Jones, Jonathan (2011), "Occupy's *V for Vendetta* Protest Mask Is a Symbol of Festive Citizenship." *The Guardian*, November 4. https://www.theguardian.com /commentisfree/2011/nov/04/occupy-movement-guy-fawkes-mask.

Kart, Larry (1987), "A Comic Book as Gripping as Dickens." *Chicago Tribune*, December 2. https://www.chicagotribune.com/news/ct-xpm-1987-12-02-8 703300496-story.html.

Kérchy, Anna (2014), "Picturebooks Challenging Sexual Politics: Pro-Porn Feminist Comics and the Case of Melinda Gebbie and Alan Moore's 'Lost Girls.'" *Hungarian Journal of English and American Studies*, vol. 20, no. 2, | pp. 121–42.

Khoury, George (1999), "The Supreme Writer: Alan Moore." *The Kirby Collector*, https://www.twomorrows.com/kirby/articles/30moore.html.

Khoury, George (2008), *The Extraordinary Works of Alan Moore: Indispensable Edition*. Raleigh, NC: TwoMorrows.

Kidd, Kenneth (2007). "Down the Rabbit Hole." *ImageText*, vol. 3, no. 3, http://imagetext.english.ufl.edu/archives/v3_3/lost_girls/kidd.shtml.

Kidder, Orion Ussner (2010), "Historicization in Alan Moore's 'Supreme' and Warren Ellis/John Cassady's 'Planetary.'" *Journal of the Fantastic in the Arts*, vol. 21, no. 1, pp. 77–96.

Killjoy, Margart (2009), "Mythmakers and Lawbreakers: Alan Moore on Anarchism." *Margaret Killjoy*, February 11. http://birdsbeforethestorm.net/2009 /02/mythmakers-lawbreakers-alan-moore-on-anarchism/.

Klock, Geoff (2003), *How to Read Superhero Comics and Why*. London: Continuum.

Kozaczka, Adam (2015), "Too Much Sex, and Now Enough: Alan Moore's Playfully Repressive Hypothesis." *Journal of the Fantastic in the Arts*, vol. 26, no. 3, pp. 489–511.

Kraemer, Christine Hoff, and J. Lawton Winslade (2010), "'The Magic Circus of the Mind': Alan Moore's *Promethea* and the Transformation of Consciousness through Comics." *Graven Images: Religion in Comic Books and Graphic Novels*, eds. A. David Lewis and Christine Hoff Kraemer, London: Continuum, pp. 274–91.

Krauthammer, Charles (1990), "The Unipolar Moment." *Washington Post*, July 20. https://www.washingtonpost.com/archive/opinions/1990/07/20/the-unipolar -moment/62867add-2fe9-493f-a0c9-4bfba1ec23bd/.

Kristeva, Julia (1986), "Word, Dialogue and the Novel." *The Kristeva Reader*, ed. Toril Moi. New York: Columbia University Press, pp. 34–61.

Kukkonen, Karin (2010), "Navigating Infinite Earths: Readers, Mental Models, and the Multiverse of Superhero Comics." *Storyworlds: A Journal of Narrative Studies*, vol. 2, pp. 39–58.

Kukkonen, Karin (2013), *Contemporary Comics Storytelling*. Lincoln, NE: University of Nebraska Press.

LaRocque, Shantel and Denis Kitchen, eds. (2016), *Will Eisner's The Spirit: The New Adventures*, Milwaukie, OR: Dark Horse Books.

Lawley, Guy and Steve Whitaker (2012), "Alan Moore." Bertatsky, pp. 26–43.

"Legendary Comics Writer Alan Moore on Superheroes, *The League*, and Making Magic" (2009), *Wired*, February 23. https://www.wired.com/2009 /02/ff-moore-qa/.

Levy, Matthew and Heather Mathews (2013), "The Abyss Gazes Also: The Self-Referential Cynicism of *Watchmen*." *ImageText*, vol. 7, no. 2. http://imagetext .english.ufl.edu/archives/v7_2/levy/.

Lindelof, Damon, creator (2019), *Watchmen*. White Rabbit, Paramount Television, DC Entertainment, Warner Bros. Television.

Maes, Hans (2011), "Art or Porn: Clear Division or False Dilemma?" *Philosophy and Literature*, vol. 35, no. 1, pp. 51–64.

Mahmutović, Adnan (2018), "Chronotope in Moore and Gibbons's *Watchmen*." *Studies in the Novel*, vol. 50, no. 2, pp. 255–76.

Marchese, David (2016), "Alan Moore on Why Superhero Fans Need to Grow Up, Brexit, and His Massive New Novel." *Vulture*, September 12. https://www.vul ture.com/2016/09/alan-moore-jerusalem-comics-writer.html.

Martin, Karl (2012), "The Love of Nationalism, Internationalism and Sacred Space in *Watchmen*." Comer and Sommers, pp. 65–74.

Materer, Timothy (1996), *Modernist Alchemy: Poetry and the Occult*. Ithaca: Cornell University Press.

McCloud, Scott (1993), *Understanding Comics: The Invisible Art*. New York: Harper Perennial.

Millidge, Gary Spencer (2011), *Alan Moore: Storyteller*. New York: Universe.

The Mindscape of Alan Moore (2008), directed by DeZ Vylenz, performances by Alan Moore, Dave Gibbons, David Lloyd, Melinda Gebbie, Kevin O'Neill, and Jose Villarubia. Shadowsnake Films.

Moore, Alan, writer (1983a), "Grit!" Art by Mike Collins. *The Daredevils*, no. 8, August.

Moore, Alan, writer (1983b), "The Importance of Being Frank." *The Daredevils*, no. 1.

Moore, Alan, writer (1983c), "Invisible Girls and Phantom Ladies." Part One. *The Daredevils*, no. 4, pp. 18–20.

Moore, Alan, writer (1983d), "Invisible Girls and Phantom Ladies." Part Two. *The Daredevils*, no. 5, pp. 18–20.

Moore, Alan, writer (1983e), "Invisible Girls and Phantom Ladies." Part Three. *The Daredevils*, no. 6, pp. 15–18.

Moore, Alan (1986), *Alan Moore's Maxwell the Magic Cat*. Vol I. Acme.

Work Cited

Moore, Alan (1987a), *Alan Moore's Maxwell the Magic Cat*. Vol II. Acme.

Moore, Alan (1987b), *Alan Moore's Maxwell the Magic Cat*. Vol. III. Acme.

Moore, Alan, writer (1987c), "The Politics and Morality of Rating and Self-Censorship." *The Comics Journal*, no. 117, pp. 35–62.

Moore, Alan, writer (1987d), *Watchmen*. Art by Dave Gibbons. DC Comics.

Moore, Alan, writer (1988a), "Batman: The Killing Joke." Art by Brian Boland. DC Comics.

Moore, Alan, writer (1988b), "The Mirror of Love." Art by Steve Bissette and Rick Veitch. *Artists Against Rampant Government Homophobia*. Mad Love, pp. 2–9.

Moore, Alan (1988c), "Twilight of the Superheroes: An Interminable Ramble." Unpublished series proposal, Internet Archive, https://archive.org/stream/Twi lightOfTheSuperheroes/TwilightOfTheSuperheroes_djvu.txt.

Moore, Alan (1989a), "The Mark of Batman." *The Complete Frank Miller Batman*. Longmeadow.

Moore, Alan, writer (1989b), "Shadowplay." Art by Bill Sienkiewicz. *Brought to Light: A Graphic Docudrama*. Eclipse.

Moore, Alan, writer (1990a), "Behind the Painted Smile. Reprinted in *V for Vendetta* by Alan Moore and Dave Lloyd. DC Comics, pp. 267–76.

Moore, Alan, writer (1990b), "One." Art by Bill Sienkiewicz. *Big Numbers*, no. 1, Mad Love.

Moore, Alan, writer (1990c), "Two." Art by Bill Sienkiewicz. *Big Numbers*, no. 2, Mad Love.

Moore, Alan, writer (1990d), *V for Vendetta*. Art by David Lloyd. DC Comics.

Moore, Alan, writer (1993a), "Mayhem on Mystery Mile!" Art by Rick Veitch. *1963*, no. 1, Image, April.

Moore, Alan, writer (1993b), "When Wakes the Warbeast!" Art by Steve Bissette. *1963*, no. 2, Image, May.

Moore, Alan, writer (1993c), "Double Deal in Dallas!" Art by Rick Veitch. *1963*, no. 3, Image, June.

Moore, Alan, writer (1993d), "Showdown in the Shimmering Zone!" Art by Jim Valentino. *1963*, no. 4, Image, July.

Moore, Alan, writer (1993e), "Twelve Hours to Dawn!" Art by Rick Veitch. *1963*, no. 5, Image, August.

Moore, Alan, writer (1993f), "From Here to Alternity!" Art by Rick Veitch. *1963*, no. 6, Image, October.

Moore, Alan, writer (1994a), "The World, Part 1." Art by Greg Capullo and Bart Sears. *Violator*, no. 1, Image, May.

Moore, Alan, writer (1994b), "The World, Part 2." Art by Greg Capullo and Bart Sears. *Violator*, no. 2, Image, June.

Moore, Alan, writer (1994c), "The World, Part 3." Art by Greg Capullo. *Violator*, no. 3, Image, Jul.

Moore, Alan, writer (1995a), "Rocks and Hard Places." Part One. Art by Brian Denham. *Violator vs. Badrock*, no. 1, Image, May.

Moore, Alan, writer (1995b), "Rocks and Hard Places." Part Two. Art by Brian Denham. *Violator vs. Badrock*, no. 2, Image, June.

Moore, Alan, writer (1995c), "Rocks and Hard Places." Part Three. Art by Brian Denham. *Violator vs. Badrock*, no. 3, Image, July.

Moore, Alan, writer (1995d), "Rocks and Hard Places." Part Four. Art by Brian Denham. *Violator vs. Badrock*, no. 4, Image, August.

Moore, Alan, writer (1999a), *The Birth Caul*. Art by Eddie Campbell. Top Shelf.

Moore, Alan, writer (1999b), "The Radiant, Heavenly City." Art by J. H. Williams III. *Promethea*, no. 1, America's Best Comics, August.

Moore, Alan, writer (1999c), "How Tom Strong Got Started." Art by Chris Sprouse. *Tom Strong*, no. 1, America's Best Comics, June.

Moore, Alan, writer (1999d), "Return of the Modular Man." Art by Chris Sprouse. *Tom Strong*, no. 2, America's Best Comics, July.

Moore, Alan, writer (1999e), "Swastika Girls!." Art by Chris Sprouse. *Tom Strong*, no. 4, America's Best Comics, October.

Moore, Alan, writer (1999f), "Smalltown Stardom." Art by Kevin Nowlan. *Tomorrow Stories*, no. 1, America's Best Comics, October.

Moore, Alan, writer (1999g), "How Things Work Out." Art by Rick Veitch. *Tomorrow Stories*, no. 2, America's Best Comics, November.

Moore, Alan, writer (1999h), "Top 10." Art by Gene Ha. *Top 10*, no. 1, America's Best Comics, September.

Moore, Alan, writer (1999i), "Blind Justice." Art by Gene Ha. *Top 10*, no. 2, America's Best Comics, October.

Moore, Alan, writer (1999j), "Internal Affairs." Art by Gene Ha. *Top 10*, no. 3, America's Best Comics, November.

Moore, Alan, writer (2000a), "Rocks and Hard Places." Art by J. H. Williams III. *Promethea*, no. 7, America's Best Comics, April.

Moore, Alan, writer (2000b), "Sex, Stars and Serpents." Art by J. H. William III. *Promethea*, no. 10, America's Best Comics, November.

Moore, Alan, writer (2000c), "Pseunami." Art by J. H. Williams III. *Promthea*, no. 11, America' Best Comics, December.

Moore, Alan, writer (2000d), "Li'l Cobweb." Art by Melinda Gebbie. *Tomorrow Stories*, no. 4, America's Best Comics, January.

Moore, Alan, writer (2001), "Promethea." Art by J. H. Williams III. *Promethea*, no. 12, America's Best Comics, February.

Moore, Alan, writer (2002a), *Captain Britain*. Art by Alan Davis. Marvel.

Moore, Alan, writer (2002b), *The League of Extraordinary Gentlemen*. Volume I. Art by Kevin O'Neill. America's Best Comics.

Moore, Alan, writer (2002c), *Supreme: The Story of the Year*. Art by Joe Bennett and Rick Veitch. Checker.

Moore, Alan, writer (2003a), "Alan Moore on Supreme." Preface to *Supreme: The Return*. Checker.

Moore, Alan, writer (2003b), *Judgment Day*. Art by Rob Liefeld and Gil Kane. Checker.

Moore, Alan, writer (2003c), "Isn't It Good to Be Lost in the Wood . . ." Art by Zander Cannon. *Smax*, no. 1, America's Best Comics, October.

Moore, Alan, writer (2003d), *Supreme: The Return*. Art by Chris Sprouse and Rick Veitch. Checker.

Moore, Alan, writer (2003e), "How Tom Stone Got Started: Chapter One." Art by Jerry Ordway. *Tom Strong*, no. 20, America's Best Comics, June.

Moore, Alan, writer (2003f), "How Tom Stone Got Started: Chapter Two." Art by Jerry Ordway. *Tom Strong*, no. 21, America's Best Comics, October.

Moore, Alan, writer (2003g), "How Tom Stone Got Started: Chapter Three." Art by Jerry Ordway. *Tom Strong*, no. 22, America's Best Comics, December.

Moore, Alan, writer (2004a), *The League of Extraordinary Gentlemen*. Volume II. Art by Kevin O'Neill. America's Best Comics.

Moore, Alan, writer (2004b), *The Mirror of Love*. Art by José Villarrubia. Top Shelf.

Moore, Alan, writer (2004c), "The Radiant, Heavenly City." Art by J. H. Williams III. *Promethea*, no. 31, America's Best Comics, October.

Moore, Alan, writer (2004d), "Please Leave Us Here, Close the Door . . ." Art by Zander Cannon. *Smax*, no. 5, America's Best Comics, May.

Moore, Alan, writer (2005a), "Wrap Party." Art by J. H. Williams III. *Promethea*, no. 32, America's Best Comics, April.

Moore, Alan, writer (2005b), *Skizz*. Art by Jim Baikie. DC Comics.

Moore, Alan, writer (2005c), *Top 10: The Forty-Niners*. Art by Gene Ha. La Jolla, CA: WildStorm.

Moore, Alan, writer (2006a), *From Hell: Being a Melodrama in Sixteen Parts*. Art by Eddie Campbell. Top Shelf.

Moore, Alan, writer (2006b), *Lost Girls*. Art by Melinda Gebbie. Top Shelf.

Moore, Alan, writer (2007a), *Alan Moore's Complete Wild C.A.T.S.* Art by various. WildStorm.

Moore, Alan, writer (2007b), *Wild Worlds*. Art by various. Wild Storm.

Moore, Alan, writer (2008), *The League of Extraordinary Gentlemen: Black Dossier*. Art by Kevin O'Neill. America's Best Comics.

Moore, Alan, writer (2009a), *25,000 Years of Erotic Freedom*. Abrams.

Moore, Alan, writer (2009b), *Alan Moore's The Courtyard*. Adapted to comics by Antony Johnson. Art by Jacen Burrows. Avatar.

Moore, Alan, writer (2009c), "Three." Art by Bill Sienkiewicz. Unpublished *Big Numbers*, no. 3. Posted to "Big Numbers #3." *Glycon Live Journal*, March 26. https://glycon.livejournal.com/11817.html.

Moore, Alan, writer (2009d), *The Saga of the Swamp Thing*. Book One. Art by Stephen Bissette and John Totleben. DC Comics.

Moore, Alan, writer (2009e), *The Saga of the Swamp Thing*. Book Two. Art by Stephen Bissette and John Totleben. DC Comics.

Moore, Alan, writer (2010a), *The Ballad of Halo Jones*. Art by Ian Gibson. Rebellion.

Moore, Alan, writer (2010b), *The Complete D.R. and Quinch*. Art by Alan Davis. Rebellion.

Moore, Alan, writer (2010c), *The Saga of the Swamp Thing*. Book Three. Art by Stephen Bissette and John Totleben. DC Comics.

Moore, Alan, writer (2010d), *The Saga of the Swamp Thing*. Book Four. Art by Stephen Bissette and John Totleben. DC Comics.

Moore, Alan, writer (2010e), *Writing for Comics*, illustrations by Jacen Burrows. Avatar.

Moore, Alan, writer (2011a), *DC Universe by Alan Moore*. Art by various. DC Comics.

Moore, Alan, writer (2011b), "For the Man Who Has Everything." Art by Dave Gibbons. *DC Universe by Alan Moore*, DC Comics, pp. 5–46.

Moore, Alan, writer (2011c), "The Jungle Line." Art by Rick Veitch. DC Universe by Alan Moore. DC Comics, pp. 125–40.

Moore, Alan, writer (2011d), *The League of Extraordinary Gentlemen: Century, 1969*. Art by Kevin O'Neill. Top Shelf.

Moore, Alan, writer (2011e), "Mortal Clay." Art by John L. Byrne. DC Universe by Alan Moore, DC Comics, pp. 180–203.

Moore, Alan, writer (2011f), *Neonomicon*. Art by Jacen Burrows. Avatar.

Moore, Alan, writer (2011g), "The Reversible Man." Art by Mike White. *The Complete Alan Moore Future Shocks*. Rebellion.

Moore, Alan, writer (2011h), *The Saga of the Swamp Thing*. Book Five. Art by Rick Veitch and John Totleben. DC Comics.

Moore, Alan, writer (2011i), *A Small Killing*. Art by Oscar Zárate. Avatar.

Moore, Alan, writer (2011j), *Whatever Happened to the Man of Tomorrow?* Art by Dave Gibbons. *DC Universe by Alan Moore*, DC Comics, pp. 204–53.

Moore, Alan, writer (2012a), "Blinded by the Hype: An Affectionate Character Assassination." Republished in "Alan Moore's Lost Stan Lee Essay." September 25. *Geek Tyrant*. https://geektyrant.com/news/2012/9/25/alan-moores-lost-stan-lee-essay.html.

Moore, Alan, writer (2012b), *The League of Extraordinary Gentlemen: Century, 2009*. Art by Kevin O'Neill. Top Shelf.

Moore, Alan, writer (2013), *The League of Extraordinary Gentlemen: Nemo: Heart of Ice*. Art by Kevil O'Neill. Top Shelf.

Moore, Alan, writer (2014a), *The Bojeffries Saga*. Art by Steve Parkhouse. Top Shelf.

Moore, Alan, writer (2014b), "Buster Brown at the Barricades." *Occupy Comics*, ed. Matt Pizzolo. Black Mask.

Moore, Alan, writer (2014c), *The League of Extraordinary Gentlemen: The Roses of Berlin*. Art by Kevil O'Neill. Top Shelf.

Moore, Alan, writer (2014d), *Miracleman*. Book One: *A Dream of Flying*. Art by Garry Leach and Alan Davis. Marvel.

Moore, Alan, writer (2014e), *Miracleman*. Book Two: *The Red King Syndrome*. Art by Alan Davis, John Ridgway, Chuck Austen, and Rick Veitch. Marvel.

Moore, Alan, writer (2014f), *The Saga of the Swamp Thing*. Book Six. Art by Rick Veitch and John Totleben. New York: DC Comics.

Moore, Alan, writer (2015a), *Crossed + 100*. Art by Gabriel Andrade. Vol. 1, Avatar.

Moore, Alan, writer (2015b), *The League of Extraordinary Gentlemen: Nemo: River of Ghosts*. Art by Kevil O'Neill. Top Shelf.

Moore, Alan, writer (2015c), *Miracleman*. Book Three: *Olympus*. Art by John Totleben. Marvel.

Moore, Alan (2016a), "Coal Memory." *Spirits of Place*, ed. John Reppion. Daily Grail, pp. 269–91.

Moore, Alan, writer (2016b), "Cinema Purgatorio." Art by Kevin O'Neill. *Cinema Purgatorio*, no. 1, Avatar, April.

Moore, Alan, writer (2016c), "Cinema Purgatorio." Art by Kevin O'Neill. *Cinema Purgatorio*, no. 4, Avatar, July.

Moore, Alan, writer (2016e), "Gossip and Gertrude Granch." Art by Dave Gibbons. LaRocque and Kitchen, pp. 25–32.

Moore, Alan, writer (2016f), "I Keep Coming Back." Art by Oscar Zárate. Sobel, pp. 96–108.

Moore, Alan, writer (2016g), "In Pictopia." Art by Don Simpson. Sobel, pp. 22–35.

Moore, Alan, writer (2016h), "Last Night I Dreamed of Dr. Cobra." Art by Daniel Torres. LaRocque and Kitchen, pp. 61–70.

Moore, Alan, writer (2016i), "The Most Important Meal." Art by Dave Gibbons. LaRocque and Kitchen, pp. 9–16.

Moore, Alan, writer (2016j) "This is Information." Art by Melinda Gebbie. Sobel, pp. 120–26.

Moore, Alan, writer (2017a), "The Book." Art by Jacen Burrows. *Providence*, no. 12, Avatar, March.

Moore, Alan, writer (2017b), "Tilotny Throws a Shape." *Star Wars: The Marvel UK Collection*. Marvel, pp. 218–23.

Moore, Alan, writer (2018a), "Cinema Purgatorio." Art by Kevin O'Neill. *Cinema Purgatorio*, no. 16, Avatar, November.

Moore, Alan, writer (2018b), "If Einstein's Right." Art by Melinda Gebbie. *24 Panels*, eds. Kieron Gillen, Steve Thompson, and Rhona Martin, Image.

Moore, Alan, writer (2019), "Cinema Purgatorio." Art by Kevin O'Neill. *Cinema Purgatorio*, no. 18, Avatar, April.

Moore, Alan, writer (2020), *The League of Extraordinary Gentlemen: The Tempest*. Art by Kevin O'Neill. Top Shelf.

"Moore on *Jerusalem*, Eternalism, Anarchy and *Herbie!*" (2019), *Alan Moore World*, November 18. https://alanmooreworld.blogspot.com/2019/11/moore-on-jerusalem-eternalism-anarchy.html.

Morrison, Grant (2012), *Supergods: What Masked Vigilantes, Miraculous Mutants, and a Sun God from Smallville Can Teach Us About Being Human*. New York: Spiegel and Grau.

Musson, Alex and Andrew O'Neill (2012), "The *Mustard* Interview: Alan Moore." Berlatsky, pp. 182–206.

Nicholson, Brian (2019), "The League of Extraordinary Gentlemen: The Tempest: A Work of Explication in Five Acts." *The Comics Journal*, July 29. http://www.tcj.com/120569-2/.

Noles, Pam (2007), "Under the Cut." *And We Shall March*, December 30. https://andweshallmarch.typepad.com/and_we_shall_march/2007/12/in-this-present.html.

Nunnally, Mya (2017), "*V for Vendetta* Gave Us A Transgender Anarchist Hero." *Comicsverse*, May 6. https://comicsverse.com/v-for-vendetta-transgender-hero/.

Ó Méalóid, Pádraig (2014), "Last Alan Moore Interview?" Slovobooks, January 9. https://slovobooks.wordpress.com/2014/01/09/last-alan-moore-interview/.

Ó Méalóid, Pádraig (2017), "The Alan Moore 2016 Christmas Interviews—Part 1." *The Beat*, June 7. https://www.comicsbeat.com/the-alan-moore-2016-christmas-interviews-part-i/.

O'Nale Jr., Robert (2014), "Creator's Bill of Rights." *Comics Through Time: A History of Icons, Idols, and Ideas*, ed. M. Keith Booker, Vol. 3, pp. 969–71.

Ough, Tom (2015), "Anonymous: How the Guy Fawkes Mask Became an Icon of the Protest Movement." *Independent*, November 4. https://www.independent.co.uk/news/uk/home-news/anonymous-how-the-guy-fawkes-mask-became-an-icon-of-the-protest-movement-a6720831.html.

Parkin, Lance (2013), *Magic Words: The Extraordinary Life of Alan Moore*. London: Aurum Press.

Pulliam-Moore, Charles (2018), "Exclusive: Grant Morrison Opens Up About Feuding With Alan Moore and Why He Still Doesn't Like *Watchmen*." *Gizmodo*, Decemebr 11. https://io9.gizmodo.com/exclusive-grant-morrison-opens-up-about-feuding-with-a-1831011198.

Rabaté, Jean-Michel (2007), *1913: The Cradle of Modernism*. Hoboken, NJ: Blackwell.

Roach, David, Andrew Jones, Simon Jowett, and Greg Hill (2012), "Garry Leach and Alan Moore." Berlatsky, pp. 8–25.

Robinson, Tasha (2011), "Alan Moore." *AV Club*, October 24. https://www.avclub.com/alan-moore-1798208192.

Robinson, Tasha (2012), "Moore in *The Onion* Edits." Berlatsky, pp. 61–94.

Rodriguez, Jaime (2011), "Anatomy of a Killing." Amended by Antony Johnson. Afterword to *A Small Killing*, by Alan Moore and Oscar Zárate. Avatar.

Sharrett, Christopher (2012), "Alan Moore." Berlatsky, pp. 44–60.

Sheehan, David (1989), "Introduction to 'Shadowplay: The Secret Team." *Brought to Light: A Graphic Docudrama*. Eclipse.

Simone, Gail (1999), *Women in Refrigerators*. https://lby3.com/wir/.

Singer, Marc (2004), "Unwrapping *The Birth Caul*: Word, Performance, and Image in the Comics Text." *International Journal of Comic Art*, vol. 6, no. 1, pp. 236–49.

Singer, Marc (2011), "*Dark Genesis*: Falls from Language and Returns to Eden from "Pog" to *Promethea*." *Studies in Comics*, vol. 2, no. 1, pp. 93–104.

Singer, Marc (2019), *Breaking the Frames*. Austin: University of Texas Press.

Sneddon, Laura (2011), "Comic Review: *Neonomicon* by Alan Moore and Jacen Burrows." *Comic Book GRRRL*, December 13. http://www.comicbookgrrrl.com/2011/12/13/comic-review-neonomicon-by-alan-moore-and-jacen-burrows/.

Sobel, Marc (2016a), "I Keep Coming Back." *Ten Short Works by Alan Moore*, ed. Marc Sobel. Uncivilized Books, pp. 109–11.

Sobel, Marc (2016b), "In Pictopia." *Ten Short Works by Alan Moore*, ed. Marc Sobel. Uncivilized Books, pp. 36–41.

Sousanis, Nick (2015), *Unflattening*. Cambridge, MA: Harvard University Press.

Souzis, A. E. (2015), "Momentary Ambiances: Psychogeography in Action." *Cultural Geographies*, vol. 22, no. 1, pp. 193–201.

Work Cited

Sragow, Michael (2009), "'Watchmen' vs. 'The Incredibles': It's Really No Contest." *The Baltimore Sun*, March 13. https://www.baltimoresun.com/news/bs-xpm -2009-03-13-0903120089-story.html.

Stork, Matthias (2014), "Assembling the Avengers: Reframing the Superhero Movie through Marvel's Cinematic Universe." *Superhero Synergies: Comic Book Characters Go Digital*, eds. James N. Gilmore and Matthias Stork. Lanham, MD: Rowman and Littlefield, pp. 77–96.

"Studio Sued over Superhero Movie" (2003), *BBC News*, 26 Sep. http://news.bbc.co .uk/2/hi/entertainment/3141720.stm.

Summers, Tim (2015), "'Sparks of Meaning': Comics, Music and Alan Moore." *Journal of the Royal Musical Association*, vol. 140, no. 1, pp. 121–62.

Tabachnick, Stephen E, ed. (2017), *The Cambridge Companion to the Graphic Novel*. Cambridge: Cambridge University Press.

Tantimedh, Adi (2010), "Alan Moore Speaks *Watchmen 2* to Adi Tantimedh." *Bleeding Cool*, September 9. https://bleedingcool.com/comics/recent-updates/ alan-moore-speaks-watchmen-2-to-adi-tantimedh/.

Teiwes, Jack (2011), "A Man of Steel (by any other name): Adaptation and Continuity in Alan Moore's 'Superman.'" *ImageText*, vol. 5, no. 4, http://ima getext.english.ufl.edu/archives/v5_4/teiwes/.

Thielman, Sam (2019), "Goodbye, Alan Moore: The King of Comics Bows Out." *The Guardian*, July 18. https://www.theguardian.com/books/2019/jul/18/good bye-alan-moore-the-king-of-comics-bows-out.

Thill, Scott (2010), "Alan Moore Gets Psychogeographical With *Unearthing*." *Wired*, August 9. https://www.wired.com/2010/08/alan-moore/.

Torner, Evan (2012), "The Poles of Wantonness: Male Asexuality in Alan Moore's Film Adaptations." Comer and Sommers, pp. 111–23.

Van Ness, Sara J. (2010), *Watchmen as Literature: A Critical Study of the Graphic Novel*. Durham, NC: McFarland.

Vollmer, Rob, int. (2016), "Northampton Calling: A Conversation with Alan Moore." *World Literature Today*, August. https://www.worldliteraturetoday.org /2017/january/northampton-calling-conversation-alan-moore-rob-vollmar.

Wanzo, Rebecca (2018), "The Normative Broken: Melinda Gebbie, Feminist Comix, and Child Sexuality Temporalities." *American Literature*, vol. 90, no. 2, pp. 347–75.

"Watchmen." DC Comics. https://www.dccomics.com/characters/watchmen.

Wegner, Philip (2010), "Alan Moore, 'Secondary Literacy,' and the Modernism of the Graphic Novel." *ImageText*, vol. 5, no. 3. http://imagetext.english.ufl.edu/ar chives/v5_3/wegner/.

Whitted, Qiana (2015), "The Blues Tragicomic: Constructing the Black Folk Subject in *Stagger Lee*." *The Blacker the Ink: Constructions of Black Identity in Comics and Sequential Art*, eds. Frances Gateward and John Jennings. New Brunswick, NJ: Rutgers University Press, pp. 235–54.

Williams, Paul (2020), *Dreaming the Graphic Novel: The Novelization of Comics*. New Brunswick, NJ: Rutgers University Press.

Wilson, Leigh (2012), *Modernism and Magic: Experiments with Spiritualism, Theosophy, and the Occult*. Edinburgh: Edinburgh University Press.

Wolk, Douglas (2003), "Please, Sir, I Want Some Moore: The Lazy British Genius Who Transformed American Comics." *Slate*, December 17. https://slate.com/culture/2003/12/how-alan-moore-transformed-american-comics.html.

Wolk, Douglas (2008), *Reading Comics: How Graphic Novels Work and What They Mean*. New York: Hachette Books.

Wright, Bradford (2001), *Comic Book Nation: The Transformation of Youth Culture in America*. Baltimore, MD: The Johns Hopkins University Press.

INDEX

Aaron, Jason   212–13
Ackroyd, Peter   218
Adams, Arthur   133
adaptation   24, 68, 84, 124, 147, 171, 194, 205, 206–11
Albuquerque, Rafael   187–8
America's Best Comics   14, 128–47, 163, 196
anarchism   50–2, 202–6
Andrade, Gabriel   153
Anglo, Mick   37–40, 114, 201
ANON   25
anonymous (hacktivist group)   204–6
Anything Goes!   117
Aragones, Sergio   133
Astro City   195
authorship   4–9, 162–4, 189–94
Avatar Press   7, 147, 153
The Avengers   211
Awesome Entertainment   110, 115

Back Street Bugle   26
Bady, Aaron   179, 196
Bagge, Peter   133
Baikie, Jim   29–32, 133, 135
Barber, Nicholas   199
Barker, Pat   218
Barks, Carl   191
Barnes, David   82
Barta, Hilary   134, 135
Batman   46, 54, 59, 64–71, 74, 77, 114, 176, 186
Beaty, Bart   1, 2, 4, 5, 6, 18, 19–20, 83, 84, 110, 115–16, 170, 191, 193, 198, 213, 218
Beck, C.C.   37
Before Watchmen   83–4, 212
Beineke, Colin   57, 210
Bender, Aimee   209
Berger, Karen   19, 58
Berlatsky, Eric   1, 24, 105, 119, 163
Bikini Kill   108

A Bill of Rights for Comics Creators, see *Creator's Bill of Rights*
Bird, Brad   194
Bissette, Stephen   53, 54, 57, 88, 105, 106, 110, 193
Bolland, Brian   19, 64–71
Boring, Wayne   128
Boys from Blackstuff   29–30
Bredehoft, Thomas   5
Brexit   150
British Council   2, 7–8
British Invasion   17–20, 53, 116, 117, 170, 215
Brooker, Will   176
Burdon, Bob   110
Burrows, Jacen   147–52, 153

Callahan, Tim   56, 116, 118–19, 136, 138, 141
Campbell, Eddie   27, 87–94, 165, 185
Cannon, Zander   138, 140, 141
Captain Marvel   37, 38, 40
Carney, Sean   2, 159, 167
Carpenter, Greg   19
censorship   14, 23, 216
Cerebus the Aardvark   21, 109
Chabon, Michael   209
Chapman, James   16, 18, 40
Charlton Comics   71–2, 84
Chaykin, Howard   121
Claus   28   47
Cline, Ernest   210
Cohen, Larry   207
Cole, Jack   118, 135
colonial   31, 124, 132–3, 181
comedy, see humor
Comer, Todd   53
Comics Buyer's Guide   200
Comics Journal   22, 87
Conan the Barbarian   140
consciousness   38, 40, 50–1, 53, 57–9, 63, 82, 91–2, 117, 119, 125, 142–4, 159, 162–8, 169, 195, 205–6, 217, 218

Conservative Party   16, 17, 152, 219
Copyright   20, 84–5, 125–8, 163–4, 208–9
Cortsen, Rikke Platz   145, 146, 151
creator rights   20–4, 36, 84–5, 105,
        107–10, 114–15, 156–7, 189–94,
        212, 216
Creator's Bill of Rights   22, 216
Creekmur, Corey   190–2, 196
Cremins, Brian   38
Crisis on Infinite Earths   54, 60–4, 67, 68,
        70–1, 113, 188
Crowell, Ellen   48
Crowley, Aleister   167
Crumb, Robert   191

Daniels, Les   22, 24
Danner, Alexander   19, 28, 77, 83, 84, 160
The Daredevils   34, 42, 135
The Dark Knight Returns   1, 83
Dark Star   26
Davis, Alan   18, 19, 32–3, 37, 42–5
DC Comics   3, 13, 14, 18, 19, 21, 22, 23,
        24, 45, 47, 52, 53, 54, 58, 60, 66, 70,
        71, 73, 83–4, 87, 128, 133, 163, 188,
        192, 193
Delano, Debbie   13
de Ray, Jill   27
Díaz, Junot   209
Di Filippo, Paul   141
Di Liddo, Annalisa   7, 46, 48, 58, 91, 122,
        134, 142, 149, 160, 162, 168, 169,
        171, 172
Dillon, Steve   19, 58
direct market   21
Disney   191, 194
Ditko, Steve   6, 71, 107
Dixon, Phyllis   12, 13
Donenfeld, Harry   21
Doomsday Clock   3, 84
Dr. Who Weekly   27
Dubord, Guy   218
dystopia   40–1, 43–4, 45–52, 127, 147–8, 150

Earth-6   16   42
Eastman, Kevin   22
EC Comics   199
Eclipse Comics   37
Eisner, Will   136–7
Eisner Award   14
Elfquest   140
Ellis, Warren   58, 117

Empire   41, 44, 97–8, 172
The Empire Strikes Back Monthly   28
English identity   17, 18, 29–32, 35–6, 43–5,
        91–4, 97–8, 98–102, 169, 170, 170–6
Ennis, Garth   58, 117, 153
Epic Comics   192
E.T.   29–30
"An Evening with Alan Moore"   176
Extreme Studios   110

Fables   210
Falk, Lee   118
Falklands War   32
fascism   39–42, 42–4, 45–52, 72, 75–7, 133
Fawaz, Ramzi   48–9, 140
The Flaming Carrot   110
Fornés, Jorge   84
Frank, Gary   84
From Hell (film)   207

Gabilliet, Jean-Paul   199
Gaiman, Neil   19, 58
Gallagher, Catherine   44
Gardner, Jared   210–11
Gebbie, Melinda   13, 119–23, 133, 135–6,
        201–2, 203, 204
Genette, Gérard   218
George, Joe   78
Gibbons, Dave   1, 6, 8, 13, 19, 58–60,
        71–86, 105, 133, 136, 195, 197
Gibson, Ian   33–5
Giordiano, Dick   71
Golliwog   3, 176, 177–8
Grahame-Smith, Seth   210
Gray, Maggie   25, 26, 29
Grenfell Tower   204
Griffith, D. W.   178
"Grim and gritty"   63, 110, 116, 197
Grimm   210
Groenstein, Thierry   5
Guerra, Pia   58

Ha, Gene   138–41
Hague, Ian   106
Hall, Stuart   15, 16
Harris-Fain, Darren   195
Hatfield, Charles   9, 21, 85, 121, 203
Henderson Buell, Marjorie   135
Hernandez, Jaime   133
Hernandez Brothers   191
Heroes   218

Index

history   20–1, 60–8, 70–1, 73, 77, 81, 85, 87–104, 107–8, 110–13, 130–1, 137, 159–60, 196, 201, 202–3
Ho, Elizabeth   91, 169
Hoberek, Andrew   9, 16, 17, 20, 54, 58, 73, 82, 85, 107, 192, 203, 208–9
Hogan, Peter   133
Hollywood   156–7, 185, 206–11
horror   53–8, 88–9, 103–4, 147–57, 168
Hughes, Mark   208–9
humor   27, 32–3, 35, 114, 116, 134–5, 139, 174, 183–4, 185, 196, 218

Ideaspace   115, 117–28, 141–7, 162–4, 217
image   14, 23, 24, 105–7, 109–10, 115–17, 193, 196, 217
imperialism   32, 123–4, 130, 170–3, 179, 184
The Incredibles   194–5
Inge, M. Thomas   8
intertextuality   39–40, 45–7, 62–4, 67–8, 70–1, 117–28, 138, 149–50, 162–4
ironic counterpoint   78, 100, 121, 122
Irons, Jeremy   213

Jackson, Ben   15
Jacques, Martin   15
Jaye, Bernie   18
Jenkins, Henry   1
Jenkins, Mitch   169
Johns, Geoff   84
Johnston, Antony   147, 149
Jones, Gerard   21
Jones, Jonathan   205
Joshi, S. T.   150–1

Kaluta, Michael   133
Kane, Bob   67
Kart, Larry   73
Kérchy, Anna   135
Khoury, George   186
Kidd, Kenneth   202
Kidder, Orion Ussner   110
Killing Joke (animated film)   187
King, Tom   84
Kingdom Come   195
Kirby, Jack   6, 54, 107, 109, 115, 191
Kirkman, Robert   217
Kitchen Sink Press   88, 136
Klock, Geoff   84, 110, 138, 142–3, 195
Knight, Steven   88

Kozaczka, Adam   148, 149
Kraemer, Christine Hoff   141, 144
Kristeva, Julia   162–4
Kukkonen, Karin   44, 131
Kurtzman, Harvey   38, 135, 195

Labour Party   16, 17, 91, 151
Laird, Peter   22
Leach, Garry   37
League of Extraordinary Gentlemen / LXG (film)   207
Lee, Jim   14, 105, 106, 115, 128
Lee, Stan   6, 18, 107, 108–9, 191
Levy, Matthew   78, 198
Liefeld, Rob   105, 110, 116
Lindelof, Damon   84
literature/literary   1, 5, 6, 8–9, 20, 42, 58, 68, 70, 82–5, 116, 119, 120, 123–4, 149, 160, 161, 166, 171, 172, 192, 193, 199, 200, 202, 203, 209–10
Lloyd, David   27, 45–52, 204–5
Love and Rockets   23
Lovecraft, H. P.   147–52, 165, 186

McCloud, Scott   5, 22, 81, 82, 99
MacFarlane, Todd   105, 115, 116
McKean, Dave   19
Mad   38, 135, 195
Mad Love   13
Maes, Hans   120
magic   13–14, 90–2, 117, 119, 141–7, 165–8, 217
Mahmutović, Adam   82
manga   218
Marvel Cinematic Universe   210–11
Marvel Comics   3, 6–7, 18, 22, 23, 24, 37, 42, 53, 105–10, 192
Marvel Superheroes   42
Marvel UK   18, 42–5, 135
Marxism Today   15
Materer, Timothy   165
Mathews, Heather   78, 198
mature readers   197–202, 215
Maus   1, 23, 83
The Maximortal   110
Mazur, Dan   19, 28, 77, 83, 84, 160
The Mighty World of Marvel   42
Millar, Mark   117
Miller, Frank   1, 83, 109, 135, 192, 200
Millidge, Gary Spencer   35

Mindscape of Alan Moore   53, 165
misogyny   34–5, 40, 56, 72, 124, 143, 149, 152, 167, 176, 177, 185, 186–8
modernism   58, 120, 166, 198, 202
Moldoff, Sheldon   67
Moore, Alan—works
   1963   105–10, 114, 115, 119, 124, 163, 193, 196
   25,000 Years of Erotic Freedom   121
   Act of Faith   176
   "After They Were Famous"   174
   Albion   133, 170
   American Flagg   121
   Angel Passage   165
   "Anon E. Mouse"   25
   Artists Against Rampant Government Homophobia (AARGH!)   47, 181, 204
   The Ballad of Halo Jones   33–5, 44, 168
   "Batfishing in Suburbia"   174–5
   Batman: The Killing Joke   64–71, 114, 176, 186–8, 196, 201, 211
   "Behind the Painted Smile"   46
   Big Numbers   98–102, 105, 106, 160, 169, 170
   The Birth Caul   10, 165
   "Black Legacy"   27
   "Blinded by the Hype: An Affectionate Character Assassination"   18, 109
   The Bojeffries Saga   35–6, 134, 171, 173–6
   Brought to Light   102–4
   "Buster Brown at the Barricades"   21, 202–3, 204, 206
   Captain Britain   18, 42–5, 52, 163, 170
   "Coal Memory"   168, 169
   Cobweb   133, 135–6, 146
   Cinema Purgatorio   155–7
   The Courtyard   147–52, 165
   Crossed + 100   153–5, 186
   Deathblow by Blow   116
   Dodgem Logic   170
   D.R. & Quinch   32–3, 106, 134
   Dr. Who   27–8
   Fashion Beast   10
   First American   133, 135
   "For the Man Who Has Everything" 58–60, 196

From Hell   14, 87–94, 97, 105, 119, 144, 163, 165, 166, 167, 169, 170, 185
Future Shocks   28, 116
Greyshirt   134, 136–7, 160
"Grit!"   135
The Highbury Working   165
"If Einstein's Right"   204
"I Keep Coming Back"   94–5
"The Importance of Being Frank"   135
"In Pictopia"   117–19, 139, 163
"Invisible Girls and Phantom Ladies" 34–5
Jack B. Quick   133, 134, 136
Jerusalem   170
Jimmy's End   176
Judgment Day   115, 116
"The Jungle Line"   58–9
"Last Night I Dreamed of Dr. Cobra" |136–7
League of Extraordinary Gentlemen (comics franchise)   3, 14, 20, 26, 123–8, 133, 138, 155, 161, 163, 165, 171–3, 176, 177, 207, 208–9, 211
League of Extraordinary Gentlemen Black Dossier   125–6, 161, 163, 164, 171–3, 177, 178, 185, 186, 211
League of Extraordinary Gentlemen Century   125, 126, 173
League of Extraordinary Gentlemen: Nemo: Heart of Ice   126–7
League of Extraordinary Gentlemen: Nemo: River of Ghosts   126–7
League of Extraordinary Gentlemen: Nemo: The Roses of Berlin   126–7
League of Extraordinary Gentlemen Tempest   3, 127–8, 129, 157, 164, 211
League of Extraordinary Gentlemen Volume I   123–5, 171–3
League of Extraordinary Gentlemen Volume II   123–5, 171–3, 177
Lost Girls   119–23, 146, 160, 163, 185, 201–2, 203, 211
"Majestic: The Bill Chill"   116
Marvelman (see Miracleman)
Maxwell the Magic Cat   26–7
Miracleman   3, 13, 15, 16, 36–42, 45, 52, 57, 72, 114, 119, 121, 135, 150, 163, 170, 180, 186, 195–6, 199, 200–1
"The Mirror of Love"   181

Index

The Moon and Serpent Grand Egyptian Theatre of Marvels 165
"Mortal Clay" 64
Neonomicon 147–52, 153, 165, 186
Night Raven 18, 46
"The Politics and Morality of Rating and Self-Censorship" 23
Promethea 141–7, 163, 165, 166, 181, 185, 211
Providence 147–52, 165, 181
"Raoul's Night Out" 173
"The Rentman Cometh" 36
"The Reversible Man" 28–30
Roscoe Moscow 26
The Saga of the Swamp Thing 13, 19, 52–8, 88, 121, 165, 168, 180, 193
"Shadowplay" 102–4
The Show 170
Skizz 29–32, 135, 168
A Small Killing 7, 95–8, 104, 170
Smax 140–1
Snakes and Ladders 165
Spawn 116
Spawn: Blood Feud 115
Splash Brannigan 134, 135
The Spirit 136–7
The Stars My Degradation 26, 29
Star Wars 27–8
Supreme 14, 71, 110–15, 116, 119, 130, 163, 180–1, 196, 211
"This is Information" 204
"Tilotny Throws a Shape" 28
Time Twisters 28–30, 32
Tomorrow Stories 133–7, 160
Tom Strong 71, 128, 130–3, 142, 145, 181
Tom Strong's Terrific Tales 133
Top Ten 137–41, 181
Top Ten: The Forty-Niners 139
"Twilight of the Superheroes" 63, 68, 70–1, 113
Unearthing 169
V for Vendetta 13, 16, 26, 28, 45–52, 121, 150, 171, 180, 181, 186, 204–6
Violator 116
Violator vs. Badrock 116
Voice of the Fire 170
Voodoo 116
Watchmen 1, 3, 6, 8, 13, 14, 16, 17, 26, 29, 42, 52, 57, 71–86, 87, 95, 104, 107, 114, 119, 121, 135, 136, 142, 150, 160, 161, 163, 178–80, 181–5, 192, 195–6, 197, 198–200, 201, 208–9, 213
Whatever Happened to the Man of Tomorrow? 58–64, 66, 70–1, 113, 196
WildC.A.T.S 115, 116, 117
Writing for Comics 6, 189–90
Youngblood 115
Yuggoth Creatures and Other Growths 147
Moore, Leah 133, 170
Moore, Steve 36, 133, 169
Morrison, Grant 19, 83, 84, 197
Multiversity 84

Nedor Comics 133
neoliberalism 17, 203
New Musical Express 26
Nicholson, Brian 127
9/11 204
Noles, Pam 3, 176, 177–8
Northampton 11–14, 25, 26–7, 35–6, 97, 98, 170
The Northants Post 26, 27
Nostalgia 52, 64, 78, 81, 106, 108, 156–7, 171, 173, 176
Nowlan, Kevin 133, 136

Occupy 21, 204
Ó Méalóid, Pádraig 177
O'Nale, Robert 22
Once Upon a Time 210
O'Neill, Kevin 123–8, 155–7, 171, 177
Ordway, Jerry 141
Orwell, George 44, 46, 70
Ostrander, John 66
Ough, Tom 205

Parker, Bill 37
Parkhouse, Steve 35–6, 134
Parkin, Lance 7, 15, 46–7, 54, 71, 73, 160, 161, 162–3, 168, 171, 173, 174, 176, 205
parody 26, 32, 38–9, 108, 114, 116, 124, 134–5, 162, 164, 195, 217
Pax Americana 84
Penny Dreadful 201
Perez, George 60
Place, *see* psychogeography

Planetary 195
Poll, Martin 207
pornography 70, 119–23, 202–3
Preacher 59
psychogeography 100–2, 168–70, 218

Quality Communications 37
queerness 47–52, 76–7, 139–41,
    146–7, 181–2
Quitely, Frank 84

Rabaté, Jean-Michel 202
race/racism 3, 31, 39–40, 51, 75–7, 84,
    124, 132–3, 139, 141, 148, 149, 150,
    152, 173, 177–81
realism 73–4, 107, 118, 196
revisionism 19, 21, 36, 38–42, 45, 53–8,
    60–4, 66–71, 105, 110–15, 118–19,
    120, 128, 131, 134–5, 150, 194–6,
    198, 211, 215, 216, 218
Robertson, Darick 58
Ronin 192
Rorschach 84

Sandman 58
Saunders, Robert 15
Self, Will 218
sexism, *see* misogyny
sex/sexuality 40, 41, 48–50, 57, 66, 76–7,
    85, 115, 116, 117, 119–23, 135–6,
    139–41, 146–7, 149, 153–4, 159,
    176, 178, 181–5, 196, 197–202, 204
sexual violence 34, 35, 49, 56, 65–6,
    122–3, 148–50, 153, 154, 176,
    184–8, 196
Shuster, Joe 21, 111
Siegel, Jerry 21, 111
Sienkiewicz, Bill 98–104
Silver Age 61, 64, 68, 70, 108, 109, 111
Sim, Dave 22, 109
Simone, Gail 66, 187
Simpson, Don 117
Sin City 110
Sinclair, Iain 169, 218
Singer, Marc 3, 9, 20, 122, 144, 145, 163,
    173, 177, 178, 186, 209
Skinn, Dez 36–7
Sneddon, Laura 176, 185, 186
Snyder, Zack 84, 194–5, 210
Sobel, Marc 118, 119
Sounds 12, 26, 29

Sousanis, Nick 145
Souzis, A. E. 168
Spawn 23, 115
Spiegelman, Art 1, 26, 83
Spielberg, Steven 210
The Spirit 136–7
Sprouse, Chris 128, 129–33
Sragow, Michael 194–5
Star Wars Weekly 28
Stork, Matthias 211
Summers, Tim 199
Superman 21, 38, 54, 58–64, 91, 110–15,
    128, 156–7, 196, 200
Swan, Curt 58–64, 128

Taboo 88
Tales from the Crypt 199
Teenage Mutant Ninja Turtle 21
Teiwes, Jack 197
Telgemeier, Raina 218
Terra Obscura 133
The Terrifics 133
Thatcherism 14–17, 29–32, 41, 46–52,
    91–2, 98–102, 171, 203, 219
Thorpe, Dave 42–3
Time 82
Top Shelf Productions 2
Top 10: Beyond the Farthest Precinct 141
Top 10: Season Two 141
Torner, Evan 140
Torres, Daniel 136
Totleben, John 37, 39, 53, 57, 105, 193
Trans identity 49–50, 146–7
Transmetropolitan 58
24 Panels 204
2000 A.D. 13, 18, 19, 26, 28–35, 71, 116,
    134, 168
Tyrant 110

Upton, Florence Kate 177, 178

Van Ness, Sara 82, 160
Vaughn, Brian 58
Veitch, Rick 37, 53, 58–9, 105, 106, 110,
    134, 136–7
Vertigo Comics 58
V for Vendetta (film) 171, 204, 206, 207
Vile, Curt 26
violence 31, 38–9, 51–2, 61–4, 65, 67–8, 89,
    95, 97, 115, 116, 117, 126, 153, 156–7,
    182–3, 184, 185–8, 196, 197–202

Index

Wanzo, Rebecca   135
Ware, Chris   191
Warrior   13, 19, 36–7, 45, 47, 134
Watchmen (film)   84, 194–5, 207, 210
Watchmen (television series)   84, 178,
   207, 213
Wegner, Philip   161
Wein, Len   18–19, 52
White, Mike   29–30
whiteness (of the superhero)   39, 48,
   132–3, 180–1
Whitted, Qiana   179
Wildstorm   14, 115, 116, 128, 133, 141
Williams, Paul   6
Williams III, J. H.   141–7, 166
Willingham, Bill   210

Wilson, Leigh   166
Winslade, J. Lawton   141, 144
Wolfman, Marv   60
Wolk, Douglas   3–4, 160, 163, 193, 208
Woo, Benjamin   1, 2, 4, 5, 6, 18, 19–20, 83,
   84, 110, 115–16, 170, 193, 197–8, 213
Wood, Wally   38
Wright, Bradford   77, 83
Wrightson, Bernie   53

X-Men   26

Youngblood   23, 106, 110
Y: The Last Man   58

Zárate, Oscar   7, 94–8